DEVELOPING INDIGENOUS LEADERS

Other Titles in the SEANET Series

Volume 10 in the SEANET Series

DEVELOPING INDIGENOUS LEADERS

LESSONS IN MISSION FROM BUDDHIST ASIA

PAUL H. DE NEUI, EDITOR

WILLIAM CAREY
LIBRARY

www.missionbooks.org

Published by William Carey Library
1605 E. Elizabeth Street
Pasadena, CA 91104 | www.missionbooks.org

Francesca Gacho, editor
Cheryl Warner, copyeditor
Hugh Pindur, graphic design
Rose Lee-Norman, indexer

William Carey Library is a ministry of the
U.S. Center for World Mission
Pasadena, CA | www.uscwm.org

Printed in the United States of America
17 16 15 14 13 5 4 3 2 1 BP800

Library of Congress Cataloging-in-Publication Data

Developing indigenous leaders : lessons in mission from Buddhist Asia / Paul H. De Neui, editor.
    p. cm. -- (SEANET series)
  Includes indexes.
  ISBN 978-0-87808-040-3
  1. Christian leadership--Asia. 2. Church work--Asia. 3. Christianity and other religions--Buddhism. 4. Buddhism--Relations--Christianity. I. De Neui, Paul H.
  BV652.1.D475 2012
  266.088'2943--dc23
                          2012037693

Contents

Introduction

If we read our scriptures carefully we must admit that God's methods for developing leaders are very unusual. First of all, the selection of women and men whom the world would never have otherwise chosen points to the primary power source in mission. First Corinthians 1:26 tells us, "Not many of you were wise by human standards; not many were influential; not many were of noble birth." To this list of disclaimers we could also add, "Not many of you were willing, not many considered yourselves capable, and not many ever imagined that you would someday end up doing this."

It is time for us to consider God's process for selecting and developing leaders. For far too long, social status, external education, and personal charisma have been the standards used for leadership selection in Christian ministry and mission at home and abroad. God's mission uses the weak, the preliterate, the marginalized. The day has come when outsiders must admit that we do not have the answers for the insiders' context. The growth of the church in the global south has shown that God is doing something new in mission today. Indigenous leaders are rising up who know the cultural context and who have remained closely connected with it in strategic ways. God is using such women and men to transform societies and to bring the Kingdom on earth in formerly unreached places.

SEANET is proud to present this collection of ten articles from ten practitioners serving within the Buddhist world. These authors bring expertise, advice, and humble witness to what God has done to change their thinking and practice. We thank each of the authors for their thoughtful contributions. Thanks also to Melissa Millis for her detailed editing assistance and to the encouraging staff of William Carey Library for their invaluable assistance in bringing this book to print.

Let us listen with open hearts so that our world may be changed to God's standards. Let the mission begin in our own hearts and minds first of all, and from there move outward following God's own irresistible and unusual methodologies.

Paul H. De Neui
January 2013

"This is what the Lord says:

" 'I will restore the fortunes of Jacob's tents
and have compassion on his dwellings;
the city will be rebuilt on her ruins,
and the palace will stand in its proper place.
From them will come songs of thanksgiving and the sound of
rejoicing.
I will add to their numbers, and they will not be decreased;
I will bring them honor, and they will not be disdained.
Their children will be as in days of old,
and their community will be established before me;
I will punish all who oppress them.
Their leader will be one of their own;
their ruler will arise from among them.
I will bring him near and he will come close to me—
for who is he who will devote himself to be close to me?' declares
the Lord.
" 'So you will be my people, and I will be your God. ' "

JEREMIAH 30:18-22

Contributors

Russell Bowers earned his PhD in systematic theology from Dallas Theological Seminary. His published dissertation compared the thought of Keiji Nishitani of Japan's Kyoto School of Philosophy with that of historical Christianity. He has pastored two churches in the USA, worked in Christian leadership development for six and a half years in Cambodia, and taught at the undergraduate and graduate levels in Singapore and the USA for four and a half years. He and his wife, Glenna, live in Texas. They have three married children, five grandchildren, and two foster-grandchildren.

Steve Evans is a cultural researcher and cross-cultural communications specialist affiliated with the International Center for Ethnographic Studies in Atlanta, Georgia, USA. He specializes in the role of oral communication and storytelling in affecting cultural transformation and values. His undergraduate studies were in biblical studies and journalism at Howard Payne University in Brownwood, Texas, and he did his graduate studies at Southwestern Baptist Theological Seminary in Ft. Worth, Texas, and at East Tennessee State University in Johnson City, Tennessee, where his research focused on storytelling and cultural transformation in the Buddhist Kingdom of Bhutan. He has published extensively in academic journals and book chapters on the topics of orality and storytelling, biblical storytelling, and orality and the Bible in the Buddhist world. He served as co-convener of the Lausanne Committee for World Evangelization (LCWE) special interest group on orality and as a founding officer of the International Orality Network (ION). In addition, he serves as a trainer in orality and Bible storying for numerous organizations and agencies around the world. He interned at the Center for Bhutan Studies and was awarded the prestigious Brimstone Award for Applied Storytelling for his work in Bhutan. An American, he has lived and served in Africa, the Middle East, and South Asia. He is currently based in London, England. He is married with three grown children.

Mitsuo Fukuda is an equipper of disciple-makers and founder of Rethinking Authentic Christianity Network, which has provided mission strategies and grassroots training systems for the body of Christ in Japan, as well as in other Asian nations. After he graduated from Kwansei Gakuin Graduate School of Theology in Japan, he researched missiology at Fuller Theological School (on the Fulbright Scholarship) and earned a ThM degree, as well as a Doctor of Missiology degree. He has authored *Upward, Outward, Inward; Mentoring Like Barnabas; Paradigm Shift in Contextualization; Readings in Missiology: Japanese Culture and Christianity;* and *Developing a Contextualized Church as a Bridge to Christianity in Japan.*

Carolyn S. Johnson is from the United States. She served with Covenant World Mission as a missionary to Thailand from 1986 to 2007, living and working in the Northeast region, also known as Isaan. Her ministry included training church leaders, developing a Bible study curriculum in Thai, counseling married couples, mentoring church planters, and serving as the mission country coordinator. Dr. Johnson graduated with a BA from Mills College, an MDiv from Fuller Theological Seminary, and a DMiss from Western Seminary. She was ordained by the Evangelical Covenant Church in 1991. She is currently an adjunct professor at North Park Theological Seminary. She and her husband, Doug, have been married since 1982 and have two daughters and two sons.

David S. Lim is from the Philippines. He has served as academic dean at Asian Theological Seminary in the Philippines and Oxford Centre for Mission Studies in the UK. His PhD in theology (New Testament) was earned from Fuller Theological Seminary. He now serves as the president of the Asian School of Development and Cross-cultural Studies, the National Director of the Philippine Missions Association, and president of China Ministries International–Philippines that recruits Filipino missionaries for China. He is the author of several books and articles on non-Western missiology, theological contextualization, and transformational development.

J. N. Manokaran is ordained in the Anglican Church of India and serves as a speaker, teacher, trainer, and writer based in Chennai, India. He received his BD from India Theological Seminary, MTh in Missiology from Hindustan Bible Institute, and PhD from International Institute of Church Management. Within India he has served as a cross-cultural missionary, serving in the Northern part of India (Haryana). He serves as visiting faculty to a few institutions in India and abroad and also is a resource person for several organizations. He travels widely in India, Asia, and other countries to conduct seminars and conferences. God has given him the opportunity to minister in over 150 cities in India and forty cities overseas. He has authored five books, edited others, and written over 300 articles in various magazines and journals. Currently he is helping Community Bible Study International to launch Bible study groups in India and Asia. His wife, Rosy, is involved in ministry with him. They have a son, Thambos, who is studying information technology in college.

Chansamone Saiyasak is a former Buddhist from Northeast Thailand who resettled in Nashville, Tennessee, USA, in 1979 where he became a Christian. He received his PhD (religious studies & missiology) from Evangelische Theologische Faculteit, Leuven, Belgium, and his DMin and MDiv (theology/religion) from Mid-America Baptist Theological Seminary, Tennessee, USA. His doctoral dissertation was entitled *A Study of the Belief Systems and Decision Making of the Isan People of Northeast Thailand with a View Towards Making Use of These Insights in Christian Evangelism.* In 1992, he returned to Thailand to establish mission work in Northeast Thailand and Laos. He is the founder and president of Mekong Evangelical Mission (US/Thailand) and president of Mekong Bible Seminary (Thailand). He also serves as professor of missiology and Asian studies at Olivet University, San Francisco, California; president of Asia Society of Missiology, Pasadena, California; director of military students at Army Reserve Command; vice president at the League of Foundation of Thailand under the Royal Patronage of H.M The King, Ubon Ratchatani; serves on the Commission for Private Education of the Ministry of Education, Ubon Ratchatani; founder and advisor of Evangelical Fellowship of Laos;

president of the Association for Christian Ministries and Workers of Ubon Ratchani; director of Mercy Christian School; president and chairman of Mercy Foundation; and cofounder and vice president of Global Foundation. He has also published articles on mission history in Southeast Asia. He and his wife, Piyapon Saiyasak, live and minister together in Ubonratchatan, Thailand. They have three children—Alex, Nathan, and Umalai.

Alexander G. Smith was born and raised in Australia. He graduated from the International Institute of Christian Communication in Kenya and Prairie Bible College in Canada. He earned graduate degrees from Western Evangelical and Fuller Theological Seminary. He is a veteran missionary to Thailand, and founder of the Thailand Church Growth Committee and cofounder of SEANET. He served as adjunct faculty at Multnomah University for eighteen years. Presently he is a minister-at-large for Overseas Missionary Fellowship International, under which he has served for forty-seven years. He has published numerous books and articles on ministry in the Buddhist world. He resides with his wife in Portland, Oregon.

G. P. V. Somaratna is from Sri Lanka. He has a PhD in South Asian history from the University of London. He served as professor of modern history at the University of Colombo, Sri Lanka, and is now serving as senior research professor at Colombo Theological Seminary. He has published numerous articles and books on the history of Sri Lanka and the impact of Christianity upon Sri Lankan Buddhism. He is widely regarded as one of Sri Lanka's leading scholars on Ceylonese history. He and his wife reside in Colombo, Sri Lanka, and have two children and eight grandchildren.

Peter Thein Nyunt was born on Manaung Island, Rakhine state, Myanmar. He was brought up in a Buddhist family and was a Buddhist monk before he found faith in Christ in 1990. He earned a BA in theology from ICI University (now Global University), Texas, which incorporated with Evangel Bible College, Yangon, in 1995. After his graduation, he started Bethel Assembly of God among the Burmese Buddhist community in Yangon. He completed his MDiv in theology in 2001 from Myanmar Evangelical Graduate School of Theology (MEGST). In 2003, he earned an MTh in missiology from Nustantra Bible Seminary, Malang, Indonesia, and his PhD in missiology in 2010 from South Asia Institute of Advanced Christian Studies, Bangalore. While serving MEGST as head of missions studies and pastoring Bethel Assembly of God, he is also leading Jesus Movements in Rakhine state. He is married to Roi Bu, and they have three growing children, John Patrick Brang Nan, Esther Hkawn San Aung, and James Sut Aung Ja. They live in Yangon City, Myanmar.

1

More Pro-Jesus than Anti-Buddha: Developing Positive Leaders

RUSSELL H. BOWERS JR.

Ministry is more sharing the good news about Jesus than it is lamenting the bad news about anyone else. It is the effort by those who have come to know the Lord to encourage others to understand, trust, and follow him as well, both as individuals and as churches. They do so out of love—because in him they have found forgiveness, acceptance, beauty, meaning, hope, healing, and truth—and out of obedience to his command. Ministry is one beggar telling another where to find rice, not bemoaning how hungry we all are before we find any.

Since 1990, a major hindrance to widespread acceptance of Christ in Cambodia has been the negative orientation of many pastors. A "ministry" characterized more by the ridicule and rejection of what it does not believe than by the exposition and celebration of what it does results not in joy and effective witness, but rather in unnecessary ghettoization and opposition. Unfortunately, many young pastors strike separatistic stances because their mentors have warned that adopting Christianity requires severing all ties with Buddhism—its principles, practices, and proponents. Hence, for a Cambodian to convert to Christianity means that she or he must abandon long-standing bonds to family, community, and nation. Monks are mocked, community contacts curtailed, families fragmented. To do less constitutes compromise, Timothys are told.

But is that so? It is true that in its atheism, orientation toward emptiness, cyclical view of history, and rejection of revelation, Buddhism represents the opposite of Christianity more than does any other major religion. Nevertheless there is still much that Christians can acclaim in the doctrines and doings of the dharma. To reject all carte blanche is wrong, both factually and missiologically. Therefore this chapter will attempt to show that biblical ministry is more positive than negative; that despite core differences, Christians can find and acknowledge much good in the Buddha and Buddhism; that while Christians must not embrace errant ideas or engage in anti-biblical behavior, they do interact in significant ways with non-Christian people; and that good examples can be found of how Christians may meaningfully and positively interact with their Buddhist neighbors.

BIBLICAL MINISTRY IS MORE POSITIVE THAN NEGATIVE

When Jesus introduced his ministry in Nazareth, he read from Isaiah 61:

> The Spirit of the Lord is on me, because he has anointed me to preach good news to the poor. He has sent me to proclaim freedom for the prisoners and recovery of sight for the blind, to release the oppressed, to proclaim the year of the Lord's favor. (Luke 4:18–19, citing Isa 61:1–2)

Significantly, Jesus stopped in the middle of a sentence, asserting that his present mission introduced the positive "year of the Lord's favor" but not the negative "day of vengeance of our God." He did so because "God did not send his Son into the world to condemn the world, but to save the world through him" (John 3:17). Jesus will judge someday, but not now (John 5:27–30).

When Matthew sought a text to characterize Jesus' ministry, he chose Isaiah 42:

> Here is my servant whom I have chosen, the one I love, in whom I delight; I will put my Spirit on him, and he will proclaim justice to the nations. He will not quarrel or cry out; no one will hear his voice in the streets. A bruised reed he will not

break, and a smoldering wick he will not snuff out, till he leads justice to victory. In his name the nations will put their hope.

(Matt 12:18–21, citing Isa 42:1–4)

This is the longest Old Testament quotation in Matthew, a gospel replete with them. Matthew (following the Septuagint) uses *pais mou* to translate the Hebrew *'abdi*; both mean "my servant," but the Greek can also mean "my child." *Pais* when meaning "servant" implies a closer relationship and a more kindly regard than do *diakonos* or *doulos*; the second line of verse 18 underscores these feelings. Interestingly, Matthew uses *paidion*, "little child," a diminutive form of *pais*, to refer to the young Jesus nine times in chapter two. He is a *pais*, not a crusader. The child/servant's ministry will be characterized by unambiguous proclamation: he will neither avoid nor dilute the truth. But he will make this proclamation gently, not brashly, sarcastically, or arrogantly. "What is pictured is a ministry so gentle and compassionate that the weak are not trampled on and crushed till justice, the full righteousness of God, triumphs. And for such a Messiah most Jews were little prepared" (Carson 1984, 287).

Jesus did not ... stay around "to show them" who is lord or to flaunt his divinely given powers. ... He is not the kind of person who seeks dramatic confrontations for the glory of God. ... He prefers to do his work quietly and inconspicuously. This is the way *God's* Messiah works, in contrast to all false Messiahs. ...

Jesus' quiet tactics have turned people away from John's day to ours. But maybe Jesus' way, beautifully outlined for us in this Isaiah quote, has more to suggest for revolution and reform than we credit. To be sure, its failure "to shout and scream," as revolutionaries and the Spirit-filled of all times are wont to do, its failure to work in the middle of the streets (as contemporary revolutionary and revivalist strategies both advise), and its strange penchant for working with bruised rather than with polished reeds, with flickering rather than with glowing flames, will often turn some people away from Jesus. ...

Jesus' method clear to the end will be the method of quiet revolution, the unlikely tactic of treating persons with great respect—the method of gentleness. There is nothing sensational or special about this method—but it has been determined ever since his baptism at least that this is the way Jesus will go, and Matthew now certifies this way as the *prophetic* way. ... And though Matthew's emphasis in the last two verses (following Isaiah) has been on what the Servant of the Lord will *not* do (stressed no less than four times), nevertheless, this Servant will never rest in his nonviolent zeal until he brings *justice* to earth. ... The Servant is quiet but not quietistic; nonviolent but not noninvolved; gentle but passionate for justice—a justice, we are promised, that he shall one day successfully bring to victory. (Bruner 1987, 453–54)

To be sure, there were times when Jesus spoke and acted strongly, and was moved by deep emotion (Matt 23; John 2:14–17; Mark 3:5). But these occasions occurred in confrontations with those who had the Scriptures and should have known better. When the Romans nailed him to the cross, Jesus neither excoriated (as in Matt 23) nor acted (as in John 2) nor gave in to anger (as in Mark 3) but prayed, "Father, forgive them, for they do not know what they are doing" (Luke 23:34). Strong reactions were exceptions; the characteristic of Jesus' ministry was the gentleness of Matthew 12. Examples could be multiplied: when persecuted he practiced and counseled not fighting but fleeing (Matt 10:23); he rejected James and John's suggestion to call down fire and destroy the inhospitable (Luke 9:51–56); Peter summarized Jesus' career for Cornelius by describing "how he went around doing good and healing" (Acts 10:38). Jesus intends to draw all people to himself (John 12:32), not drive them away from others. The combined testimony of these texts is that Jesus' ministry was overwhelmingly positive and noncombative.

So it is not surprising that the rest of the New Testament prescribes a similar straightforward but nevertheless respectful demeanor on the part of Christ's ambassadors. Key passages include 2 Timothy 2:24–25 ("And the Lord's servant must not be quarrelsome but must be kind to everyone, able to teach, not resentful. Opponents must be gently instructed"); 1 Peter 3:15–16 ("Always be prepared to give an answer to everyone who asks you to give the reason for the hope that you have. But do this with gentleness and respect, keeping a clear conscience"); and James 3:17–18 ("the wisdom that comes from heaven is first of all pure; then peace-loving, considerate, submissive, full of mercy and good fruit, impartial and sincere. Peacemakers who sow in peace raise a harvest of righteousness"). (For further discussion see Bowers 2004, 41–59, 71–79.)

DESPITE CORE DIFFERENCES, CHRISTIANS CAN FIND AND ACKNOWLEDGE MUCH GOOD IN THE BUDDHA AND BUDDHISM

Paul began his address to the Epicurean and Stoic philosophers in Athens by commenting on their altar to an unknown god. He agreed that there was such a god, proposed to introduce him, and went on to approvingly quote Aratus and Cleanthes. His doing so implied neither that the apostle endorsed all that these poets said, nor that he was compromising Christian faith. A dozen times the Old Testament describes creation in terms of Near Eastern myths: a repressive monster (Leviathan or Rahab) restrains creation, a heroic god defeats the monster, releases the forces necessary for life, and ultimately controls these forces. This does not mean that the Old Testament writers accepted these myths as factual. Jesus illustrated biblical truth by talking about an unjust steward and a judge who neither feared God nor cared about people. He said that sometimes nonbelievers act more prudently than do people of the light, and on one occasion urged his hearers to follow his enemies' words though not their behaviors (Luke 16:1–9; 18:1–8; Matt 23:2–3). From these examples we must conclude that it is wrong to automatically and uncritically reject all that non-Christian people think and do as if it were evil. It is not. Pretending otherwise aids neither our own walk with the Lord, nor our invitation to others to join in following him. By contrast, honest assessment that is willing to acknowledge strengths is more likely to be heeded when it does uncover weaknesses, and can pinpoint these more precisely.

With this in mind it might be helpful for Christians ministering to Buddhists to open-mindedly evaluate the Buddha and his message. We may learn from and applaud what he said and did well before zeroing in on where we differ and why we believe there is a better Way. Without attempting to be exhaustive in either the number or description of some positives, I shall simply mention a few:

1) He was neither a materialist nor a hedonist. If, as seems reasonable, we accept the traditional outlines of Siddhartha Gautama's biography, in his early years he enjoyed a life of wealth, power, pleasure, and ease. Most people who have these seek nothing more. But when confronted with the realities of disease, age, and death, the prince admitted that his privileges neither ultimately satisfied nor represented life's summum bonum. One is reminded of Qoheleth, the author of Ecclesiastes, who after "[denying] myself nothing my eyes desired" and "[refusing] my heart no pleasure" concluded that "everything was meaningless, a chasing after the wind" (Eccl 2:10–11).

2) He was sincere and wholehearted in his search for truth. We may disagree, for example, with the way Siddhartha abandoned his wife and son, but must admit the sincerity of his search for truth. Convinced that there must be a way to surmount inevitable suffering and death, the twenty-nine-year-old prince decisively abandoned his assets to discover it. He was not one who put his hand to the plow and then looked back (Luke 9:62). He was following the repeated advice in Proverbs to cry out for insight and value wisdom above silver and gold, and when he found what he considered the pearl of great price he sold all he owned to buy it (Prov 2:1–5; 3:13–18; 16:16; Matt 13:45–46). Many Christians would do well to emulate his priorities, single-mindedness, and sincerity.

3) He was willing to admit when he was wrong and change course. Abandoning princely power and position at age twenty-nine was not the only time Siddhartha renounced his previous ideology and practice. After devoting six years to rigorous ascetic practice that nearly starved him, Siddhartha realized that spiritual reality was not to be found in this extreme any more than it had been in indulgence. So at age thirty-five he turned once again from that to which he had so deeply devoted himself and adopted a "middle way." His rejection of asceticism constituted a tacit admission that for six years he had been wrong. When

he did so his five companions turned from him as a compromiser. The fear of man is a snare, and it is disastrous to love human praise more than praise from the divine (Prov 29:25; John 12:43). Obviously Siddhartha was not seeking praise from God. But he was at least seeking to understand and practice truth, and once he realized that he was not on the right path, he did not allow the fear of his fellows or rejection by former compatriots to deter him from pursuing a new direction. Christians similarly must turn from beliefs or practices—even of fellow believers—that prove unbiblical, and be willing to be misconstrued as compromisers when they do. Buddhists likewise can be reminded that recognizing the error of a way long followed and turning from it is a very Buddhist thing to do.

4) He acted on what he believed. Many people, Christians included, say they believe one thing, but act in another way. Jesus asked, "Why do you call me, 'Lord, Lord,' and do not do what I say?" (Luke 6:46). When Siddhartha came to believe that he must find a way out of suffering, and then realized that asceticism was not that way, he acted on what he believed.

5) Once enlightened, he selflessly taught others. Siddhartha's struggle for enlightenment had been long and hard. The new understanding that came to him under the *bodhi* tree had been difficult to attain and grasp. He therefore concluded, "If I were to teach the Dharma, others would not understand me, and that would be wearying and troublesome for me." As he thus considered keeping to and enjoying for himself the truth he had uncovered, Sahampati Brahmā, probably the most important god of that time, appeared and urged, "Let the Blessed One teach the dharma, let the Sublime One teach the Dharma. There are beings with little dust in their eyes who are wasting [or "perishing"] through not hearing the Dharma. There will be those who will understand" (*MN* i.168). And so, moved by compassion for the unenlightened, the Buddha devoted the remaining forty-five years of his life to traveling, teaching the Dharma, and training disciples. There are, by contrast, Christians who do little or nothing with the good news that has brought them salvation. Around them are beings who are perishing through not hearing the gospel. The Buddha resembles Paul, who selfishly speaking would

have preferred dying and being with Christ, but knew that his staying and serving on earth would be more helpful to others (Phil 1:21–26).

6) He urged his followers to think, not just accept his word. "Enlightenment," the goal of all Buddhists, is the emancipation of one's mind from false ideas and one's practice from impurities. It is understanding and embracing things as they really are.

> To attain liberation, we first have to examine things closely in order to come to know and understand their true nature. Then we have to behave in a way appropriate to that true nature. This is the Buddhist teaching; this we must know and bear in mind. Buddhism has nothing to do with prostrating oneself and deferring to awesome things. It sets no store by rites and ceremonies such as making libations of holy water, or any externals whatsoever, spirits and celestial beings included. On the contrary, it depends on reason and insight. Buddhism does not demand conjecture or supposition; it demands that we act in accordance with what our own insight reveals and not take anyone else's word for anything. If someone comes and tells us something, we must not believe him without question. We must listen to his statement and examine it. Then if we find it reasonable, we may accept it provisionally and set about trying to verify it for ourselves. (Buddhadasa n.d., 13–14)

Many Buddhists today might be surprised at this description. But the mind was important to the Buddha, and he urged his hearers to take not even his own statements for granted, but to test matters for themselves. The Noble Eightfold Path is usually divided into the categories of insight, morality, and concentration (*prajñā, śīla, samādhi*). But the first two steps on that Path—right understanding and right thought (that is, accepting the Four Noble Truths and deciding to live in accordance with them)—are initially matters of faith. A person hears the dharma and decides to provisionally accept and live by it. Later, after having proven for him or herself its validity, right understanding and right thought become matters of the practitioner's own insight (*prajñā*). The Path and Truths are thereafter no longer matters of faith in someone else's word. At any rate, Buddhadasa's description of Buddhism parallels the Apostle Paul's advice to the Thessalonians: "Do not treat prophecies with contempt but test them all; hold on to what is good, reject whatever is harmful" (1 Thess 5:20–22). In other words, listen to input from others, but do not accept it uncritically. Test for yourself what is said; hold onto what is true, and reject what is false. Christians may (and do) question whether the Buddhist dharma in fact describes "things as they really are." But we agree that trying to discover and base one's life on "true truth" is essential, and that blind acceptance of someone's speech is not the way to find out what it is.

7) He was a master teacher. The Pali sutras record the Buddha's interactions with a wide variety of inquirers who either craved his counsel or derided his dharma. In most of these encounters the Buddha showed himself to be a master teacher. He knew what he believed and was never shaken or sidetracked from it. Rather than always lecture his interviewer he often, like Socrates, asked questions. He adapted his method to the capacities of and issues important to the one(s) who sat before him or respectfully to one side. Indeed, a value of the later Mahāyāna tradition is *upāya* or skillful means, the adaptation of the message to the audience. In employing *upāya* the Buddha implied that his students' learning was more important than his speaking. While it is possible to take exception to some of the content that he taught, or even the central thrust of that content, the impartial observer will acknowledge that Siddhartha Gautama's method was skilled and insightful.

8) He led by example. He taught that possessions do not satisfy, and did not himself labor to acquire them. He taught the importance of meditation, and regularly meditated. He continued to personally collect alms. The Buddha thus remained centered and true to his own dharma throughout his forty-five years of teaching, and had no reason to advise his followers, "Do as I say, not as I do." One is reminded of Jesus (John 13:15; 1 Pet 2:21) and Paul (1 Cor 11:1; Phil 3:17; 2 Thess 3:7).

9) He taught some good principles. Up until now we have considered the man. This paper cannot attempt to evaluate his entire system, or even outline all that is admirable within it. Suffice it to say that some at least of what the Buddha taught is quite commendable. The Five Precepts (though not all ten), in both their negative and positive thrusts,

urge basic biblical morality. The four illimitables (S. *apramāna*; P. *appamañña*) or qualities of which there can never be enough—"loving kindness" (the wish for all beings, oneself and others, to be well and happy), "compassion" (the wish for the sufferings of all beings to cease), "sympathetic joy" (delight in the good fortune of others and the wish for it to continue), and "equanimity" (calm balance or evenness of mind, especially under stress)—are noble aspirations. Simple honesty seems to require that we freely acknowledge that some of what the Buddha urged is very good. Doing so implies neither disloyalty to Christ, nor that one is a Buddhist.

WHILE CHRISTIANS MUST NOT EMBRACE ERRANT IDEAS OR ENGAGE IN ANTI-BIBLICAL BEHAVIOR, THEY DO INTERACT IN SIGNIFICANT WAYS WITH NON-CHRISTIAN PEOPLE

I am not assuming or arguing for the first point—that Christians must neither endorse anti-Christian thought nor engage in anti-biblical deeds. We do not do evil that good may come, or compromise where Scripture speaks clearly. However, on matters on which the Bible is silent, we often find not only permission to participate with non-Christians but even positive encouragement to do so.

Paul's encounter with the Athenians has already been mentioned. His address was given in a non-Christian setting (the *Areios Pagos*, named in honor of the Greek god of war), described God in universal rather than specifically Judeo-Christian terms ("the God who made the world and everything in it"), and approvingly cited nonbiblical sources for support (Aratus and Cleanthes). These contrast sharply with an earlier gospel presentation, which was similar in essential message and purpose, but verbalized differently because it was made to Jews in Pisidian Antioch (synagogue, "The God of the people of Israel," Psalms and Isaiah). The literary parallels between Acts 13 and 17 strongly suggest equal Lukan approval of both messages. Before addressing the Areopagus, Paul had invested the time not only to observe (*theōreō*), but to examine carefully (*anatheōreō*) the Athenians' objects of worship, so that he could understand local ideology and be able to incisively evaluate it (Bowers 2005, 79–81). His doing so reflected his philosophy of ministry of becoming "like one not having the law ... so as to win those not having the law" (1 Cor 9:21). The point for us is that the apostle did not dismiss all non-Christian thought or religion out-of-hand, but salvaged what he could to enable himself to connect with his audience, stimulate their understanding, and win some who heard him.

Similarly, one of the least-compromising Old Testament heroes, Daniel, studied long and hard to acquire skill in "the language and literature of the Babylonians" and therefore qualify himself to serve in Nebuchadnezzar's pagan court. The literature he learned was undoubtedly laced with Babylonian mythology and gods. He and his friends mastered their material to the point that they proved "ten times better than all the magicians and enchanters in [Nebuchadnezzar's] whole kingdom" (Dan 1:4, 17–20). Without this expertise in non-Jewish thought, none of the four would have earned a platform from which to testify of Yahweh before the most powerful regional king of that time. Their experience recalls that of Moses who, before God commissioned him to lead the Exodus and convey the Torah, "was educated in all the wisdom of the Egyptians" (Acts 7:22). Following Daniel's example, Christian workers might do well if they knew more of Buddhism than do the Buddhists to whom they minister, enabling them to speak intelligently to the more thoughtful.

The Bible not only commends such interaction with non-Christian thought, it goes so far as to itself employ pagan myths to express its ideology. As already mentioned, a dozen times the Old Testament refers to God's primeval battle to subdue the chaotic sea monster and thereby establish creation. Such images come from neighboring mythologies (Bowers 2006, 1–2). The Bible's use of them does not imply that its writers thought that God literally conquered such dragons in order to establish the world.

It is easy and comfortable to mingle only with others of like mind, but that is not God's agenda for the church. We are commissioned to go; God used persecution to scatter believers who were slow to go (Acts 1:8; 8:1); Peter learned through a repeated vision that "God does not show favoritism but accepts [people] from every nation" (Acts 10:34–35), and that he therefore should socialize with them despite Jewish scruples; the Holy Spirit commissioned emissaries to take the message far from Jerusalem and Judaism (Acts 13:2). It is clear that God does not intend Christians to camp in enclaves where they wait for outsiders to approach and ask admission. We are to be proactive with peoples, philosophies, and cultures that at first seem diametrically opposed to Christian faith. This may require adopting some of their diction and demeanors, where these do not violate Scripture, to make the message meaningful.

This is what Jesus did. He told stories with which others immediately identified. Opponents ostracized him for eating with tax collectors and sinners, but he replied that it is the sick who require a physician. Contrary to Pharisaic scruples, Jesus did not believe he compromised himself by eating their meals in their homes. And on at least one occasion, Jesus told a questioner, "You are not far from the kingdom of God" (Mark 12:34). Why should not Jesus' followers today find others who are "not far" in their thought and practice, and rather than unthinkingly and uniformly berating their blindness, help them to see what they do not yet see so that they may come in?

Naaman, an Aramean convert to faith in Yahweh, asked indulgence for external "worship" of another god while performing his official government function:

> [Y]our servant will never again make burnt offerings and sacrifices to any other god but the LORD. But may the LORD forgive your servant for this one thing: When my master enters the temple of Rimmon to bow down and he is leaning on my arm and I have to bow there also—when I bow down in the temple of Rimmon, may THE LORD forgive your servant for this. (2 Kgs 5:17–18)

Elisha's reply was, "Go in peace." While not an enthusiastic endorsement, Elisha's words grant tacit approval. Evidently, courtesy to the king who would be leaning on his arm permitted Naaman to bow with him to Rimmon (Hadad, the storm god of Damascus, equivalent to the Canaanite god Baal), since in his heart he would not be doing so.

It would be to the king in the course of his official duties that Naaman would be showing loyalty, not to Rimmon as a worshiper. This token respect differs from the genuine worship implied and required in Nebuchadnezzar's command in Daniel 3. Nigerian church leader Musa Gotom comments that in allowing Naaman to go in peace,

> Elisha was not accepting that Rimmon was worthy of worship but was recognizing Naaman's level of growth. Naaman had just realized that only Yahweh is God, and Elisha was now letting the rest play out as Naaman grew in understanding of what that meant. When we deal with people, it is important to remember that spiritual growth is gradual and that we should not expect perfection as soon as someone comes to faith. (Gotom 2006, 448)

Perhaps this passage and principle help us understand Acts 19:17–19, in which only at some point after initially believing did new Christians renounce their former practices and burn their scrolls. It was of course important for these believers eventually to sever their allegiance to sorcery. But the text does not indicate that insistence on their doing so was the focus of the apostle's teaching. Their public, decisive break with the past came about only after, in God's way and time, events dramatically convinced them of the power and holiness of Jesus' name.

THERE ARE EXAMPLES OF HOW CHRISTIANS CAN MEANINGFULLY AND POSITIVELY INTERACT WITH THEIR BUDDHIST NEIGHBORS

Here at the heart of the paper, where we try to understand in specific examples how to apply these principles, I as a Westerner who has spent too little time in Asia must fall silent, except to commend some of my more culturally aware sisters and brothers who have wisely led the way.

One of Thailand's most recognized and picturesque festivals is Loy Krathong. On the night of the twelfth full moon, Thai people float downriver little banana-leaf boats laden with food, betel nuts, flowers, coins, lighted candles, and joss sticks as offerings to Mae Khongkha, goddess of the waters, to ask her forgiveness for having polluted the water during the previous year. By extension, doing so symbolizes the wish to send away all sins and misfortune. The ceremony has roots in and significance to several religious traditions: animism (honor of water spirits), Hinduism (coinciding with Diwali, and lights in honor of Rama and Sita; Khongkha is the old Thai pronunciation of Ganges), and Buddhism (in honor of the Buddha's golden bowl floating upstream prior to his enlightenment. Gerson 1996, 44–47). While some Christians believe they should therefore shun Loy Krathong, Davis suggests that it can be "*reinvested with redemptive meaning* to declare the other Way of removing sins." Thanks can be given to God rather than river spirits; a cross as well as a candle can be floated downstream in the *krathong*. Doing so could "evoke questions about the meaning of the cross—and how it is through the cross that sins are taken away." Participating in such a manner would allow Christians to simultaneously present the gospel and "show social and cultural solidarity with their own people during this important time" (Davis 1998, 141–42).

A conundrum faced by many Southeast Asian Christians is how to respond to Buddhist monks who stand in front of their homes seeking alms. Not a few Christian leaders encourage their flocks to disregard them, as donating rice would be seen as affirming Buddhism, under-writing its continuation, and attempting to earn merit. One of the most senior Cambodian Christian leaders, however, has taken an opposite tack. Mam Barnabas was for years a Buddhist, the son of a master of ceremonies. He became a Christian shortly before the Pol Pot era, and has gone on to start and lead many significant ministries in Cambodia. His response to mendicant monks who, it is thought, bless those who donate, is to turn the tables. As he spoons rice into their bowls, Barnabas will say, "Jesus Christ blesses you!" Thus, instead of the monks bless-ing him, he is blessing them; instead of the Buddha being the ultimate source of blessing (through the sutras the monks chant), Jesus Christ is; instead of attempting to earn merit, Barnabas is showing grace; instead of isolating himself from his Buddhist neighbors, he is including them in his community circle. The monks' response to this approach has been very positive. All Christians might not agree with this way of interacting with the monks or feel comfortable doing so themselves. But it is a suggestion that comes from a Southeast Asian leader who obviously knows the culture, knows Buddhism, and is in no way a compromiser. It strikes me, as a Westerner, as being profoundly wise, gracious, and Christian. It certainly opens more doors to communicate the gospel than do coldly ignoring or ridiculing the monks.

A regional cliché says that Buddhism is Asian and Christianity Western. That, of course, is wrong. Christianity started in Asia, and when properly practiced transcends cultures. Buddhism emerged in India and Nepal, also in Asia but far from Southeast Asia. Nevertheless, that misperception runs deep. An example of how it can be unmasked is provided by two women—one Cambodian and one Western. Noren Vann Kim and Gioia Michellotti teamed to found the Cambodian Christian Arts Ministry (CCAM). Its goal is to take in orphaned and impoverished children, provide them a home, teach basic skills, and train them in traditional arts. During the Pol Pot era, much of Cambodian culture was not only neglected but purposely destroyed. CCAM has taken upon itself the task of training a new generation in the beautiful, traditional Cambodian dance, with its costumes and gestures and storytelling. In short, here is a Christian organization taking the lead in restoring a sadly battered Asian art form. The school sets high standards for its dancers, who have performed for high government officials. Some have commented that the children do a better job than do the university students. Thus CCAM, by inculcating a sense of pride and skill in traditional dance, has profoundly challenged the misconception that Christianity is intrinsically non-Asian (Kim 2003, 137–170; Michelotti and Kim 2004, 1–11).

As my Cambodian associate Uon Seila and I dirt-biked into a rural village over badly neglected dikes separating rice paddies, Seila described how when he was a child, before the communists crushed all community consciousness in his country, the villagers would annually collaborate to repair and maintain the dikes. Elders would organize all, including schoolchildren, so that the task was enjoyably completed in a few days' time. But the Khmer Rouge destroyed both infrastructure and interpersonal camaraderie, so that in the decades since, villagers rarely if ever work together on such projects. The dikes disintegrate and everybody suffers. What might happen if the Christian churches in various villages sat down with (Buddhist) village elders to again organize such communal projects and help them succeed?

Ram Gidoomal became a Christian not from a Buddhist but from a Hindu background. Nevertheless, his story may prove parallel and helpful for our purposes. He describes the foreignness of his first church experience:

> I recall my first visit to church here [in London], my first church ever, St. Paul's Onslow Square. I went to the evening service, so none of my friends or relations would see me going. The first thing I looked for on walking in was the shoebox. I wanted to take my shoes off: *This is holy ground, and you're asking me to come in with my dirty, filthy feet and go into the presence of God? This is not right; this is not holy. I must take my shoes off.* But they told me there was no place for shoes. So I went to sit on the floor, in the proper position of respect, and the usher said to sit on the wooden bench. Then the organ blasted out, and I thought, *Who has died?* Because organ music was just for funerals in my mind. It was an alien experience. There's a whole lot of unlearning to be done in asking how we can communicate the message of Jesus with simplicity [in a way] that will take these barriers away. (Crouch 2007, 36 Author's italics)

One of the ways Gidoomal has himself tried to remove those foreign barriers has been to adopt and adapt his Hindu vocabulary to express Christian truth. He refers to Jesus as the *sanatan sat guru* ("eternal true living way"), "the *bodhisattva* who fulfilled his *dharma* to pay for my karma to negate *samsara* and achieve *nirvana!*" (Crouch 2007, 36). There are, of course, dangers in employing vocabulary laden with unwanted connotations. But before we discard the idea entirely, it may be helpful to remember that the Old Testament uses such words as *baal* to refer to the God of Israel (e.g., 2 Sam 5:20), despite its use as the name of the Canaanite storm god. It is arguably more dangerous to use foreign terms that convey no meaning than to adopt familiar terms that communicate key ideas, even though their definitions may need to be tweaked.

These are but a sample of suggestions on how the church might integrate with and minister positively to their neighbors, rather than remaining aloof or critical. The most appropriate and effective ideas will come from those who know their own communities. The principle to remember, as stated by African leader Lawrence Lasisi, is that "there is nothing wrong theologically and missiologically with integrating culture and the gospel as long as the finality and supremacy of Jesus Christ alone as our Lord and Saviour is not sacrificed" (Lasisi 2006, 900).

CONCLUSION

Biblical Christian ministry is overwhelmingly positive.

[O]ur message to you is not "Yes" and "No." For the Son of God, Jesus Christ, who was preached among you by us—by me and Silas and Timothy—was not "Yes" and "No," but in him it has always been "Yes." For no matter how many promises God has made, they are "Yes" in Christ. (2 Cor 1:18–20)

The gospel invites people to come to a great feast, not to flee from famine. It is a call to the thirsty to drink (Isa 55:1; John 7:37; Rev 22:17). It is good news—an *evangelion*—not bad. Now is the day of salvation. Certainly Christians who minister in Southeast Asia are neither unaware of nor do they wish to minimize "the negative aspects of non-Christian religions under which many Asians are suffering and from which they would like to be liberated" (Ho 1998, 31). They will address these negative aspects when necessary. And individual Christians will struggle with how far to participate in non-Christian rituals, as did Jeffrey and Carol Oh after the death of her parents (Oh 2002, 189–200). But primarily our call is a positive one to turn to God through Christ. When one turns to God he or she will in doing so automatically turn from idols, but turning from idols does not necessarily mean one has turned to God (1 Thess 1:9). It is possible to exorcise evil spirits, but unless they are replaced with something positive—the spirit of God—seven who are worse may take their place (Matt 12:43–45). We are not competent to pull only weeds and not destroy some wheat at the same time (Matt 13:24–30). We therefore need to train pastors who lead their congregations into becoming positive, outgoing, overflowing communities of faith.

If we will love Jesus, love people, and seek to win, we will do so. If we love Jesus, people will see that and ask, "How is your beloved better than others?" (Song 5:9). If we love Jesus we will love people because he loves them. They are not the enemy—Satan and wrong ideas are. If we love people we will seek to win them over to the Kingdom, as Paul did in 1 Corinthians 9. Seeking to win requires more than merely being faithful (though it includes that), and more than just giving out the message (though it includes that). Winning means adapting ourselves and our presentation so that both are comprehensible and attractive. We want to catch fish, not merely wet our lines or nets. A fisher of men who is trying to win (that is, catch fish) will use bait that is familiar and appealing.

> He drew a circle that shut me out—
> Heretic, rebel, a thing to flout.
> But love and I had the wit to win:
> We drew a circle and took him in!
>
> —Edwin Markham, "Outwitted"

References

Bowers, Jr., Russell H. 2004. Gentle strength and *Upāya*: Christian and Buddhist ministry models. *Palm Tree Theology*: 41–75. Phnom Penh: by the author.

_____. 2005. The value and limits to dialogue. In *Sharing Jesus holistically with the Buddhist world*, ed. David Lim and Steve Spaulding, 71–97. Pasadena: William Carey Library.

_____. 2006. The sufficiency of the Bible and the utility of the Bibles: Why read the Qur'ān and the Bhagavad Gītā? Paper presented at the regional meeting of the Evangelical Theological Society, March 24–25, in Fort Worth, Texas.

Bruner, Frederick Dale. 1987. *The Christbook: A historical/theological commentary*. Waco, Texas: Word.

Buddhadasa Bhikkhu. n.d. *Handbook for mankind*. Bangkok: Mahachula Buddhist University Press.

Carson, D. A. 1984. Matthew. In *The expositor's Bible commentary*, gen. ed. Frank E. Gaebelein. Vol. 8: *Matthew, Mark, Luke*, 1–599. Grand Rapids: Zondervan.

Crouch, Andy. 2007. Christ, my bodhisattva [Interview with Ram Gidoomal]. *Christianity Today*, May.

Gerson, Ruth. 1996. *Traditional festivals in Thailand*. Kuala Lumpur: Oxford University Press.

Gotom, Musa. 2006. "1 and 2 Kings." In *Africa Bible commentary*, gen. ed. Tokunboh Adeyemo, 409–466. Grand Rapids: Zondervan.

Ho Jin Jun. 1998. Evangelical challenges to religious pluralism in Asian contexts. *Torch Trinity Review* 1(1): 29–61.

Kim, Noren Vann. 2003. How God turned my mourning into dancing. *Honeycomb* 4(1): Khmer 117–157; English 158–170.

Lasisi, Lawrence. 2006. Syncretism. In *Africa Bible commentary*, gen. ed. Tokunboh Adeyemo, 409–66. Grand Rapids: Zondervan.

Michelotti, Gioia, and Noren Vann Kim. 2004. Glorifying the Creator with our creativity. *Honeycomb* 5(1): English 1–4; Khmer 5–11.

Nanamoli, Bhikkhu, and Bhikkhu Bodhi, trans. 2009. *The middle length discourses of the Buddha: A translation of the Majjhima Nikaya [MN]*, 4th ed. Boston: Wisdom Publications.

Oh, Jeffrey. 2002. The gospel-culture encounter at Chinese funeral rites. *Journal of Asian Mission* 4(2): 189–200.

2

"You Think in Lines, We Think in Circles": Oral Communication Implications in the Training of Indigenous Leaders

STEVE EVANS

Appropriate learning styles must be taken into consideration when training indigenous leaders. This chapter focuses on the differences in leadership training between oral-circular cultures and linear-abstract cultures, with a particular interest in storytelling. It looks at Jesus' teaching methods and who he chose to train as leaders. The article takes a look at storytelling in the Buddhist world and concludes with a case study on the successful training of leaders among a circular-thinking, oral culture.

INTRODUCTION: CIRCULAR VS. LINEAR THINKING

The schoolteacher with a master's degree in education stood up to address the American workshop leader. She was participating in a multinational training on Sunday school curriculum production for developing nations. The instructor had just finished going over the outlines for three months' worth of lessons. "You think in lines, we think in circles," the participant said. She then walked to the board and drew two illustrations. The first resembled an outline with points, sub-points, an introduction, and conclusion. "You think like this," she said. The second illustration was a large circle surrounded by a series of smaller ones. There were lines like spokes connecting the smaller circles to the larger one. "We think like this."

The participant then went on to explain that in many non-Western cultures a lesson is learned through the telling of stories. A main story is told illustrating the lesson or point to be conveyed, followed by any number of smaller stories to reinforce the main one. What she described was the natural and common way of conveying and understanding information for most of the world's seven billion people. They are concrete-circular thinkers versus abstract-linear thinkers. The concrete thinker processes information in terms of what has been experienced or what is real, while the abstract thinker uses formulas, proposition, and deductive reasoning to convey and process information.

Interestingly enough, the arrival of the digital age has contributed to the morphing of some abstract-thinking cultures to concrete ones. "The ability for abstract reasoning is diminishing in our time," said Christian apologist Ravi Zacharias in an address entitled "Mind Games in a World of Images" (1993):

> When you really start to argue with somebody and start with a minor premise and a major premise, build a syllogism and enter into a deduction, the average person loses you halfway through, because they ... come to their conclusions on the basis of images. Their capacity for abstract reasoning is gone. (ibid.)

Concrete thinkers are oral communicators, while abstract thinkers are literate communicators. Oral communicators learn best through means that are not tied to or dependent on print. The definition, however, is somewhat flexible. At minimum the term *oral communicator* refers to people who are illiterate. Many, though, who are functionally illiterate or semiliterate express a strong preference for oral communication as opposed to literate or print-based communication. When they are included in the definition of oral communicator, the combined total clearly makes up a majority of the world's population—those who are oral communicators by necessity or preference. However, preferences for oral communication span all demographic levels. It can be noted that many literates around the world express strong preferences for oral communication as well when tested by appropriate tools to identify their communication patterns and choices. One academic dean and a professor of a Christian college and seminary, both with advanced degrees, were surprised to learn that their results showed oral preferences, but were also quick to agree with the findings.

Primarily through story, proverb, poetry, drama, and song, oral communicators encapsulate their knowledge, information, teachings, concepts, and ideas in narrative presentations that can be easily understood, remembered, and reproduced. Oral people think in terms of these stories, and not in outlines, principles, points, steps, concepts, or propositions, which are largely foreign to their way of learning and communicating. If they have a teaching, a concept, or a principle they want to remember or convey, they do it through story.

Oral cultures are centered in the practice of storytelling. It is their primary means of communicating ideas, normally done in their heart language. They prefer this holistic way of learning rather than the fragmenting, analytical approaches that are common in contemporary education. Western-style education emphasizes analysis—breaking things apart and focusing on extracted principles. Oral communicators prefer holistic learning, keeping principles embedded in the narratives that transmit them. Both learning approaches deal with propositional truth, but oral communicators keep the propositions closely tied to the events in which those truths emerge. People who are steeped in literacy can more easily detach the propositions and deal with them as abstract ideas. In both cases people are learning truth, but the way the truth is packaged and presented differs dramatically.

Those of a literate-print culture mistakenly believe that if they can outline information or put it into a series of steps or principles, anyone, including oral communicators, can understand and recall it. Most oral communicators, however, do not understand outlines, steps, or principles, and cannot remember them. For oral communicators, life lessons are processed by observation, participation, and stories. It is through oral histories, sayings and proverbs, genealogies, dramas, songs, and stories that knowledge, understanding, and life application are expressed and shared, and by which new information is processed and assimilated.

THE ROLE OF STORY IN BUDDHIST CULTURE

Buddhist cultures have rich traditions of conveying truth and morals through their ancient and modern folktales, wisdom tales, and Zen tales, including those categorized as foolish wisdom. Across the ages, these stories entertained people around a campfire at night, as they sat with a mother or a favorite uncle, or with a visitor in front of a hearth. But in reality these stories didn't just entertain; they connected the deep things of life and the values and morals of Buddhist society and culture to everyday living. On one side they made the listener content with life and the everyday world around him, and on the other side they invited the listener into a world larger than the one he presently lived in—pulling him in as a participant and not a mere spectator. More often than not, the intent of these stories was for them to become imbedded in the consciousness of the listener and subtly provide new insights and new perspectives. They had the power to shake one's very foundations, causing him to seek further wisdom and better understanding.

Meme Haylay Haylay and His Turquoise
A Tale of Foolish Wisdom from Bhutan

RETOLD BY STEVE EVANS

One time long ago there lived a poor old man named Meme Haylay Haylay. One day he went to his fields to prepare them for planting, and as he uprooted a clump of very stubborn weeds, he found a huge blue turquoise stone buried in the dirt. It was so heavy that a man his age could hardly lift it.

Because of his good fortune, he decided to stop working and go home. On the way he met a man leading a horse with a rope. "Hey, what are you doing there,

Meme Haylay Haylay?" the horseman asked. "To-day I am no longer a poor old man," Meme Haylay Haylay replied, "because today I struck it rich! As I was digging in my fields, I found this huge valuable turquoise." But before the horseman could utter a word, Meme Haylay Haylay put forth a proposal, "Will you exchange your horse for this stone?" "Don't joke with me, Meme Haylay Haylay! Your turquoise is priceless, and in comparison my horse is worthless," the horseman replied. "Priceless or worthless, if you are for the trade, take this turquoise and hand over the rope," Meme Haylay Haylay said. The horseman lost no time in throwing over the rope and went his way carrying the stone, feeling happy. Meme Haylay Haylay went his way feeling happier than the horseman.

But that was not the end of Meme Haylay Haylay's business. On the way, he met a man with an ox. "Hey, Meme Haylay Haylay. What are you doing there?" the ox-man asked. "Today I am no longer a poor old man, but a rich man," Meme Haylay Haylay replied. "As I was digging in my fields, I found a huge valu-able turquoise stone and I traded it for this horse." He then asked the ox-man, "Would you trade your ox for this horse?" "I certainly would," the man with the ox replied, and the man went away with the horse feeling very happy. Meme Haylay Haylay went his way feeling happier.

Then Meme Haylay traded the ox for a sheep, and the sheep for a goat, and the goat for a rooster. And after each transaction, the others walked away feeling happy, but Meme Haylay Haylay walked away feeling happier. Finally Meme Haylay Haylay heard someone singing a beautiful song, and tears of happiness filled his eyes as he listened to it. "I feel so happy just listening to the song," he thought. "How much happier I would be if I could sing it myself." Just then the singer spied Meme Heylay Heylay and asked, "Hey, Meme Haylay Haylay, what are you doing there?" "Today I am no longer a poor old man, but a rich man," Meme Haylay Haylay replied. "As I was digging in my fields, I found a huge valuable turquoise stone and I traded it for a horse, then I traded the horse for an ox, the ox for a sheep, the sheep for a goat, and the goat for this rooster. Here, take this rooster and teach me how to sing your song. I like it so much."

After learning the song, Meme Haylay Haylay gave away his rooster and went home singing the song, feeling the happiest, richest and most successful businessman in the world.

"These tales magnify our foibles and folly, our appetites, impulses, and delusions, and serve as useful and accurate mirrors of our human condition." So state Tanahashi and Levitt in their book *Flock of Fools: Ancient Buddhist Tales of Wisdom and Laughter*. "As we witness the silly, crazy, and sometimes hurtful things these fools say, think, and do, we laugh at them or shake our heads in disbelief." Often laughter and horror turn into recognition and insight upon reading these Buddhist tales, the authors say. "Since these parables are able to inspire such recognition, they help us to cultivate wisdom and compassion as we seek to develop real understanding and 'do no harm' in the world" (2004, 9).

In *Zen Flesh and Zen Bones*, Reps and Senzaki say that for Buddhists, who are more interested in just being rather than being busy, the self-discovered person is one most worthy of respect. "These are stories about such self-discoveries" (1985, 17). These stories evolved from actual life experiences over the ages, the book said, and it suggests that those who encounter them today can vicariously relive the same events and learn the same lessons.

Just as Buddhism over the ages used foolish wisdom to shape the hearts and minds of its adherents, God uses the foolish, the weak, the lowly, and the despised to accomplish his purposes and establish his kingdom. Acts chapter 4 tells of Peter and John's arrest after the healing of a crippled beggar. The next day they stood before the religious council, responding to questions and accusations put to them. The leaders were amazed at the depth and the clarity of the responses they heard, particularly because they knew these two were ordinary men, unschooled and with no special training in the Scriptures. They could tell, however, that these two men had been with Jesus.

A BIBLICAL FOUNDATION

By selecting his disciples, Jesus used twelve ordinary men to do extraordinary things. None of them were scholars or theologians. In fact, there is no indication that they were even very religious. Several were fishermen; all had mundane occupations. Yet Christ called, discipled, and empowered them with the Holy Spirit to fulfill his mission. He was with them less than two years, then left them with the task. There was no backup plan. Should they fail, the mission would fail. Christ knew what he was doing, though, because the real measure of success depended on the Holy Spirit working in these men and not on the men themselves.

> With all their faults and character flaws—as remarkably ordinary as they were—the men carried on a ministry after Jesus' ascension that left an indelible impact on the world. Their ministry continues to influence us even today. God graciously empowered and used these men to inaugurate the spread of the gospel message and to turn the world upside down (Acts 17:6). Ordinary men—people like you and me—became instruments by which Christ's message was carried to the ends of the earth. (MacArthur 2006, xiii)

Jesus spent time with his disciples. He walked with them, ate with them, spent time day and night with them, and even told them stories.

One day, when Jesus saw the crowds of people who sought him out, he went up on a mountainside, sat down with his disciples, and began to teach them. When he was nearly finished, he said:

> "These words I speak to you are not incidental additions to your life, homeowner improvements to your standard of living. They are foundational words, words to build a life on. If you work these words into your life, you are like a smart carpenter who built his house on solid rock. Rain poured down, the river flooded, a tornado hit—but nothing moved that house. It was fixed to the rock. But if you just use my words in Bible studies and don't work them into your life, you are like a stupid carpenter who built his house on the sandy beach. When a storm rolled in and the waves came up, it collapsed like a house of cards." (Matt 7:24–27, MSG)

When Jesus finished with these words, "the crowds were amazed at his teaching, because he taught as one who had authority" (Matt 7:28).

So it is that whenever Jesus taught, he used stories and parables. One day the crowds that followed Jesus got so big that he got into a boat and pushed out into the water while the crowds remained on the shore. Using stories and parables, he began teaching them many things. He said:

> "What do you make of this? A farmer planted seed. As he scattered the seed, some of it fell on the road, and birds ate it. Some fell in the gravel; it sprouted quickly but didn't put down roots, so when the sun came up it withered just as quickly. Some fell in the weeds; as it came up, it was strangled by the weeds. Some fell on good earth, and produced a harvest beyond his wildest dreams. Are you listening to this? Really listening?" (Matt 13:3–8)

When they were off by themselves, those who were close to him, along with the Twelve, asked about the stories. He told them, "You've been given insight into God's kingdom—you know how it works. But to those who can't see it yet, everything comes in stories, creating readiness, nudging them toward receptive insight." ..."Do you see how this story works? All my stories work this way."

"The farmer plants the Word. Some people are like the seed that falls on the hardened soil of the road. No sooner do they hear the Word than Satan snatches away what has been planted in them. And some are like the seed that lands in the gravel. When they first hear the Word, they respond with great enthusiasm. But there is such shallow soil of character that when the emotions wear off and some difficulty arrives, there is nothing to show for it. The seed cast in the weeds represents the ones who hear the kingdom news but are overwhelmed with worries about all the things they have to do and all the things they want to get. The stress strangles what they heard, and nothing comes of it. But the seed planted in the good earth represents those who hear the Word, embrace it, and produce a harvest beyond their wildest dreams." (Mark 4:10–20)

A CASE STUDY:
TELL THE GENERATIONS—AN EXPERIMENT IN ORALITY FOR THEOLOGICAL EDUCATION AND PASTORAL TRAINING

One special day seventeen young men tucked away in a small town in some corner of the world—many of whom could barely read or write, and some not at all—received certificates from one of the world's largest evangelical seminaries. Though each might find it difficult to read the certificate he held in his hands, they all received above average marks on their final exam, qualifying them to graduate.

A legacy had just been born, the first fruits of an associate professor of preaching who lived and taught half a world away. Dr. Grant Lovejoy had dreamed of this day and had worked hard for it, confident it would come. He knew there had to be a way to effectively address the theological education and pastoral training needs of oral cultures.

To address the situation, Lovejoy and the academic institution he represented developed a plan based on the concept of Chronological Bible Storying (CBS). He partnered with a large international mission sending organization and its national or local colleagues.

"There are many ways to prepare people for leading in Christian ministry," Lovejoy said (2001).

Probably the oldest way is to live with, learn from, and work alongside an accomplished leader. Jesus used this approach with the Twelve. Like apprentices to a master craftsman, they learned by close observation of his life and work and by his evaluation of their lives and work. This apprentice model of training and learning is ancient and used worldwide. (ibid.)

It was this method of instruction that Lovejoy wanted to try, coupled with the concepts of CBS. He developed a program called Tell the Generations, agreeing to issue certificates to those who qualified, according to criteria set up by Lovejoy and approved by the seminary he represented. He said,

Chronological Bible Storying, which was developed to address the needs of oral communicators, has a demonstrated effectiveness in teaching oral communicators Scripture in ways that enhance their understanding of the Bible, theology, and its relevance to their lives. It also gives oral communicators new confidence to share their faith, because they can do it in a culturally appropriate form, through storytelling. (ibid.)

Four years prior to the seventeen men receiving their certificates, a local center to train evangelists had been established by a partnering organization. Something wasn't working, however, and leadership was frustrated. Missionaries in the area agreed to help by providing curriculum and teachers. Through missionary contacts, Lovejoy became involved. They agreed to implement a curriculum that used an approach modeled on Chronological Bible Storying. A missionary, a pastor from a neighboring country, and Lovejoy initiated the teaching. The best-educated students had about ten years of schooling, but the area's schools often met sporadically and without the benefit of books or qualified teachers. Several students had had little or no previous schooling.

Lovejoy and the missionary left after about a week, leaving the new program in the hands of the pastor and another missionary who joined him.

By the end of their training, students admitted that they began their training with little Bible knowledge. For example, various students acknowledged that they entered knowing little of the Old Testament, did not understand the relationship between God and Jesus, did not know the characteristics of God, did not know that God created the angelic beings, had not heard of being born again, and did not know that Christians should not seek help from local deities. (ibid.)

He said that these students were unable to communicate the Christian faith to other people. "By the time the training was over they had dramatically improved their understanding of all of these matters and many more" (ibid.).

Over the next two years the training took place under adverse circumstances related to war, drought-related hunger, and the absence of medical care. Students were noticeably thinner than they had been two years before when the training began. Two students dropped out because of poor health. The host school failed to keep its commitment to feed the students, because a famine had made it difficult for the churches to fulfill their promise—the church members themselves were hungry. Furthermore, oppressive heat made learning difficult much of the time; sluggishness set in as the morning sun beat down on the class. Later Lovejoy noted, "The students' accomplishments are all the more admirable, coming as they did under these difficult circumstances." After an initial rocky six months trying to establish an appropriate teaching pattern, it became apparent that the approach being used was too literate, both in aim and in methodology. The first missionary returned for a visit and changes were initiated—changes designed to restore a more oral, functional approach.

In an informal discussion this missionary heard reports that villagers had recently killed a hyena, a cause of great celebration. At the celebration the villagers sang a song they composed to celebrate the event. They also created a dance that communicated what had happened. They did the same with respect to a conflict over water that had recently been resolved in their favor. With these two recent cultural events as examples, the leaders of the training were able to guide students to create a song and drama to reinforce the learning and communication of each biblical story they learned—now three stories per week. The fact that it was familiar culturally made it easier for students to do it and also made it easier for the teachers to demand it as part of the learning process.

Within a matter of weeks the introduction of song brought a new zest to the daily classroom sessions. "Students were finding learning fun. Moreover, the songs made the learning easier as well. People in the area were glad to hear the songs, so this made it much easier for students to initiate opportunities to share what they were learning" (ibid.). Students, however, were slower to develop effective dramas, but with extensive coaching by their teachers, they gradually developed this as well. Students then learned to tell each story, create at least one song to teach each story, and create dramas of the stories. They discussed the meaning of the stories and interpreted them in light of God's unfolding redemptive plan.

The students shared Bible stories and story-songs spontaneously in their communities, with rapid, massive spread of the biblical message a likely consequence. During one month-long break, villagers were so eager to learn the songs and stories from the visiting students that they sat up far into the night—even all night—to hear the songs and stories. Many wanted to hear the stories and songs repeatedly so that they could learn them well.

"Listeners were more likely to repeat the song accurately than they were the stories. Students agreed unanimously that it was best to initiate the Word in a village via the story-songs because the music is very popular" (ibid.). Students then used the learned Bible stories to clarify what the songs meant. They were able to answer questions about the stories, reporting that they did what they had learned in training—to answer biblically if possible, but if the Scriptures did not give the answer, they simply said so.

"Students reported seeing evidence that the biblical stories were producing changed lives," Lovejoy said, "such as people praying to God for healing instead of visiting a local magician. Students reported using biblical stories at funerals to correct the common practice of using magic to determine whom to hold responsible for the death of the one being buried." (ibid.)

The students learned to organize and tell the stories in chronological clusters: Creation, judgment, the Exodus, etc. Teachers taught students the stories orally, dialogued at length with students about the stories, and then evaluated each student carefully as the students told and sang the stories and performed the dramas. Each week the teachers evaluated how the students handled the new stories introduced that week. The weekly schedule also included extensive periods of reviewing earlier stories and occasionally involved weekend trips to use what they were learning. This pattern continued until the end of training.

Finally, after two years of hard work, the students were ready to be put to the test. A team of seminary educators, along with missionaries, was sent to evaluate the success of the program and the accomplishments of the students. Lovejoy was part of that team. Over a period of four days the visiting team interviewed at length the teachers, members of the training center's board of governors, the students, and the local chief. Then the students underwent a six-hour oral exam.

Students achieved knowledge of approximately 135 biblical stories in their correct chronological sequence, spanning from Genesis to Revelation. They were able to tell the stories, sing songs that told the stories, and enact dramas about each of the stories. Students could tell the stories singly or in clusters—such as the "creation cluster"—dealing with the creation of the spirit world, creation of heavens and earth, and the creation of man and woman. ... They demonstrated the ability to answer questions about both the facts and theology of the stories. They showed an excellent grasp of the gospel message, the nature of God, and their new life in Christ. Students drew quickly and skillfully on the stories to answer a variety of theological questions. Given a theological theme, they could quickly and accurately name multiple biblical stories in which that theme occurs. If asked, they could tell each story and elaborate on how it addresses the theme. (ibid.)

Lovejoy concluded,

In six hours of oral examination and interviews, the 17 graduating students answered 70 questions dealing with factual matters, plus another 50 open-ended questions such as, "How will you use what you have learned?" Students answered the 70 factual questions correctly more than 85% of the time. (ibid.)

The storying approach received an excellent response from the unbelieving members of the local people, including adults and children alike. The songs have already become a part of the general culture. At the graduation ceremony a representative of the chief exhorted the crowd not to let the ceremony degenerate into violence since it was customary for major cultural events to include a volatile mix of alcohol and insulting songs.

In fact, one observer said it was rare to have a cultural event that did not end with bloodshed. The day after the graduation, the chief, who is not a Christian, paid a visit. When asked by the team for his evaluation of the training program, he said he was not the one to evaluate the doctrine being taught, but that he had noticed adults and children in the villages singing the Bible songs and that this was a good thing because it gave them something constructive to sing in lieu of insult songs. (ibid.)

In addition, members of the center's board of governors reported that this group of students has far better biblical knowledge than the members of the board do, including the ordained members of the board.

> The board chairman said that he wished members of the board of governors could take the training. He said he and the older members of the board are too old for that, but that the younger ones could participate. The training process has successfully achieved its goals of enabling students to tell a large number of biblical stories accurately, to have a good understanding of those stories and the theology that they convey, and to have an eagerness to share the Christian message. ... The community received the stories and story-songs enthusiastically and have made them part of the culture and church life alike. ... Despite some deficiencies in the training process, students told of using their training effectively during vacation periods and seeing lives changed in their communities. They also expressed confidence in using biblical stories in ministry and articulated plans for using their training in the various ministry situations to which they will go after graduation. The pattern modeled in the classroom was very appropriate for the culture. Local members of the board praised the students' biblical knowledge. (ibid.)

Lovejoy concluded, "It seems readily apparent that students have grown dramatically in their biblical and theological knowledge, their capacity to share their faith, and their grasp of the Christian life. As members of the board pointed out, everything that they have seen thus far is positive, but the final evaluation depends on seeing what happens when students go to their churches and serve" (ibid.).

DEVELOPING INDIGENOUS CHRISTIAN LEADERS IN THE BUDDHIST WORLD

God continues to use ordinary people to do extraordinary things. His Word is adequate to equip and train his servants empowered by the

Holy Spirit to carry out his mission. Those involved in the development of indigenous Christian leaders must learn to trust these two ultimate resources: God's Word and his Spirit. At the same time, effort must be taken to expose these leaders-in-the-making to God's Word in ways that are culturally and educationally appropriate for them to hear, understand, use, and reproduce. It is too easy for one to fall back on learning and teaching styles with which he is most familiar and comfortable. It it necessary, though, to step out of comfort zones and approach teaching and disciple-making from the perspective of the learner and disciple.

Jesus used ordinary men (and women) to change the world, to "turn the world upside down," in fact. Much of his training methodology was through the telling of parables and stories. He then empowered his disciples and sent them out. This tried-and-true method has proven effective through the generations, from then until today. In today's world, with the spread of the gospel to difficult and sometimes even hostile places, careful consideration must be given to how today's leaders will be developed, equipped, and trained. In addition, it must be decided who will be selected as those leaders. Is it too risky to follow the example of Jesus? To use ordinary people and equip them in simple and approproriate ways to do extraordianry things for the Kingdom? Is it worth the chance?

References

Christian Book Summaries. 2007. *Twelve ordinary men.* Vol. 3, Issue 37, September.

Lovejoy, Grant. 2001. Tell the generations. *Providing Theological Education for Oral Communicators: Southwestern Seminary's Role.* Fourth Edition, Southwestern Baptist Theological Seminary, January 26.

MacArthur, John. 2006. *Twelve ordinary men.* Nashville: Thomas Nelson.

Reps, Paul, and Nyogen Senzaki, eds. 1985. *Zen flesh and Zen bones: A collection of Zen and pre-Zen writings.* Tokyo: Tuttle Publishing, Tokyo.

Stringer, Stephen, ed. 2010. *S-T4T: Storying and church formation training for trainers*. Richmond: WIGTake Resources, LLC. http://www.movements.net/wp-content/uploads/2010/09/Storying-Church-Formation-2010.pdf.

Tanahashi, Kazuaki, and Peter Levitt, trans. 2004. *A flock of fools: Ancient Buddhist tales of wisdom and laughter from the one hundred parable sutra*. New York: Grove Press.

Zacharias, Ravi. 1993. *Mind games in a world of images*. Norcross, Georgia: Ravi Zacharias International Ministries, Compact disc.

3

Empowering Fourth Generation Disciples: Grassroots Leadership Training in Japan and Beyond

MITSUO FUKUDA

Japan is a highly Westernized nation with a deeply animistic worldview. A good illustration of this is the Shinto shrine wherein the founder of the Japanese electronics corporation Panasonic has been elevated to the level of a Kami, a deity. Toyota Motor Corporation, Mitsubishi Companies, and many other big enterprises in Japan also have their own shrines in order to be protected by their guardian deities.

Shinto and Buddhism are clearly different in their functions. But the rituals and practices of both religions express the inner animistic assumption of the Japanese that one is able to control the spirit world in order to obtain well-being for the present and the future. Shinto is concerned with happiness and prosperity in this world. Buddhism, for the Japanese, relates to maintaining peace for the souls of the deceased in the afterlife. Managing ancestral spirits properly through Buddhist rituals is vital in order to insure good fortune and to insure protection from less benevolent spirits.

On the other hand, Japanese society also has a group-oriented value system. *Time* magazine reported how Japanese coped with the tsunami tragedy in the following manner:

> Even though basic supplies are running low, lines at gas stations and grocery stores are orderly. There have been no reports of looting. Rationing of everything from petrol to water has generally been accepted with nary a complaint or raised voice; the idea is that everybody has to share the pain equally. (Beech 2011)

Japanese society's emphasis is on the group and its "others-oriented motivation" system. It is very different from a Western individualistic worldview.

Japan's value orientation is also very different from that of Western missionaries. In this chapter, I will examine the ineffectiveness of the Western school type approach for Japanese people in relation to the development of indigenous leaders. I will also affirm an Asian family type approach in terms of a sustainable disciple-making movement. The biblical foundation of this approach is Jesus' model project of sending out seventy-two disciples, as described in Luke chapter 10. Jesus assumed that his disciples would meet those who would promote peace (cf. Luke 10:6). This person was called a "man of peace," a person of influence not only in his household but also in the local town or village. He would be the first domino in a disciple-making movement if he was a worthy person (cf. Matt 10:11).

THE MEANING OF THE SENDING EVENT FOR THE SEVENTY-TWO DISCIPLES

There are two places in the New Testament where Jesus sent out his disciples. First was the sending event of the Twelve in Matthew 10. Another one was the sending of the seventy-two in Luke 10. In the latter case, the Twelve were not sent out with the seventy-two. In the Luke account, the twelve disciples experienced being on the "sending" side, not on the side of the "sent." It was very important for the Twelve to experience both sides. Jesus was teaching vital truths not only by his speech, but also by his actions. His teaching was that the sent one should become one who sends, so that workers are continuously sent out from the very cities where workers were once only received.

Another point in this series of sending events is that the disciples multiplied each time. The first number was twelve and the second number was seventy-two, which is six times as large as twelve. It is like a family tree. Jesus and the Holy Spirit raised twelve children, and then the twelve children, that means six pairs, raised seventy-two children. David Lim assumes that the seventy-two children, which means thirty-six pairs, raised 432 children, which is six times as large as seventy-two. The total of the numbers 432 and seventy-two is the number of disciples whom the risen Jesus met, which was over 500. Peter baptized about 3,000 men on Pentecost. This number was also about six times bigger than 500 (Lim 2003, 75–76). The growth of the disciple-making pairs did not happen by addition, but was exponential through multiplication. The disciples were reproduced six times by disciple-making pairs who were continually sent out. This is the New Testament version of the first command to human beings, "Be fruitful and increase in number; fill the earth and subdue it" (Gen 1:28).

Without this kind of multiplication, there will be no hope of seeing disciples who will fill the earth and govern it. Our focus is not on how many disciples were raised up by one great person, but upon how many generations of a disciple-making series we can observe in such a movement. In 1993, a famous Japanese evangelist, Mr. Akira Takimoto, and friends had a series of big evangelistic meetings, called the "Koshien Revival Mission," and had a total of 124,000 attendees in three days. The next year, in 1994, the Billy Graham Evangelistic Association held a bigger meeting in Tokyo and had a total of 130,000 attendees; and out of that, there were 52,000 converts in four days. However, no one knows where the majority of the converts went during these last twenty years. We need to confess that the Japanese Christian population is still less than 1 percent. Makito Goto assumes that the number of active Christians who are going to church on a given Sunday in Japan would be 140,000 or 150,000, which is just beyond 0.1% of the whole population (Goto 2011, 15). Our evangelistic focus was on the second generation, and this generation has not stayed in the church.

FOURTH GENERATION DISCIPLES

Contrary to current methods, Jesus' objective was wide enough to equip fourth generation disciples. Of course, his final objective was to disciple whole nations. The first instructions he gave at the sending event for the seventy-two was to pray for harvesters. "The harvest is plentiful, but the workers are few. Ask the Lord of the harvest, therefore, to send out workers into his harvest field" (Luke 10:2). This did not mean that the project should be postponed until a third worker joined the pair. Jesus gave them this instruction at the time of their dispatch. Jesus expected that new workers would emerge from the harvest field and that they would be equipped by the seventy-two. The workers were the previously mentioned men of peace, their extended families, and even the slaves living together in their houses. We can think of Jesus as the first generation, the twelve disciples as the second generation, the seventy-two disciples as the third generation, and finally the man of peace and his household in the mission field as the fourth generation. Jesus considered the emerging man of peace and his household as workers for the harvest in the thirty-six plus towns and villages where the seventy-two traveled (seventy-two divided by two equals thirty-six).

The Apostle Paul also had the same scope in his ministry. Paul wrote a letter to Timothy saying, "The things you have heard me say in the presence of many witnesses entrust to reliable people who will also be qualified to teach others" (2 Tim 2:2). If we recognize Paul as the first generation, Timothy as the second generation, reliable people as the third generation, then "others" mentioned in this verse would be the fourth generation. This indicates that mentoring is intended as a multiplying movement. More experienced workers help less experienced workers pass the baton of disciple-making on to those who will do the same in the future (Fukuda 2011).

Some years ago, I met a couple in East Asia who were leading a huge movement where about 1,500 new churches had been planted each week. They said that they could recognize the fifteenth generation of disciple-making series where the baton had been passed. When we can envision the fifteenth generation of spiritual grandchildren, then we can also envision future disciples who will fill the areas around us—districts and even nations.

REPRODUCIBLE DNA

In this kind of disciple-making movement, there are three important characteristics. The first characteristic is that **first generation spiritual parents are encouraged to have fourth generation descendants.** Parents have not only their spiritual children, but also their spiritual grandchildren who can bring up the great-grandchildren. It is like Paul, who had spiritual fourth generation descendants through his "son," Timothy, and reliable people who became his "grandchildren." It is unusual in normal family settings to have great-grandchildren, even if the generations are not living together at the same time. However it happens in spiritual families because the period between spiritual generations is shorter than natural ones. Sometimes a new spiritual parent has great-grandchildren within a month.

The second characteristic is that **first generation parents give the DNA of equipping fourth generation descendants to second generation parents.** For example, when Paul succeeded in teaching truths to his fourth generation disciples, the next task he had to do was plant the DNA of equipping the fourth generation workers through Timothy. If Paul failed to do this, multiplication would stop. Timothy was encouraged to view his spiritual great-grandchildren as the children of "others."

The third characteristic is that **this reproducible DNA of getting to the fourth generation is passed on from generation to generation.** Every spiritual parent instills in their spiritual children the vision of discipling for future fourth generations. This is the meaning of the promise to Abraham, when the Lord took Abram "outside and said to him, 'Look up at the heavens and count the stars—if indeed you can count them.' Then he said to him, 'So shall your offspring be' " (Gen 15:5). Abraham believed that God would give him a son who would produce the wide-ranging family tree. Like Abraham, we first need to look up to the sky and count the stars; then we need to believe that each of us will have a child who will give us an extensive family tree. This is the way to fulfill the Great Commission in our generation.

The chart below reflects the evangelistic potential of disciple-making. Assume that an evangelist sees one soul turn to Christ each day, then he or she will have 12,045 (365 times 33) converts in thirty-three years. On the other hand, a disciple-maker equips one disciple-maker a year, and in the second year, each disciple-maker equips other disciple-makers, then in the third year, all of the four disciple-makers equip another four disciple-makers, and so on. We can calculate that the disciple-makers will have 8,589,924,592 disciples by the thirty-third year. The chart below shows the potential power of multiplication.

	EVANGELIST	DISCIPLE-MAKER
YEAR	1 SOUL / DAY	1 DISCIPLE / YEAR
1	365	2
2	730	4
3	1,095	8
4	1,460	16
5	1,825	32
6	2,190	64
7	2,555	128
8	2,920	256
9	3,285	512
10	3,650	1,024
11	4,015	2,048
12	4,380	4,096
13	4,745	8,192
14	5,110	16,384
15	5,475	32,768
16	5,840	65,536
17	6,205	131,072
18	6,570	262,144
19	6,935	524,288
20	7,300	1,048,576
21	7,665	2,097,152
22	8,030	4,194,304
23	8,395	8,388,608
24	8,760	16,777,216
25	9,125	33,554,432
26	9,490	67,108,864
27	9,855	134,217,728
28	10,220	268,435,456
29	10,585	536,870,912
30	10,950	1,073,741,824
31	11,315	2,147,483,648
32	11,680	4,294,967,296
33	12,045	8,589,934,592

Figure 1
How Disciple-Making Gets the Job Done
(Mission Africa 2005)

WHAT WAS THE COMMISSION OF THE SEVENTY-TWO DISCIPLES?

Jesus himself traveled through all the towns and villages, teaching in the synagogues and announcing the good news about the Kingdom. And he healed every kind of disease and illness. However, people's needs were too massive for response by just one person. Jesus was not a soloist, but like a chorus master. He wanted to hear the unique voice of each disciple and invited each to his works. After some time of training in a group, the point came when he had to release the twelve disciples into ministry.

He appointed the twelve disciples for two reasons. The first was to continue to be with them. The second was to send them out to preach as apostles, giving them authority to cast out demons (cf. Mark 3:14–15). He modeled beforehand what his sent ones would do in the new towns and villages, by traveling with them. Disciples watched what Jesus did, and sometimes, they themselves were given certain responsibilities to execute Kingdom works, such as baptisms (John 4:2), casting out demons, and healings (Luke 9:40, Mark 9:38). In the meantime, the period of the "on-the-job-training" with the Master had passed and they were ready to do the same works of Jesus on their own, in pairs, in unknown places.

Weep for the Lost

The most important part of the on-the-job-training for the disciples was to watch Jesus' compassion. "When he saw the crowds, he had compassion on them, because they were harassed and helpless, like sheep without a shepherd" (Matt 9:36). The faithful shepherd, by day and by night, was with his flock. He protected it, made it rest in green meadows, and led it beside peaceful streams. Without the shepherd's care, the sheep would be lost. They were in danger of wild beasts because they had no fangs, no claws, no guards, no teamwork, and no strategies. Their eyes were weak and they did not know where to go. No wonder that gentle Jesus was moved with compassion for them.

The word *compassion* is the English translation of a Greek word, σπλαγχνιζομαι (*splanchnizomai*). It is a strong word. Literally, it means to be moved with pity from the very inmost bowels. Jesus' bowels, which mean the innermost parts of his heart, yearned for the people who were harassed and helpless. *Splanchnizomai* is used uniquely to express God's deep feelings. Take, for example, the father's love and compassion when he ran to his son the prodigal, embraced him, and kissed him (Luke 15:20); or the compassion of the good Samaritan, when he saw a traveler half dead beside the road (Luke 10:33). So also was the pity of a king who released a servant and forgave his debt (Matt 18:27), or Jesus' compassion on the huge crowd (Matt 14:14) that followed him on foot from many towns. Of course, Jesus healed their sick.

The disciples were sent out having Jesus' *splanchnizomai* in their hearts. For this reason, they were brave enough to go into unknown towns and villages without bringing any money with them, nor a traveler's bag, nor an extra pair of sandals. Jesus said to them, "Go! I am sending you out like lambs among wolves" (Luke 10:3). What a briefing session with Jesus! The battle went against them. The places where they would go were very dangerous, with no guarantee of life or safety. Knowing that they were going to be at a disadvantage, they went because their hearts were deeply impressed with Jesus' compassion for the lost.

Some adventurous people want to get thrills and suspense, and other task-oriented people want to prove their power. However, if they don't weep for the souls who are going to the eternal judgment, their motivation is not from Jesus' love. The unreached people are not playmates, nor field test samples. They are people whom Jesus so loved that he gave his life for them. So also, we as workers need to do the Lord's work humbly and with many tears. Our roots should grow down into God's love (Eph 3:17).

Listen and Obey

The sending mission was successful. We know it because the seventy-two disciples returned and joyfully reported to Jesus (Luke 10:17). Their success did not come from well-planned, detailed strategies; rather, Jesus' instructions were so simple that uneducated fishermen could understand. The disciples did not read thick manuals. They were "unschooled, ordinary men" (Acts 4:13). All their instructions were like simple memos without further explanation. These instructions were as simple as pray, eat, heal, and proclaim. In truth, genuinely effective strategies are always simple.

There are at least three reasons why Jesus' instructions were so simple. First, they were given not only for gifted workers, but were simple enough so that anybody could follow them. Jesus wanted to invite all the disciples to participate in his harvest works. It was easy to pass on these simple batons to other ordinary workers. To be simple is the foundational element for multiplication.

Secondly, the disciples already knew how to do it. The seventy-two learned directly from Jesus, the best example, as well as from the Twelve, who had already had the experience of being sent. They were empowered by the first generation leaders as well as by the second generation leaders, who were traveling with them. The instructions, "pray, eat, heal, and proclaim," were familiar to the third generation leaders (the seventy-two), because they had been with mentors before being sent out.

Thirdly, they could listen to God, so they did not need more details. Jesus taught the disciples, "When they arrest you, do not worry about what to say or how to say it. At that time you will be given what to say, for it will not be you speaking, but the Spirit of your Father speaking through you" (Matt 10:19–20). Not only in urgent situations like this, but at all times, listening to God was the standard for the disciples.

The center of Jesus' training was to recognize the shepherd's voice and to follow him.

The one who enters by the gate is the shepherd of the sheep. The gatekeeper opens the gate for him, and the sheep listen to his voice. He calls his own sheep by name and leads them out. When he has brought out all his own, he goes on ahead of them, and his sheep follow him because they know his voice. But they will never follow a stranger; in fact, they will run away from him because they do not recognize a stranger's voice. (John 10:2–5)

The disciples knew how Jesus prioritized his conversations with the Father. Some of them had even heard a physical voice from heaven (Luke 3:22). They knew the result of walking in the guidance of the Holy Spirit through the lifestyle of Jesus. They themselves had experienced the Holy Spirit working through them when they drove out demons and healed the sick.

Jesus' simple instruction was like a map, and the Holy Spirit was like a GPS unit. The seventy-two disciples had both the map and the GPS, but still they had the freedom of choice not to follow the map or use the GPS. However, they followed intentionally and knew that they had authority over the evil spirits. More important, their names were written in heaven (Luke 10:20). They followed the shepherd, who enabled them to recognize his voice. The way to follow the shepherd is neither easy nor safe. One day Jesus turned around and said to the large crowd following him, "If anyone comes to me and does not hate father and mother, wife and children, brothers and sisters—yes, even life itself—such a person cannot be my disciple. And whoever does not carry their cross and follow me cannot be my disciple" (Luke 14:26–27). The disciples could not stay in a safe place. Jesus was leading them on a wild adventure to transform the world. They watched how Jesus lived, which was expressed in the following statement:

> Who, being in very nature God, did not consider equality with God something to be used to his own advantage; rather, he made himself nothing by taking the very nature of a servant, being made in human likeness. And being found in appearance as a human being, he humbled himself by becoming obedient to death—even death on a cross! (Phil 2:6–8)

The disciples noticed how much it cost when they decided to follow the shepherd.

AFTER MEETING THE PERSON OF PEACE

What were the seventy-two disciples instructed to do for the man of peace and his household?

Pray for the House

The first instruction after meeting a man of peace was, "When you enter a house, first say, 'Peace to this house' " (Luke 10:5). Praying for peace on the house had at least three meanings. First was to express their love to the people. The cultural diversity of each community was relatively rich at that time, as they did not have television, Internet services, or a strong government that tried to standardize the local cultures. The seventy-two must have experienced culture shock when they visited these mission fields. It was easy for naive travelers to despise foreign cultures, so Jesus told them to respect unknown cultures and to embrace them by praying for peace.

The second meaning of praying for peace was that people should receive this peace practically. The disciples could execute the authority of the Creator as Kingdom agents. In the same way when God said, "Let there be light" (Gen 1:3), and there was light, the disciples acted for the Creator. Through the announcement of peace, the disciples were used to rescue people from the kingdom of darkness and transfer them into the kingdom of the Son (Col 1:13). The people actually received blessings when the disciples prayed for them. If that house deserved to receive the peace, they got it, as did Potiphar's house in the story of Joseph: "The LORD blessed the household of the Egyptian because of Joseph. The blessing of the LORD was on everything Potiphar had, both in the house and in the field" (Gen 39:5).

The third meaning of praying for peace was to discern if the household deserved to receive the peace. It was easy to discern this because Jesus foretold, "If the head of the house loves peace, your peace will rest on that house; if not, it will return to you." (Luke 10:6). I believe that if the peace returned to the disciples, the disciples quit approaching the house. Their purpose in stopping was to reach not only that house but also the whole town, because Jesus urged, "Stay there, eating and drinking whatever they give you, for workers deserve their wages. Do not move around from house to house."(Luke 10:7). If a house refused to welcome the disciples, it meant that the town refused the kingdom. The disciples should then "go into its streets and say, 'Even the dust of your town we wipe from our feet as a warning to you. Yet be sure of this: The kingdom of God has come near' " (Luke 10:10–11).

The mission of the disciples was not sowing, but harvesting. It is unnecessary to sow seeds in a field full of mature plants ready to be harvested. The disciples were told that if they discerned that the first house they visited was not the right one, they should give up approaching the town and move on to another town. If they did not, they would lose the harvest in the other towns, because "The fields are already ripe for harvest" (John 4:35 NLT). Through praying for peace, the disciples knew where the right field was.

Eat Whatever Is Set Before You

"Eat what is set before you" (Luke 10:8 TNIV) was the next instruction. In this short paragraph, Jesus twice told them to "eat." The brevity of the command indicates the importance of this instruction. To eat with others indicates an acceptance of the culture and the people in a mission field. If you find a missionary eating the traditional food that is foreign to the missionary's culture, the people know that this foreigner loves them and they will begin to trust him or her.

Here is a good place to insert a story from Ethiopia. Tenalem Mulugeta, the hero of this story, is an Ethiopian evangelist.

> Tenalem set off on the long journey to Mira, on the Sudanese border. On his arrival there, five men from the Opo tribe came to him, and asked him three times whether he really had come because he loved them. Tenalem told them yes, he had come because he loved them. They decided to test him, saying that if he really loved them, then he would eat their food. If he did that, they would believe him, otherwise they would kill him. It was a hard test, because the food was mice and rats, which Tenalem had never eaten. He asked to be allowed to pray before the meal, and was then able to eat the 'regional speciality'. Following his successful completion of the test, the tribesmen were convinced that he really loved them, and hugged him. Some

100 people gathered to hear the gospel, and accepted Jesus as their saviour. (DAWN Fridayfax 2001)

Jesus did not own a house. He said, "Foxes have holes and birds have nests, but the Son of Man has no place to lay his head" (Luke 9:58). He could not host a home party, so he went to someone else's house to eat dinner, and most probably stayed the night there. The conversion story of Zacchaeus, the chief tax collector in Jericho (cf. Luke 19), was a typical story that expressed Jesus' everyday life. The seventy-two disciples reproduced the dinner fellowship with Jesus in the houses of peace they discovered. Through the honest, transparent, interactive, family-like communication over the dinner table, the disciples would naturally share a Christ-following lifestyle. Eating local foods together would develop an intimate fellowship where every participant would think, "Your fight is my fight and your victory is my victory."

The seventy-two may have wondered initially why they were called to seek out these so-called "men of peace." We are told they later reported what they had seen and heard, which was "The blind receive sight, the lame walk, those who have leprosy are cleansed, the deaf hear, the dead are raised, and the good news is proclaimed to the poor" (Luke 7:22). In addition, they must have shared their personal testimonies. As Jesus told the former demon-possessed man in the region of the Gerasenes, the disciples told everything God had done for them personally (cf. Luke 8:39). Moreover, I believe that the Holy Spirit showed the disciples something in the household supernaturally as Jesus did for a Samaritan woman at a well, because they were trained to listen to the Father.

Heal the Sick

Jesus' command was not to pray for the sick, but to heal the sick. Wherever Jesus went, healing and casting out demons accompanied the proclamation of the Kingdom. There were a few exceptions, like the time when he went back to his hometown, but almost always Jesus demonstrated his healing powers to the people. There were two reasons why so many healings happened. One is that the Father was so merciful in having Jesus heal the sick. Jesus was "a man of suffering, and familiar with pain" (Isaiah 53:3). He was filled with pity for the sick and healed them. Another reason why multiple healings occurred was that his healing ministry was the sign of his being the anointed one. Jesus replied to Philip, "Believe me when I say that I am in the Father and the Father is in me; or at least believe on the evidence of the works themselves" (John 14:11).

The disciples were sent out after they had been empowered to cast out all demons and heal all diseases (cf. Luke 9:1). The purpose of their being sent out was twofold: first, to tell everyone about the kingdom of God, and second, to heal the sick. Healing of the sick served to prove the message of the Kingdom. The disciples shared the work of Jesus with the men of peace at dinner and confirmed what they said by many miraculous signs (cf. Mark 16:20). The people knew that what they were hearing was not simply an old wives' tale, but a reality in their own time, so that they could see with their own eyes and they could touch with their own hands (cf. 1 John 1:1; Job 42:5).

The men of peace recognized that the King was working through the Kingdom armies, because healing was the demonstration that the King had defeated the enemy. The King freed the people from the bondage of Satan, and one of the results of the King's victory over the enemy's power was healing. Jesus once said to a religious leader about an old lady who was healed by Jesus, "Then should not this woman, a daughter of Abraham, whom Satan has kept bound for eighteen long years, be set free on the Sabbath day from what bound her?" (Luke 13:16). The men of peace experienced the progress of the spiritual warfare that was going on in their own towns.

Proclaim

Jesus' first act of his public life was to announce, "The kingdom of God has come near. Repent and believe the good news!" (Mark 1:15). "People are destined to die once, and after that to face judgment" (Heb 9:27). The disciples were sent out to warn people to repent and respond to the good news to avoid punishment. If people could accept the peace, then they would eat food with the disciples and be healed; if they did not repent and believe, their final destiny would be eternal hell. The kingdom of God has come near, so that everyone should prepare to stand at the divine court.

Driving out demons was a very crucial sign for the coming judgment day. Jesus made an important statement: "If I drive out demons by the finger of God, then the kingdom of God has come upon you" (Luke 11:20). Jesus was invading the enemy's territory with Kingdom authority, and he was restoring the original order of his creation. In the near future, the King will come with his full authority and judge the world finally. All people need to repent and accept the reign of King Jesus, dying to self to serve God and neighbors with all their heart. Otherwise, they will be judged like Sodom. "The Judge is standing at the door!" (Jas 5:9).

Those who welcomed the disciples knew the heart of Jesus for the lost. They were trained to listen and obey God in blessing others, to eat with neighbors, to heal the sick, and to proclaim the King's coming. They became the disciples and disciple-makers, and later trainers of disciple-makers to equip to the fourth generation of workers. The man of peace would be the first to start the chain reaction of the disciple-making movement. On the other hand, those who refused the disciples would be warned to repent due to the coming judgment day.

UOI TRAINING

Nine years ago, I started a church planters' training program. The material of the training was original. I didn't want to learn from materials others had created until I could get some results of my own. I was afraid of just copying foreign strategies. After experiencing some failures, students started to plant house churches, and an exciting chain reaction of disciple-making happened. So, I went overseas to observe other similar grassroots disciple-making trainings: Greenhouse in California, Luke 10 Training in Texas, and the Tentmaker's training in Manila, Philippines. Learning from other trainers' designs, I composed a more systematic training than my original one. At that time, it took seventeen hours to cover all the materials. I coined the name "Catalyst Training." In some ways it worked; I could see fifth generation disciples. However, it was still too complicated.

I have continued through much trial and error to eventually make the training simple and practical. Now I have a revised Catalyst Training, called "Upward, Outward, Inward Training" (UOI Training). The training material is divided into two parts which I call the first story and the second story. It takes six hours to cover the material of the first story and four to five hours for the second part. It includes many role-plays, exercises, and homework. The first part is designed to train new believers immediately after their conversion. The second part is designed to send disciple-makers to unfamiliar groups domestically, as well as internationally. Only the students who do the six- to seven-item homework from the first part can be trained for the second part. If you are interested in learning more details of the training, please refer to "Upward, Outward, Inward: Passing on the Batons of Discipleship" (Fukuda, 2010) listed in the reference section of this chapter.

There are two ways to use this training. One is to provide different opportunities for traditional churchgoers to obey their King in their daily contexts, out of the context of a church building. We presently have five trainer teams in Japan, and they hold training seminars periodically. It is an infrastructure through which the body of Christ in Japan can access resources in order to become more decentralized, prophetic, and relational. We also have several indigenous training teams overseas.

Another way to use this training is to train new converts in a grass-roots setting within the first forty-eight hours after their conversion. In this case, two hours are enough to cover the first part, including baptism. Friends in South Asia are using this training to reach unreached tribes. When the tribal people accept Christ, they train new converts using the UOI Training, on that day. Then the next day, they take these trained workers to reach the next tribe and do the same things there as the former day.

UOI Training facilitates three kinds of relationship. We call them "Upward, Outward, Inward." Upward represents the relationship with God, while Outward represents the relationship with nonbelievers, and Inward represents the relationship with self and Christian brothers and sisters. Briefly speaking, this training is intended to help participants listen to God, equip them to reach the world, and facilitate organic fellowships among believers.

Listening to God and obeying his guidance not only takes skill, but also impacts the very lifestyle of every disciple. As it is written in the Bible, "the sheep listen to his voice. He calls his own sheep by name and leads them out" (John 10:3). Jesus calls my name and speaks to me. We have many different thoughts in our minds, and they come and go continuously. However, among those many thoughts we have "the word God has planted in [our] hearts" (Jas 1:21 NLT) and "the desire and the power to do what pleases him" (Phil 2:13 NLT). Thus "listening to God's voice" means discerning which thoughts in our heart are from God. Through some exercises, ninety percent of the participants start to listen to God by themselves. These prophetic words are for themselves, for the unbelievers around them, and for their Christian friends.

To equip the new believers to reach the secular world, we teach them four things. The first is that the believers' lifestyle testifies to God. Their joy, conviction, kindness, involvement, honesty, and fellowship will be a great attraction for unbelievers. The second is for them to get ready to share their own stories. Through some role-playing, they will be able to tell their stories of "before" and "after" knowing Jesus by choosing key words that explain their experiences. Third is to give prophetic words to unbelievers. Jesus saved a whole family through Zacchaeus (Luke 19:5) and an entire town through the woman at the well (John 4:28–30). There is potential for entire families and cities to come to Christ through the person who receives the words of God, if we deliver God's message. The fourth one is to manage money. It is impossible to serve God wholeheartedly while your heart is obsessed with money (cf. Matt 6:24). Therefore, it is critical to teach and encourage new believers, just after their conversion, to let go of pursuing material success and to choose to serve God wholeheartedly instead.

For catalyzing the organic fellowship for new Christians, we introduce two kinds of accountability groups and one interactive Bible study group: "As iron sharpens iron, so one person sharpens a friend" (Prov 27:17 TNIV). In a family-like fellowship, people share honestly their struggles, sins, and victories. In this transparent relationship, people will learn the truths from the real stories where Jesus is leading in the partners' lives. It would be great encouragement for any disciples to have fellowship, supporting each other in prayer and challenging each other by confirming action steps to obey Jesus.

The following chart shows steps for the reproduction of these types of disciples.

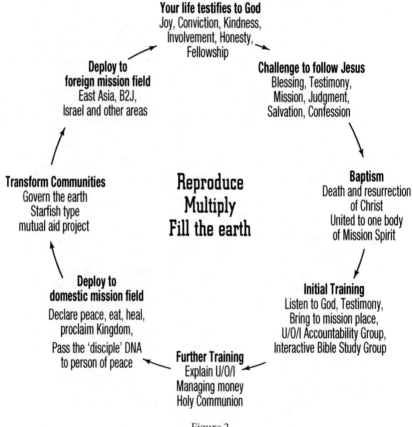

Figure 2
Steps for the Reproduction of Disciples

WESTERN SCHOOL VS. ASIAN FAMILY

The qualifications of Christian leaders are different between the West and Asia. In Western institutional churches, teaching the genuine truth from the Bible is the central skill for the pastors; but in Asia, catching the spiritual guidance in applying Scripture to the contexts of people's lives is more important. While evangelistic meetings and distributing tracts are the major evangelistic tools of Western conventional churches, housewives who are gossiping the stories of Jesus are the major evangelistic force in the Asian context. Leaders who have degrees and publish books are admired in the West, but the leaders who function as spiritual parents will be respected in Asia.

Teach vs. Listen

Paul Hiebert analyzes the middle level of the supernatural, yet "this-worldly" beings are excluded from a Western two-tiered view of reality. The upper zone, the world of transcendence, is either missing or largely absent from a traditional Japanese worldview (see Figures 3 and 4).

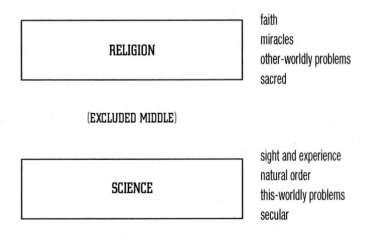

RELIGION

faith
miracles
other-worldly problems
sacred

(EXCLUDED MIDDLE)

SCIENCE

sight and experience
natural order
this-worldly problems
secular

Figure 3
A Western Two-Tiered View of Reality
(Hiebert 1982, 44)

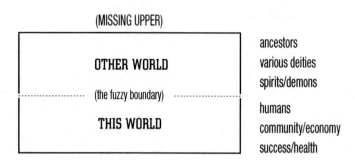

Figure 4
A Japanese Two-Tiered View of Reality
(Fukuda 1992)

The emphasis of Westernized Christianity is on its theology and doctrine. It is rational, logical, and morally oriented, but it has often excluded areas of the supernatural, such as prophecy, casting out demons, healings, miracles, signs, and wonders. It is this spiritual dimension which most Asian people, including Japanese, stress. This is not something good or bad, but a worldview issue. It is an advantage for the Japanese to sense spiritual messages, because there is a possibility for them to listen to God naturally due to their sensitive receptors to the spiritual world. However, educated, evangelical Western missionaries tend to make them stop hearing the voice from the spiritual world, because their worldview does not have the capacity to understand the middle zone.

Of course there is a danger of hearing the noise and/or the messages from the enemy, but we need to trust God, who wants to interact with his beloved children. An example would be the way toddlers learn to walk. They must keep trying even if they continue to fall down. No parent would make them stop walking because of their failures. It is good for educated, evangelical Western missionaries to emphasize Bible study in the classroom setting for themselves, but they don't have to apply their cultural behaviors to the Asian context. The UOI Training also values Bible study, but our focus is not in understanding sound doctrines, rather in listening to God speak from the Bible, in order to obey Jesus in our real life contexts.

The fundamental qualification for leaders is the ability to listen to God on their own, in their daily lives, and help others listen to God. They can go anywhere God commands them to go in pairs and impact the mission field. "As they pass through the Valley of Baka, they make it a place of springs; the autumn rains also cover it with pools" (Ps 84:6 TNIV). "Swarms of living creatures will live wherever the river flows. There will be large numbers of fish, because this water flows there and makes the salt water fresh; so where the river flows everything will live" (Ezek 47:9).

Event vs. Gossip

The Western-educated, evangelical missionaries serving in Japan tend to explain the structure of salvation in the Western theological order: God, sin, and salvation. Japanese are not very interested in a transcendent event. There is no unique, absolute God, nor an unchangeable divinity in the Japanese worldview. So, if they do not understand a unique absolute personal God, there is no way to understand sin as rebellion against God or to accept salvation as reconciliation with God. Most evangelistic events have been ineffective because they are just soft approaches to explain God, sin, and salvation, using good music and inspiring messages.

The assumption of Western institutionalized training is that "knowledge is power." A teacher leads a "one-man show" for transmitting knowledge to passive students in a classroom setting. Even if the teacher is exceptional and the educational system is perfect, our minds quickly forget the knowledge that has been instilled in us. Jesus told us not only to listen to him, but also to obey him. Once we know his will, we should obey consistently by producing lasting behavioral change. We need to intentionally focus on what pleases God in our daily lives. We should say, "Focus is power" (cf. Rock 2006), in order to see new divine customs take root in our lives.

Leaders need to obey Jesus, focusing on spiritual guidance in everyday life, and help others obey the King through their example and encouragement. The capability to plan a "one-man show" is not so important. The leader's function is not to be spotlighted, but to weep for souls. Paul declared to the elders of the church at Ephesus, "When they arrived, he said to them: 'You know how I lived the whole time I was with you, from the first day I came into the province of Asia. I served the Lord with great humility and with tears and in the midst of severe testing by the plots of the Jews' " (Acts 20:18–19). The essential weapon against cult attacks on the church is a humble leader's example, where a leader can say, "Be on your guard! Remember that for three years I never stopped warning each of you night and day with tears" (Acts 20:31).

When people really experience the fruit of repentance, obedience, and faith by doing God's will, they cannot stop witnessing to it. The gossip of ordinary believers will be the mission force for the spontaneous expansion of the gospel, as the Samaritan woman at the well was for the whole village of Sychar (cf. John 4:1–42).

School vs. Family

Japan's new prime minister, Yoshihiko Noda, spoke to Democratic lawmakers about his choices for a new executive party lineup. Noda said on August 31, 2011: "In soccer terms, I want them to be mid-fielders. There are many, including me, who want to be a centre-forward but what this party needs is a group of mid-fielders with broad views who can deliver strategic passes" (Reuters 2011). Noda's preaching was expressed as one of the ideal Japanese ideal leadership styles, namely, making harmony in a group. The mid-fielders' function is to make full use of each member's talent. They are active behind the scenes to support the strikers.

The mid-fielders are accountable to other players, both offense and defense. Without the mid-fielders' support, there will be fewer chances to score a goal. The mid-fielders' controlling power is a decisive element for the overall defense strategies of a team. They empower other members, maintaining harmony on the team, and adjusting for a difference of views in order to win the game. One of the strong points of the Japanese workers in international projects of cooperation is being the facilitator who makes a mutual agreement for the team. This function, like that of a mid-fielder in a soccer game, is also a traditional

Japanese leadership style for a family, in a local community, and even in the national government.

This capability to empower each member of a group is indispensable for the disciple-making movement, because we need to fight as a team. There is an old African proverb that says, "If you want to go fast, go alone; if you want to go far, go together." A movement needs small groups where people share each other's burdens. One of the vital qualifications of a leader in a movement is to be compatible enough to work together with an accountability partner, to lead interactive family-like small groups, and to encourage others to have such partners to lead their own groups.

A school itself, as a system, is like a coffeemaker. A coffeemaker can make coffee, but it will never be able to make another coffeemaker. In nature, however, the order of things is entirely different: a coffee plant produces coffee beans, which in turn can produce new coffee plants (cf. Schwarz 1996, 10). A family lives a life for reproduction. It is not so organized. It is rather noisy and messy. In a family-like church, you will find crying babies, fatherless young people, fighting couples, grumbling mothers-in-law, and lonely old guys, but it is a family life. "Where there are no oxen, the manger is empty, but from the strength of an ox come abundant harvests" (Prov 14:4). If you have a spiritual parent who is weeping for the family members, God will give him or her children who will become a parent of grandchildren later, and so on, to the fourth generation.

CONCLUSION

Leadership development in the context of house church movements always needs to expect to see the fourth spiritual generation disciples equipped. In the episode of sending out seventy-two disciples in Luke 10, the man of peace and his household were the fourth generation disciples because they were equipped by the seventy-two who had been equipped by the Twelve, who had been equipped by Jesus. Jesus was the first generation leader, passing on the baton of reproducible DNA. The DNA consists of two characteristics: 1) weeping for the lost, 2) listening and obeying; and four skills: 1) praying for the peace, 2) eating whatever is set before them, 3) healing the sick, and 4) proclaiming the King's coming. In Japan, we employ the Upward, Outward Inward Training (UOI Training) to equip the new converts to listen to God, to reach the world, and to catalyze organic fellowships. This training is not the Western school type, but the Asian family type, where it qualifies the disciples: 1) to listen to God by themselves and help others listen to God, 2) to gossip about their personal stories of their own repentance, obedience, and faith, and 3) to empower each member of a family-like group to have spiritual great-grandchildren.

References

Beech, Hannah. 2011. *How Japan copes with tragedy: A lesson in the art of endurance.* http://globalspin.blogs.time.com/2011/03/14/how-japan-copes-with-tragedy-a-lesson-in-the-art-of-endurance/#ixzz1hyyGOBuF (accessed January 2, 2012).

DAWN Fridayfax 2001. *Ethiopia: Moslem walks again.* http://www.jesus.org.uk/dawn/2001/dawn25.html (accessed January 2, 2012).

Fukuda, Mitsuo. 1992. Developing a contextualized church as a bridge to Christianity in Japan. PhD diss., Fuller Theological Seminary. (Published in Japanese in 1993.)

_____. 2010. *Upward, outward, inward: Passing the baton of discipleship.* Gloucester: Wide Margin. (Originally published in Japanese in 2010.)

Fukuda, Mitsuo. 2011. *Mentoring like Barnabas.* Gloucester: Wide Margin. (Originally Published in Japanese in 2002.)

Goto, Makito. 2011. *Nihon Senkyo-ron (Missiology in Japan).* Tokyo: E-Grape.

Hiebert, Paul G. 1982. The flaw of the excluded middle. *Missiology.* 10(1): 35–47.

Lim, David. 2003. Towards a radical contextualization paradigm in evangelizing Buddhists. In *Sharing Jesus in the Buddhist world,* ed. David Lim and Steve Spaulding, 71–94. Pasadena: William Carey Library.

Mission Africa. 2005. *How disciple-making gets the job done.* http://www.macmtm.com/making_disciples-e.html (accessed January 2, 2012).

Reuters. August 31, 2011. *Japan's new PM uses sports talk to calm party feuds.* http://in.reuters.com/article/2011/08/31/idINIndia-59070120110831 (accessed January 2, 2012).

Rock, David. 2006. *Quiet leadership: Six steps to transforming performance at work.* New York: Collins.

Schwarz, Christian A. 1996. *Natural church development: A guide to eight essential qualities of healthy churches.* Saint Charles, IL: Churchsmart Resources.

4

Developing Church Leaders Through Apprenticeship

CAROLYN S. JOHNSON

With fellow believers and family members gathered on the shore, Mr. Ahn stood in the shallows and asked the three teen boys to affirm their faith in Jesus. Having done so, the four moved into deeper water where Mr. Ahn baptized the boys in the name of the Father, Son, and Holy Spirit. They descended into the water with their hands in the traditional Thai gesture of respect, the *wai*, and came out with big smiles on their faces.

This baptism was significant for Mr. Ahn as it was the first at which he officiated. The previous afternoon, he had met with his mentor, who reviewed with him the Isaan baptismal ceremony and how to lead it. During the baptism itself, Ahn's mentor stood with the congregation on the shore, offering emotional support to his apprentice and ready to help if necessary.

Mr. Ahn is the primary leader of the young church of seventeen believers in his village, but he has never attended Bible school or seminary. Though he has attended a few seminars, most of his training has occurred through the regular visits of his mentor. His mentor has taught him Isaan worship songs, how to study the Bible and lead others in Bible study, how to conduct Isaan church ceremonies, and how to share the gospel. This is how leadership training is happening in rural Isaan churches, through apprenticeship.

A mentor-apprentice model of leadership training is scripturally sound, theoretically coherent, and culturally suitable in much of the Buddhist world. Apprenticeship is an appropriate and effective method of training women and men as clergy and lay leaders for churches. After looking at the limitations of formal theological education, this paper examines biblical, theoretical, and cultural perspectives of apprenticeship. An example from Northeast Thailand provides evidence of the model's effectiveness.

PERSPECTIVES ON FORMAL THEOLOGICAL EDUCATION

The most common means of training pastors worldwide is through Bible schools and theological seminaries. Most Christian denominations in Buddhist majority countries have followed this pattern. Academic institutions have a role to play in preparing church leaders, particularly in settings in which higher education is common and valued. Other models of leadership development, however, are sometimes more appropriate due to local economic, educational, and political situations. One of the alternatives is apprenticeship. Before examining the mentor-apprentice model, it is useful to consider the limitations of formal theological education.

One limitation is the cost of seminary education. When considering cost, it is not enough to consider the direct costs of tuition, books, etc. The larger cost is often lost income. The traditional approach to seminary education is full-time study, usually at a location distant from the potential leader's home. To give up one's source of income to attend school full-time is a substantial economic sacrifice. In the Buddhist world, maturity is a valued quality in leaders. It is seldom realistic to expect mature people, who typically have families to support, to give up their livelihood to attend school. An apprenticeship approach to leadership training is more feasible in these situations.

Another limitation is the educational level of church members. Seminaries and Bible schools train on an academic level of bachelor's degree or higher. In some settings this is no obstacle as the educational level of the population is high. I served for twenty-one years in Northeast Thailand, where it is a substantial obstacle, particularly for members of village churches. The Thai government has made significant improvements in the quality of education over the past two decades. By 1995 compulsory education was extended to ninth grade, and public education became available through twelfth grade. Completing twelfth grade is now common for young Thais, but as late as the mid-seventies, compulsory education extended only to fourth grade. By the mid-eighties it was sixth grade. Thus, a majority of mature adults in Thai villages have only a fourth or sixth grade formal education. This greatly affects their readiness, or lack thereof, for academically oriented instruction. Even if Bible schools and seminaries were the best way to train them, most rural church leaders lack the educational qualifications to be admitted. As the level of education rises with today's young people, future generations of leaders will be able to handle more challenging book learning alongside the direct input of their mentors.

Regulations regarding religious institutions restrict formal education for church leaders in some contexts. In a number of primarily Buddhist countries, the governments so limit church activities that seminaries are not free to operate effectively. This lack of openness is another reason that apprenticeship may be the most appropriate means to train leaders.

Another reason to consider alternatives to traditional seminary models in training church leaders in Buddhist contexts is the limitations of formal education itself. A number of authors question the value of the academic approach. The disadvantages are expounded by Charles Kraft:

> For most nonwestern churches it is standard procedure to pull potential church leaders out of their home contexts for three years for training in a traditional residential Bible school or seminary setting. This approach disrupts the students' relationships with their people, dislocates the family (if the student is married), trains them informationally rather than practically in an artificial context, often without opportunity for practice of the kind of ministry being trained for and, in many cases, is little short of disastrous personally and relationally. (Kraft 1996, 287)

Kraft accuses the schooling approach to training as lacking the cultivation of desirable behavior as it focuses on transferring knowledge; it tends to be inadequate in terms of advancement of skills.

Echoing Kraft's concerns, Robert Banks notes the failure of semi-naries to adequately prepare servant leaders for the church. He calls for more focus on spiritual formation and skill development. Banks advocates a "missional model" which involves "learning-in-ministry" as opposed to "learning-for-ministry" or "learning-alongside-ministry" (Banks 1999, 226). Mentoring by mature ministers is crucial to Banks' model of developing "head, heart, and hands for ministry" (ibid., 230). In his study of spiritual formation at Thai theological institutions, Richard Herring found that more spiritual formation occurs outside the classroom than through formal instruction. Modeling and mentoring by faculty is so significant in the spiritual formation of students that Herring identifies it as "the *single most important method of spiritual formation* at Thai theological institutions" (Herring 1999, 218). This affirms the value of informal learning, even within a formal program. The two complement one another; in situations where formal academic programs are appropriate, Bible school and seminary educators do well to integrate mentoring into their programs.

BIBLICAL FOUNDATIONS OF APPRENTICESHIP

Jesus did not open a seminary to train his disciples. He used the primary method of leadership training that we see in the Bible—apprenticeship. Jesus offers the most extensive look at this model, but he did not invent it. We see examples of leadership training by apprenticeship in both Old and New Testaments.

Apprenticeship in the Old Testament

Three examples in the Old Testament stand out. Joshua was Moses' apprentice. Elisha was Elijah's apprentice. King Joash was Johoiada's apprentice.

The first clear example of training by apprenticeship in Scripture is Moses and Joshua. Joshua first appears as a warrior, leading the battle against the Amalekites (Ex 17:9–14). He becomes Moses' assistant (Ex 24:13; 33:11). As such, Joshua goes up the mountain with Moses and remains with him while Moses receives the law (Ex 24:13–32:17). Joshua stays at the tent of meeting where God converses with Moses. He gains experience through his close relationship with Moses, as he assists him.

Joshua is clearly recognized as a leader when Moses sends men to scout Canaan (Num 13). One leader from each tribe is chosen for the scouting mission; Joshua is the leader from the tribe of Ephraim. Along with Caleb, Joshua stands up against those afraid of entering Canaan. He exhibits faith in the Lord and in God's ability to give the people the land if they will trust and obey the Lord (Num 14:6–9). His trust in God is rewarded; out of their generation, only Joshua and Caleb are allowed into the Promised Land.

Toward the end of Moses' life, God tells him to commission Joshua as his successor (Deut 3:28). This commissioning occurs in front of the entire assembly (Num 27:15–23). Joshua has served as Moses' assistant for many years. He has been a leader of his tribe for over forty years. He has proved himself faithful and is now ready to lead on his own.

The prophets give us another example of training by apprenticeship. When God commands Elijah to anoint Elisha as his successor (1 Kgs 19:16), Elijah initiates a mentoring relationship with Elisha (1 Kgs 19:19–21). Elisha becomes Elijah's servant, following him wherever he goes and learning from him. He refuses to leave his master (2 Kgs 2), staying with him until Elijah is taken up to heaven. Elisha expects to inherit Elijah's spiritual power (2 Kgs 2:9), and indeed he does (2 Kgs 2:15). From that time on, Elisha is Israel's premier prophet, as Elijah was before him.

Apprenticeship is also the manner of training a king. When his father, King Ahaziah, dies, Joash is an infant (2 Kgs 11). He is hidden for six years to protect him from his grandmother, Athaliah, who has seized power. Joash is raised in the temple, under the guidance of the priest, Jehoiada, who has Joash crowned as king of Judah when he is seven years old. He continues to mentor him throughout his life. Jehoiada desires Joash to be a godly king. At his coronation, "Jehoiada then made a covenant between the LORD and the king and people that they would be the LORD's people" (2 Kgs 11:17). His influence is shown in the summary, "Joash did what was right in the eyes of the LORD all the years Jehoiada the priest instructed him" (2 Kgs 12:2). Jehoiada's mentoring shapes Joash's leadership.

Apprenticeship in the New Testament

Apprenticeship is also the primary pattern of leadership development we see in the New Testament. It is the method Jesus uses to train the apostles. Following his example, it becomes the process by which leaders are trained in the early church.

Jesus devotes much of his ministry to mentoring the apostles, seeking to develop their potential as servant leaders. He teaches them and gives them assignments to develop their skills. The training cycle can be divided into four stages which build on one another. In the first stage, the disciples watch Jesus; this learning by observation continues until Jesus' ascension. The second stage involves the apostles assisting Jesus publicly. The third stage involves the disciples ministering with Jesus' instructions. The final stage is the transition of ministry into the hands of the disciples as Jesus prepares to return to the Father. This four-phase learning cycle is sometimes characterized from the mentor's perspective as 1) "I do, you watch"; 2) "I do, you help"; 3) "You do, I help"; 4) "You do, I watch." Greg Ogden provides a fuller description of these phases (Ogden 2003, 83–97).

Throughout these phases, Jesus exemplifies the apprenticeship learning cycle of teaching, practice, and reflection. After the disciples watch and listen to Jesus for a period of time, he sends out twelve of them to minister (Mark 6:7; cf. Matt 10 and Luke 9). The Twelve return and report what they have done and taught (Mark 6:30; Luke 9:10). Jesus takes them away to rest and gives them more teaching. On occasion he tests their understanding before giving them further teaching (Luke 9:18–27). As the apostles continue to get experience in ministry, we see another instance of debriefing in Mark 9:28–29. A similar cycle is illustrated in the sending of the seventy-two, their reporting back to Jesus, and receiving further training (Luke 10:1–23).

Jesus uses every occasion as a learning opportunity for his apprentices. He explains things to them as they walk together from place to place (Mark 8:27–33). The disciples accompany him wherever he goes. They eat together and travel together. Life together contributes to their training.

Jesus understands the value of concentrating on a small number of apprentices. That is why he chooses the twelve apostles and takes them aside to focus on them (Mark 9:30–31; 10:32). It is worth noting that Jesus' method is a group process, not one-on-one, though he does sometimes narrow his focused training to a small group. From the Twelve he chooses three to give extra attention—Peter, James, and John. These three receive the most intense training as they accompany Jesus to the mountain of transfiguration (Mark 9:2), to the healing of Jairus' daughter (Luke 8:51), and to pray with him in Gethsemane (Matt 26: 36–46; Mark 14:32–34). As one might expect, these three emerge as the leaders of the apostles in the early chapters of Acts.

The pattern of leadership training by apprenticeship continues in the early church. It appears in Acts and in Paul's letters. Paul himself has some formal theological training, studying under Gamaliel (Acts 22:3). But that is not sufficient to prepare him for his ministry. After Paul becomes a Christian, Barnabas mentors Paul. When the church is still afraid of their former persecutor, Barnabas introduces him to the apostles and speaks on his behalf (Acts 9:27). Later he seeks out Paul in Tarsus and mentors him through his early ministry in Antioch (Acts 11:24–26). By Acts chapters 13–14, Barnabas and Paul have become colleagues. We also see Barnabas mentor John Mark (Acts 12:25; 13:5; 15:37–39).

As Barnabas mentors him, so Paul in turn mentors many other emerging leaders. One that we know by name is Timothy, whose potential Paul recognizes when Timothy is still a youth, and whom he invites to accompany him (Acts 16:1–4; 18:5). By Acts 19:22, Timothy is referred to as one of Paul's helpers or assistants, sent out by Paul to minister to the church in Macedonia. In the letter to the Romans, Paul refers to Timothy as "my co-worker" (Rom 16:21). Erastus is also referred to this way; he is another of Paul's apprentices (Acts 19:22). Paul trains apprentices as they work alongside him in a team. In one case, seven of them are listed by name as accompanying Paul, who is attended by

Luke at the same time (Acts 20:4–5). Like Jesus, Paul works with groups, investing in these people, developing them as leaders for the church.

It is not clear if there is any mentoring relationship between Paul and Priscilla and Aquila or if they are colleagues from the beginning of their relationship. We do know that they live and work together (Acts 18:1–3) and they travel together (Acts 18:18–19). It is evident that Priscilla and Aquila mentor Apollos briefly (Acts 18:24–28), preparing him for a more fruitful ministry for Christ.

Paul's vision for leadership training appears also in his letters. Separated from his apprentices, he mentors them through correspondence. He tells Timothy to continue the mentor-apprentice chain by passing on to others the training he has received: "The things you have heard me say in the presence of many witnesses entrust to reliable people who will also be qualified to teach others" (2 Tim 2:2).

One aspect of leadership Paul emphasizes in his letters is leading by example. He tells Timothy to "set an example for the believers in speech, in conduct, in love, in faith and in purity" (1 Tim 4:12). Similarly he instructs Titus, "In everything set them an example by doing what is good. In your teaching show integrity, seriousness and soundness of speech that cannot be condemned" (Titus 2:7–8). Paul himself lives as a model to the churches, calling them to imitate him (1 Cor 4:16; 2 Thess 3:7). He elaborates in Philippians 4:9, "Whatever you have learned or received or heard from me, or seen in me—put it into practice." His aim is to raise up new leaders like himself.

E. Glenn Hinson's overview of spiritual formation of leaders throughout church history provides additional historical perspective (Hinson 1999). He notes that in the early church, leadership formation took place on the job. He traces the mentor-apprentice pattern from Jesus with his disciples through Paul and on for several generations, until the conversion of Constantine caused rapid expansion and a change in leadership training models.

The primary means by which biblical leaders train others is by mentoring them. We have several Old Testament examples of this mentor-apprentice model. It is also the method used by the Lord Jesus and the early church leaders. From a scriptural point of view, apprenticeship is an appropriate and effective process by which to train leaders. Training church leaders through apprenticeship has a strong biblical and historical basis.

SOCIAL SCIENCE PERSPECTIVES ON LEADERSHIP DEVELOPMENT

Having set a biblical foundation, the social sciences offer additional support for the mentor-apprentice model. Learning and communication theories are relevant, as are anthropological studies. Having spent two decades ministering in Northeast Thailand, I will detail that cultural milieu.

Learning includes the dimensions of knowledge, abilities, and attitudes. A number of authors note the importance of including all three in an educational program (Kinsler and Emery 1991; and Kraft 1996, for example). Formal education is most typically found in schools, where large groups of learners are taught according to a set program; it tends to focus on the knowledge element. Informal learning takes place through modeling, storytelling, informal talking, and doing things together; it is an excellent method of skill development. Nonformal education describes learning which is more planned than informal education, but lacks the strictures of formal education. Seminars are one form of nonformal education. As was noted above, seminaries have often focused on the knowledge element while neglecting the development of attitudes and skills. Combining formal, informal, and nonformal learning experiences maximizes learning and provides avenues for the development of "head, heart, and hands" (Conner 1997, 284; Elliston 1995, 172; Kraft 1996, 288; Patterson and Currah). George Patterson and Galen Currah note that it is not necessary to use a classroom approach to incorporate formal aspects of learning. Apprenticeship can include a formal aspect if there is either a set course sequence or a menu of courses to be completed in the order most relevant to a learner's situation.

Robert Clinton's leadership development framework is relevant here (Clinton 1988). He observes that emerging leaders in the Inner-life Growth phase will be focused more on personal spiritual development.

Those at the next stage, Ministry Maturing, need skill development. These stages may overlap one another. It is not uncommon for personal spiritual growth and ministry development to occur simultaneously in emerging leaders of new, multiplying congregations. Leadership development should provide for both and balanced according to the individual's stage of development. Such individualization is an advantage of apprenticeship. Clinton sees formal training as an optional component to leadership development, whereas informal and nonformal components are essential.

Mentoring

Secular writers affirm the value of informal and nonformal learning. Experience and mentoring are means of developing leaders in any sector. Max DePree asserts that one becomes a leader primarily through leading. DePree and John Kotter both see leadership development as a long process of increasing skill through the learning that comes from experience. In an example from Southeast Asia, David Conner affirms that mentoring is a valuable means of developing leadership in the Isaan region of Thailand.

Spiritual maturity being essential, mentoring the faith walk of emerging leaders is an important aspect of Christian leadership development, emphasized by several authors. Stacy Rinehart asserts that "a major thrust of our equipping process is to encourage an authentic relationship and intimacy with God" (Rinehart 1998, 131). Edgar Elliston calls for mentoring as a means of "relational empowerment" which will effectively develop emerging leaders (Elliston 1995, 172–173). He notes that informal mentoring has a number of advantages over formal education. Personal spiritual development is the central concern of E. Glenn Hinson (Hinson 1999), who observes that leaders minister out of who they are in Christ more than out of a set of acquired skills. Hinson believes we should return to the mentor-apprentice model used by Jesus, Paul, and the early church.

Enoch Wan proposes "relational realism" epistemology (2006, 1–4). To put it succinctly, relational realism as a theory of epistemology postulates that we come to know through relationship. We know God through what is revealed in the process of the relationship between God and humans. Our Triune God is inherently relational. Rinehart observes, "Relationship is at the core of the Godhead, and in that relationship we see the fundamental spiritual principles regarding leadership" (Rinehart 1998, 88). We know other people through our relationships with them, which often lead to opportunities for learning from one another. Communication theory supports the concept of relational realism. Donald Smith explains, "It is in the individual that the message is made visible, and through the individual that God's truth can be perceived" (1992, 115). We were created in the image of the Trinity as relational beings. That truth shapes how we know. In Smith's words,

> Sharing information—"facts"—only appears to be the primary reason for interaction. The unspoken and basic need is for relationship with people. These relationships directly and indirectly influence everything we seek to communicate. This is the *social meaning* of communication, something that lies beyond the words or signs used. (ibid., 109)

Smith also proposes that "communication is a relationship" (ibid., 39), which he sees modeled by God:

> When God wanted to speak to human beings, he did not send a tract or preach a sermon. He came in person. His life was completely involved with people, sharing their language, experience, and culture and seeing to the very core of their values and false assumptions. The incarnational model of communication that Jesus gave us needs to be carefully studied and understood; it is our pattern for effective completion of our task. (ibid., 37)

Effective communication is built on relationship. This is the reason that informal interactions between mentor and apprentice are so important. Smith's theoretical propositions, "Communication is involvement" and "Communication is a process," provide further rationale for including mentoring in a leadership development program. The mentor-apprentice model is based on the understanding that communication is a process requiring involvement and relationship.

Learning and communication theories affirm the value of mentoring, particularly a mentoring approach that combines formal, informal, and nonformal learning opportunities. It appears that apprenticeship is a theoretically coherent means of developing church leaders.

Nonformal Leadership Development Programs in Thailand

Looking more narrowly at examples in Thailand, we see that in spite of the dominance of formal academic programs, nonformal programs training leaders for rural churches have been used in several regions of the country. In their historical studies of the Thai church, both Alex Smith and Samuel Kim lament the shortcomings of leadership development programs in Thailand, particularly the tendency to follow Western academic models of training. Kim contrasts the academic seminary approach with that of the Christian Service Training Center in Northern Thailand (CSTC) (Kim 1980, 148–149). The CSTC trained leaders at a lower academic level than the seminary. The graduates fit well into the rural situation, having both the training and the attitudes necessary for leading village churches. Smith reports on a similar program used to train lay leaders in Central Thailand (Smith 1977, 221–227). Participants engaged in home study and seminar sessions, so they had a combination of methods. The training was multidimensional, focusing on four areas: biblical knowledge, evangelism, pastoral care, and leadership. Emphasis was given to putting lessons into practice from week to week. Preliminary results were evaluated as effective in training leaders for rural churches. More recently, Mark Leighton found that the Home Bible Seminary (HBS) program, centered on inductive Bible study supplemented by tutoring and seminars, was successful in increasing biblical understanding, growing spiritual life, discipline, and improving leaders' teaching (Leighton 2000). The program was determined to be weak on the practical side; only thirty-three percent of participants felt that HBS had helped them to be good church leaders. Leighton observes that the Bible study approach was particularly helpful for leaders at Inner-life Growth and Life Maturity stages of Clinton's model. Those at the Ministry Maturity stage feel a need for skills training, which was lacking in the HBS program. In Northeast Thailand, the organizations of the Thailand Covenant Church have used both TEE (theological education by extension) and district leadership training meetings as vehicles of leadership training. These methods were chosen primarily because of the failure of Bible schools to train leaders for the village churches and the effectiveness of equipping for ministry in context (De Neui 2002). In 2004, the Lower Isaan Foundation for Enablement began to use a mentor-apprentice model as the primary vehicle for leadership training.

Cultural Traditions of Apprenticeship in Northeast Thailand

Teaching through a master-apprentice relationship is an Isaan tradition. Older monks serve as master teachers for apprentices studying herbal medicine, astrology, magic, arts, or trade. The skills of the monks at a given temple determine which arts or trades are taught there. Trades passed on in this manner include carpentry, making agricultural tools, making tile or bricks, painting, and body tattooing. It is not uncommon for monks to later disrobe and earn their living as artisans.

In traditional Isaan society, young men could also train for an occupation outside the temple. They would find a master of the craft they wanted to learn and ask to be taken on as an apprentice. If they were learning from an elder in their own village, they would live with their own family. Otherwise, they would live with their master's family. The learning period differed according to the skill being learned; it could be a few days or several months. The study of herbal medicine or traditional singing, dancing, and playing musical instruments required longer training periods.

The master (*khru*) did not simply teach his apprentice a trade, but modeled the values and lifestyle appropriate to the artisan. Seri Phongphit elucidates,

> *Khru* is an essential concept in traditional village culture. As noted previously, a *khru* is not only a person who has passed knowledge to his disciples, but personifies the whole process

of the passing of wisdom, knowledge and skills through the generations. ... People who are *khru* not only 'teach', in the modern sense of the word, telling, advising and explaining to their disciple, and providing know-how, but also disseminating a 'spirit', a knowledge incorporating values and spirit, life, energy, and other forces; in fact, everything that the *khru* has and is, is given to the disciple. One might say that *khru* give their 'life' to their student followers. (1990, 75–76)

It is striking how the master-disciple relationship described by Phongphit mirrors Jesus' method of training his disciples. This type of master-apprentice relationship is less common now in Isaan, as the government schools provide education for all young people, including vocational training at the secondary school level, but it still exists in some trades. Using an apprenticeship model that was more prevalent in earlier years is one way to allow adult learners to learn at their own pace and is flexible enough to adjust to varying levels of educational background. The mentor and apprentice model of training fits Isaan culture and coincides with calls to train for ministry within the context for ministry. Banks asserts that theological education "should orient itself primarily around 'in service' ministry activities, within which intellectual, spiritual, and practical concerns form a seamless whole" (1999, 126). Apprenticeship suits these criteria beautifully.

The Experience of the Lower Isaan Foundation for Enablement

Apprenticeship appears to be appropriate for churches in the Buddhist world, but is such a model effective? In mid-2004, the Lower Isaan Foundation for Enablement (LIFE) began to use apprenticeship as the primary means of leadership training along with a two-year process of action research to evaluate its effectiveness. During that period of time, mentoring chains were developed. The LIFE staff mentored village church leaders and encouraged them to pass on what they were learning to emerging leaders in their own churches and daughter churches. Toward the end of the evaluation period, the team sensed a need to add more structure to the mentoring program and decided to use *Train and*

Multiply materials, adding a more formal element to the program but maintaining flexibility due to the menu approach of *Train and Multiply.* The process and results are detailed by Carolyn Johnson (2007, 134–164). The LIFE team saw mentoring improve leadership training as evidenced by more balance between formal, informal, and nonformal training, an increase in the number of apprentices, apprentices' growing skills in planning, and an increase in emerging leaders' pastoral activities, such as visiting sick church members and visiting seekers.

Effectiveness was confirmed by quantitative analysis. It was hypothesized that a combination of formal, informal, and nonformal learning experiences would provide the training necessary to develop effective leaders who would both empower church members and mentor new leaders. It was further hypothesized that empowered members would lead to evangelism and to new churches being planted. There was an increase in apprentices mentoring others, but it was not statistically significant. What was statistically significant was the increase in church membership. In the two years under examination, the number of churches increased from twenty-four to twenty-nine; total membership increased from 247 to 274 (ibid., 160). When mentored churches are compared to non-mentored churches there is a more striking difference (ibid., 160–163). In mentored churches, the mean membership increased from 9.3 in 2004 to 10.9 in 2006, an increase which a statistical test showed as very significant, meaning it cannot be attributed to chance. The mean membership in non-mentored churches increased from 7.9 in 2004 to 8.4 in 2006. The test did not show statistical significance, indicating that the slight increase in the membership of non-mentored churches could have occurred by chance. When we contrast the statistical analysis of churches in the mentoring chain with those not being mentored, it becomes clear that mentoring leaders has had an impact on church growth and church planting. The most striking results occurred in a church in which LIFE used a plural leadership approach. A team of mentors trained a team of local church leaders. One mentor worked with church leaders to develop their skills as Bible teachers. Another mentor, more gifted in evangelism and church planting, focused on that area. This church and its daughter churches saw the most growth. In a relatively short period of time, the effectiveness of apprenticeship was confirmed.

CONCLUSION

A mentor-apprentice model is the primary method of leadership training in the Bible and in early church history. Its viability for today is affirmed by educational theory, cultural traditions, and the effectiveness of apprenticeship in a church planting situation. Apprenticeship does face challenges in its implementation. Consistency and thoroughness require a commitment that is hard to find outside formal programs. Young churches often do best with plural leadership, with responsibilities based on spiritual gifts. A one-size-fits-all method, even a menu-based one, is probably not optimal. Mentors need to discover how to most effectively train apprentices with differing spiritual gifts, while seeing that all grow in spiritual maturity. Finally, the push for more formal education in Thailand and elsewhere causes some to doubt the value of an apprenticeship approach in spite of evidence of its effectiveness. None of these challenges is insurmountable. We need to hold on to the truth that the mentor-apprentice model is scripturally sound, theoretically coherent, culturally appropriate, and can be effective for training church leaders in the Buddhist world.

References

Banks, Robert. 1999. *Reenvisioning theological education: Exploring a missional alternative to current models.* Grand Rapids: Eerdmans.

Clinton, J. Robert. 1988. *The making of a leader.* Colorado Springs: NavPress.

Conner, David W. 1997. *Personal power, authority, and influence: Cultural foundations for leadership and leadership formation in Northeast Thailand and implications for adult leadership training.* Ann Arbor: UMI.

De Neui, Paul. 2002. The development of a multi-dimensional approach to contextualization in Northeast Thailand. ThM thesis, Fuller Seminary. http://www.thaicov.org.

Elliston, Edgar J. 1995. Developing the development worker. In *Serving with the poor in Asia,* eds. Tetsunao Yamamoni, Bryant L. Myers, and David Conner, 165–177. Monrovia: MARC.

Herring, Richard S. 1999. Spiritual formation at six Thai evangelical theological institutions. DMin thesis, Columbia Biblical Seminary and School of Missions.

Hinson, E. Glenn. 1999. *Spiritual preparation for Christian leadership.* Nashville: Upper Room Books.

Johnson, Carolyn S. 2007. Developing servant leaders in rural Isaan churches through apprenticeship. DMiss diss., Western Seminary.

Kim, Samuel I. 1980. *The unfinished mission in Thailand: The uncertain Christian impact on the Buddhist heartland.* Seoul: East-West Center for Missions Research and Development.

Kinsler, F. Ross, and James H. Emery, eds. 1991. *Opting for change: A handbook on evaluation and planning for theological education by extension.* Pasadena: William Carey Library.

Kraft, Charles H. 1996. *Anthropology for Christian witness.* Maryknoll: Orbis.

Leighton, Mark W. 2000. *Appraisal of the Home Bible Seminary: A leadership training program in Thailand.* Portland: TREN.

Ogden, Greg. 2003.*Transforming discipleship: Making disciples a few at a time.* Downers Grove: InterVarsity Press.

Patterson, George, and Galen Currah. *Classroom instruction and mentoring compared.* http://www.mentorandmultiply.com.

Phongphit, Seri, with Kevin Hewison. 1990. *Thai village life: Culture and transition in the Northeast.* Bangkok: Mooban Press.

Rinehart, Stacy T. 1998. *Upside down: The paradox of servant leadership.* Colorado Springs: NavPress.

Smith, Alex. 1977. *Strategy to multiply rural churches: A central Thailand case study.* Bangkok: OMF Publishers.

Smith, Donald K. 1992. *Creating understanding.* Grand Rapids: Zondervan.

Wan, Enoch. 2006. The paradigm of "Relational Realism." *Occasional Bulletin.* Wheaton: Evangelical Missiological Society, Spring.

5

Developing Transformational Leaders for Church Multiplication Movements in the Buddhist World

DAVID S. LIM

Evangelicals were made aware of the unreached people groups (UPGs) within nations by Dr. Ralph Winter in Lausanne 1974. Yet why, almost forty years later, have we hardly decreased the number of the unevangelized in the world today?[1] Can't we reach them more speedily and more effectively? And can we train missional Christians to do this task, especially in the Buddhist world?

This paper ventures to answer two questions: First, can the UPGs (from families to nations) be reached effectively? Our reply is that they can be evangelized rapidly through church multiplication movements (CMMs; also called church-planting movements, CPMs), especially the contextualized ones called "Jesus Movements" (JMs; also called "Insider or People Movements"). And they can also be discipled and transformed holistically through community development (CD). These two components of "Transformational Mission" (TM) constitute the vision and curricular content of "Transformational (or Integral)[2] Leadership Development" (TLD).

---

1 At the end of 2010, Joshua Project (www.joshua project.net/) reported that 6,847 of the 16,562 people groups on earth have no gospel access; that is 41.3% of all people groups are unreached. Johnson et al 2010:29 show that global Christianity (including 60% Roman Catholics) has declined slightly from 34.8% in 1910 to 33.2% in 2010; they also uncovered the facts that 86% of religionists globally do not personally know a Christian, and non-Christians in Asia are more isolated from Christians than in any other continent in the world (p. 34). And if present trends continue, 1.95 billion (24.5%) will still be unreached by 2025. Perhaps worse is the statistical trend that Christianity will only be 33.8% of the world's population in 2025, and 35% by 2050.

2 "Transformational" emphasizes the result, whereas "integral" (including ecological, sociological, anthropological, political, economic, cultural/aesthetic, spiritual and theological) stresses the nature of the training process. Cf. Gnanakan 2007.

The second question is: How can we effectively develop leaders to do such transformational mission well? Movements will grow and expand according to the rate of the development of their leaders. This work's second half will describe what the TLD methodology looks like. What we need is to replicate in each nation or people group the best practices that are already being implemented in several evangelical organizations, especially Christian development organizations (such as World Vision, Compassion, etc.), campus ministries (especially Navigators, Campus Crusade for Christ International, and International Fellowship of Evangelical Students), mission agencies (especially those linked to the International Orality Network), and particularly in the writer's institution called Asian School for Development and Cross-cultural Studies (ASDECS) in the Philippines.[3]

TLD VISION: SOCIETAL TRANSFORMATION

In recent years, especially through the Lausanne Movement, evangelicals have come to recognize a common objective for our mission: to make disciples of nations includes "teaching them to obey all that [Christ has] commanded" (Matt 28:18–20). "Transformation" is the favorite term that has surfaced to denote this goal in proclaiming the whole gospel of the kingdom of God. It means the restoration of *shalom* in the world through the establishment of Christ-centered and Bible-based communities of love, righteousness, justice, and peace (Isa 65:19–25; Rom 12:1–15:7; cf. Rev 21:24–27). It brings about harmony and reconciliation, whereby people are invited to repentance and faith in Jesus Christ, and then discipled in faith-communities that seek to build right relationships with God, their neighbors, creation, and their own selves (Matt 22:37–39; 2 Cor 10:5). Every person and community/people group will have been enabled to become what God intended each of them to be (Matt 5:1–7:12; Rom 12:1–21; Eph 2:1–10; 4:17–24).

3ASDECS is a nine-year-old Manila-based training consortium composed of 3 seminaries, 6 Christian development organizations, 4 mission agencies, 3 denominations, and 16 individuals. It offers modular courses leading to master's degrees in business administration, community development, development management, and transformational leadership. It also offers nonformal training modules through its Center for Transformational Development. Its website is www.asdecs.com.

The integral goals of transformational mission (TM) are saturation evangelism and community transformation. Whether the whole people group turns to Christ or not, we hope that the populace will have been empowered (given authority) to become mature and responsible (not dependent) adults who can make dignified and wise decisions for their individual and communal lives (including to be for or against Christ). They would be active participants (not passive spectators) in tackling issues that affect their lives and destinies in the light of God's Word.

Such lofty goals seem impossible, and indeed they are, humanly speaking. Yet the Bible reveals that our God is eager to have all peoples redeemed and transformed (1Tim 2:3–5; 2 Pet 3:9; Luke 15:3–7), and his Spirit is at work to make the "fields ripe for harvest" (John 16:7–11; cf. 4:34–38). In fact God will not end world history until this harvest is reaped (Matt 24:14). God must have intended his mission to be achieved (and soon) in simple ways, though not without cost. Christ did not intend his Great Commission to take this long to have hell filled with more people than heaven after almost 2,000 years since his salvific death on the cross. It seems clear that it is his church that has failed to follow the Spirit's movement to send more laborers into the harvest (mainly due to inertia effected by its burdensome and heavy church structures), and the few laborers have mainly failed to use the right strategies to reap this harvest. May I suggest what the two right strategies should be?

Strategy #1: Church Multiplication Movements

In recent years, especially since 1999[4], the missionary community has (re)discovered God's simple "master plan of world evangelization."[5] The secret formula is CMM through disciple-making in small groups—often called house churches.[6] The goal is to do rapid church multiplication, so that as many converts as possible are made to become quality witnesses

4We thank the Southern Baptist International Mission Board that had David Garrison research and publish a monograph (1999), which was reproduced entirely in USCWM's *Mission Frontiers* in April 2000. This has been expanded in his book (Garrison 2004), and updated recently in *Mission Frontiers* 33.2 (March–April 2011).

5Cf. Coleman 1964; Eims 1981. Also cf. Allen 1962, 1962a; Donovan 1978; and Lim 2004.

6This contrasts "church multiplication" (hence, multi-church) from "church growth" of mega-churches, cell-churches and G-12; cf. Simson 2001; Petersen 1992; Neighbor 1990; Comiskey 1999 and Zdero 2004. Also cf. Snyder 1975; Boff 1986; Ringma 1992; Lim 2001 and 2004.

and disciple-makers (servant leaders) as soon as possible. Saturation evangelism even in hostile UPGs is possible, perhaps only through CMMs. And thank God, this has been done in China and India (Garrison 2004, 49–64 and 286–291), and somewhat faintly in Cambodia (Carlton 2000, cf. Garrison 2004, 68–74), Mongolia (ibid., 65–67), Myanmar, and many places, mostly in recent years.[7]

The fastest documented strategy is "Training for Trainers" (T4T), through which an American-Chinese was able to disciple thirty believers in China to become witnesses and disciple-makers for Christ—in an amazing way! Within six months, they had more than 4,000 baptized members in 327 house churches; in twelve months, more than 12,000 baptized members in 908 house churches; and in twenty-four months, 104,542 in 9,320 house churches. He began by just training them to compose and memorize their three-minute testimonies, and then each shared his or her testimony with five family members, friends, workmates, or neighbors. Those who responded positively were invited to a cell meeting which had a six-session curriculum: 1) assurance of salvation, 2) prayer, 3) daily devotions, 4) body life in a house church, 5) understanding God and his will, and 6) witnessing, which means learning to share their testimonies with at least five people close to them and start a new house church with them also.[8]

This CMM model approximates our Lord Jesus' own strategy: To start his world transformation movement, he called twelve ordinary people (almost all rural folks) and discipled them for a while (Mark 3:13–15). Then he sent them out two by two (that's six pairs) to make twelve disciples each (Matthew 9:35–10:16). When he sent out disciples the second time, he did not commission the Twelve, but the "seventy-two others" (Luke 10:1, 17). These were sent out two by two also (that's thirty-six pairs) to make twelve disciples each, thereby making 432 new disciples in all. First Corinthians 15:6 mentions that after the resurrection, our Lord appeared to more than 500 (432 + 72 + 11) brethren. If these 500 paired up, that's 250 making twelve new disciples each, they would be able to disciple exactly 3,000 new converts, which actually hap-

---

7For a historical view, cf. Zdero 2004:59–69. For its present global scope, cf. Garrison 2004:35–168; and Zdero 2004:69–76.

8Garrison 2004:286–291 & 307-314. The best resource is Smith 2011. Also in http://t4tonline.org/wp-content/uploads/2011/02/t4tOnline-Trainers-Manual.pdf.

pened on the day of Pentecost. All converts were baptized immediately, since the apostles knew they would all be followed up and discipled in at least 250 house churches in Jerusalem ("from house to house," Acts 5:42; cf. Acts 2:41–47). No wonder their numbers increased daily.

To become a CMM leader, one just has to be a "disciple-maker"[9] who has to learn only two basic skills: friendship evangelism and leading disciple-making groups (DG). 1) She or he learns how to share the gospel and their personal testimony after establishing friendship with each of a few non-Christian relatives, friends, colleagues, and even strangers. Converts and potential converts are then brought to her or his DG, or better, encouraged to start a DG or house church at a convenient place and time.[10] And then for quality follow-up, 2) she or he also learns how to lead small group discussions, facilitating meetings in which all attendees can participate in setting their agenda and seeking the proper interpretation and application of God's Word (through *lectio divina* or the devotional use of Scripture) for the issues relevant to their personal lives and social contexts (cf. 1 Cor 14:26); hereby they learn intuitively how to meditate and listen to God regularly in their personal devotions.

Moreover, believers can also be trained to share their faith with their kin and friends wisely as soon as possible. The simplest method today is called the Viral Simple Bible Study (VSBS). It asks only three questions of any chosen text: 1) What does the text say in your own words? 2) What does God require of us from the text? And 3) Who are the three to five people you can share what we learned with before we meet again next time? The leader aims to empower each disciple to do likewise (as in 2 Tim 2:2) by leaving them as soon as possible, so she or he can make new disciples elsewhere.

Thus, the goal of transformation through saturation evangelism is made possible through CMM. Reason and experience seem to indi-

---

9 Though often used interchangeably with "disciple" and "discipleship," "disciple-maker" is used here to emphasize the qualitative maturity and the quantitative reproducing capacity of the TM worker to make disciples who will disciple others (cf. 2 Tim 2:2).

10 Those who work in oral cultures should learn to do "chronological Bible storying," cf. ION/LCWE 2010; Gauran 1991. If there is no Bible in their native tongue, the native converts should be encouraged to lead the translation efforts in close consultation with trained linguists and translators. Among nonliterates, one can also use "oral Bibles," memorization, audiovisuals, songs, and educated youth, cf. Garrison 2004:184–186. Those who believe in "spiritual warfare" can also develop "prayer walking," healing and deliverance "power ministry" skills to deal with the "spirit world" as they evangelize.

cate that such multiplication can happen only if the first converts are not brought in close contact with the traditional local churches—for obvious reasons: they will not only be exposing themselves to danger (being known as converts prematurely), but they will also become ineffective witnesses very soon, since they will be decontextualized from their culture (into a Christian subculture) rapidly (cf. Garrison 2004, 194–196 and 245–249). It is best for new converts to form new DGs or house churches.

This TM strategy of contextualized CMM has been called "insider movements" (IM).[11] Though controversial when it was first introduced in 1998 (Travis 1998 and 2000), this approach has been gradually accepted in Western—especially American—nondenominational missions, but also in Asian—including some Korean—missions, especially those in the Asia Frontier Missions Initiative (AFMI) and most recently by the Asia Missions Association (AMA) during its 10th Triennial Consultation in Jakarta in November 2010 (cf. Lim 2003 and 2008). It has entered the mainstream of evangelical missions very recently as "Jesus Movements" (JM) through the May–June 2011 (33.3) issue of *Mission Frontiers*.

Strategy #2: Community Development

Yet to be really effective, especially to disciple and transform an entire family, clan, community, or tribe, CMM/JM should be combined with the community development (CD) strategy. The process involves not only approaching the people group holistically, but also doing so in as contextual and empowering a way as possible, so as not to create dependency but rather to help the whole community grow together to its fullest potential.[12]

By holistic, we mean that the point of entry and eventual development should cover the entire range of cultural and social life of the people group. Hence missionaries can enter through any entry platform (read: area of expertise) that serves the community, either as professionals (like medical personnel, English or any teachers, managers, engineers,

---

11On the "Biblical Basis of Insider Movements," see Appendix 2.

12For secular models, cf. Andres 1988. For Christian models, cf. Bobo 1986; Linthicum 1991; Myers 1999; Samuel & Sugden 1999; Suderman 1999; Yamamori et al 1995 and 1998; and Lim 2010a.

etc.), as businesspersons (like setting up computer or language schools, travel agencies, beach resorts, etc.), or even as skilled workers (caregivers, drivers, seamen, domestic helpers, etc.). The harvest can indeed be joined through any role, as long as the worker has the right perspective and skills.

By contextual, we mean that the needs or issues to be tackled are derived from the local situation of the target group itself. Every people and community has their own unique sets of problems and aspirations; thus, rather than going among them with a preconceived message (beyond Christ and him crucified) and a prepackaged strategy, the missionary must be willing to learn from the populace, be appreciative of their culture (except perhaps for the five percent that are sinful,[13] which have to be transformed) and be flexible in her or his ways (cf. 1 Cor 9:19–23).

And by empowering, we mean that the missionary should identify herself or himself as a servant-leader and work with (not for) the people. The key is for one's ministry to have a clear commitment to encourage the local people themselves to be responsible for the welfare of their own people and community life. In the end, the people should be able to say, "We did it ourselves"! Hence we should plant indigenous simple churches (actually networks of house fellowships) which are from the start self-governing (with their own leaders), self-supporting (with their own budget and funding), self-propagating (with their own programs of action/ministry), and self-theologizing (with their own statement of faith), which aim at community conversion to Christ (not to a particular brand of Christianity) and community transformation through their obedience to Christ's law (loving one another and their neighbors and enemies to the ends of the earth) (Lim 2011, 21).

In order to achieve all these, CD consists of only two very important community organizing skills: 1) immersion, which is to spend time with the people to learn about their culture, including their language, social structure, values, beliefs, leaders, and so forth; it is best to learn basic field research techniques for this. And then 2) core group formation—upon working with the people to discern a local need or issue to tackle, the worker facilitates a process by which a leadership core is

---

[13]The sins are idolatry, individualism (pride), (personal) immorality, and (social) injustice.

formed to tackle the problem or attain their aspiration.[14] In Luke 10, Jesus taught his disciples to enter communities simply (v. 4) and just focus on finding and living with (and evangelizing the household of) a local "man of peace" (v. 6), who is usually connected if not related to the community leaders (see Appendix 1, especially step #3). Local resources are tapped and maximized before any foreign help or funds are considered. Even before the successful completion of the program or project, the missionary may be able to leave when she or he sees that the people can finish it on their own.

Through CMM/JM, the ideal of an indigenous movement that is self-governing, self-supporting, self-propagating, and self-theologizing is easily achieved. Even from the beginning, local leadership is developed and empowered to continue the multiplication of simple churches. Yet when CMM is combined with CD, the latter provides at least four more advantages: 1) It becomes possible to befriend and reach community leaders (the influencers) from the start, thereby hastening the process of societal transformation. 2) It shows Christianity's relevance to any local need or issue. 3) It avoids creating dependency, since local leadership and resources are considered first and foremost. And 4) the programs and activities are contextualized and sustainable; thus the worker can leave as soon as the momentum is discernible. Such is the wonder of TM/JM. Should these CMM and CD skills not be the main emphases in the training of Christians, especially in the Buddhist world? TM has already proven to be effective indeed in many regions in China, India, Cambodia (Sluka and Budiardjo 1995, 47–78), Sri Lanka (Stephens 1995, 103–115), and many others (Lim 2008 and 2010), which are starting to be known only in the past few years.

Even if TM has already occurred in a people group, the church will still need to be constantly in missional mode: each person and family has to be reached (can 100 percent conversion rate ever be reached?), and every child (new generation) has to be discipled. In the Old Testament, even if the whole of Israel was nominally "reached," God institutional-ized house churches (Deut 6); celebrative worship in the Temple was not weekly, but only three times a year (16:16) (cf. Appendix 2; Lim 2008 and Simson 2001). Churches among nominally "reached" peoples

---

14For more details, see Andres 1988:5–23 and 35–43.

should continue to use this TM paradigm of lay-led house fellowships lest they retrogress to become a UPG again, as has happened in many post-Christian nations today.

TLD METHODOLOGY

We proceed to delineate the training methodology that will produce effective TM leaders for ministry in Asia, especially among UPGs in the Buddhist world. What is the best training paradigm (pedagogy and programs) by which we can train missionaries who will be able to effectively bring about TM? We need to educate and train leaders with the attitudes, understanding, and skills for TM. For leadership development to be truly transformative, just as the curriculum has to be holistic, contextual, and empowering (as seen above), its training methodology should be simple, people-centered, practical, contextual, and participatory.

Simple

In order to attain the integral objectives of TLD, the methods have to be simple, so that even nonliterates (which are the majority of UPGs) can do them and replicate them. Our students should learn to define basic Christianity in simple forms that can be the basis for making contextual (read: multiform) applications, even by the poor.

All successful CMM models have developed simple training strategies to train as many believers as possible (if possible, every believer) to evangelize, disciple, and plant churches that plant churches. They include training in basic skills in friendship evangelism, leading small group discussions, hermeneutics and theologizing, and dynamics of social change,[15] learning styles of the poor, and so forth, all within the context of nonformal field ministry programs where the mentors are TM leaders themselves. The simpler the TLD, the easier and faster the

---

15 TLD must explore and develop *non-violent* means (both a Christian and a Buddhist value) to challenge oppressive structures. The choice is not between the status quo and change; it is between violent change and peaceful change. J. F. Kennedy said, "They who do not make peaceful change possible make violent change inevitable." We must seek new ways to resolve conflicts, injustice, and underdevelopment.

multiplication potential. No need to construct buildings (except homes and community service structures) nor provide subsidies to train simple folks to do TM. The use of external funding has often led to the slowing down, if not the death, of CMM/JMs.[16]

For CD, simplicity in all aspects of ministry and training is also required in order to maximize people empowerment. Even among the poor masses, indigenous leadership for community transformation can be developed from the beginning. Then each ministry can be a rapidly self-organized and self-sustaining movement that hardly needs external input and support. With simplicity in TLD, missionaries may be able to leave the area soon. In fact, the sooner they leave, the better (Garrison 2004, 186–189 and 193–194). Why? Because the new local believers will be able to do better (read: more contextualized) replication of TM among their people.

Relational

The second major mark of TLD is its people-centeredness and people-orientation. People need to see ideas lived out in practice before they can accept them. Life is relationships; all the rest are details. Moreover, as we serve in a high-tech world, we have to major in "high touch" work. To remain simple and relational, we need to resist the temptation to become too high-tech, so as not to deflect from high-touch. Sadly many training programs have not been able to win against this kind of temptation: high-tech has almost always taken away time and energy from high-touch. Hence TLD must be relational in two essential ways: the relationship of the trainer to the trainee as well as the training focus in the TM approach.

First, following recognized educational principles, TLD requires that each teacher should be a role model of TM as a CMM practitioner, a justice advocate, and/or development agent working with a team of missionaries or coworkers. This may be more popularly called a disci-

---

16Garrison 2004:249–255. It also refers to a quote of an American house church network called Church Multiplication Associates: "We must raise leaders for the harvest from the harvest, and all the resources for an abundant harvest are in the harvest" (164).

pling method, and in this article, TLD facilitators are best referred to as "disciple-makers" (servant leaders). It is said that values (and skills) are better caught than taught. Thus, while committed to the propagation of propositional truths, TM workers need to learn that their calling involves relating openly and intimately with people. Truth is not disembodied: the gospel is truth incarnated in Christ, and the Bible teaches us to follow the example of Christ and "speak the truth in love" (Eph 4:15). The message and the messenger must become one as much as possible. And in embodying (and modeling) their teaching, the TM teachers should approach their students with love and respect. Hence the best way to teach and train others (in CMM and CD) is to relate with them as persons, as friends, in close personal relationships.

Secondly, people-centeredness must be shown in the views and attitudes that are modeled before the trainees, particularly in relation to our target people. The issue in TM is our relationship with Buddhists, not with Buddhism: "It is the street-Buddhists who are the brothers and sisters whom I see, with whom I speak and with whom I live. To love them as they are in all their complexity and not just to love anthropological, sociological, theological 'formulations' of brothers and sisters is the command of God whom we have not seen (1 John 4:20)" (Koyama 1999, 151). TLD therefore emphasizes discipling one's trainees to focus on developing close, loving relationships with people; in CMM this is called "friendship evangelism," while in CD it is "immersion" or "integration."

Practical

A close corollary to the relational nature of TLD is its being field-based and action-oriented, founded on an intimate link between reflection and practice, between classroom and fieldwork. It should be conducted close to real-life situations, identifying and organizing learning resources that link the student with the actual milieu through nonformal education and community participation.

Successful CMM have been able to develop on-the-job training (OJT) programs, which train local leaders[17] and often with emphasis on lay leaders, even new believers. Such "just-in-time training" and mentoring programs aim to develop better-equipped (not necessarily better-educated, which may come later) Christians who can multiply churches that plant churches.[18] Of course, this entails a redefinition of what is leadership and leadership training: it is not the accumulation of more knowledge (one can be overeducated, miseducated, and/or mistrained), but the upgrading of actual ministry skills, which require (just enough) knowledge and wisdom (Garrison 2004, 242–243) that fit each context. OJT is also the training model of CD (cf. Elliston 1989, especially chapters 4, 12–15, 17, 19). Thus, in ASDECS we use traveling teachers and short-term modular courses with practical requirements even in our formal degree courses.

Moreover, this apprenticeship model should work very well in Asian and Buddhist contexts. It fits the traditional training practice, perhaps of most civilizations except the post-Enlightenment Western academic tradition, though that too is changing rapidly through postmodern modes of teaching, including the use of Internet and social networking. Buddhist novices and candidates for monkhood are trained even as children in practical ways, including going from house to house to solicit food, chant, meditate, and so forth. After all, learning occurs best by doing (or through experiencing).

Contextual

Further, following the incarnational pattern of God's redemptive action, TM has to use the contextual approach to leadership development. Even modern education (including theological and missionary education) has become more and more decentralized through extension centers, correspondence courses, Internet modules, and various distance learning programs. Those in CMM and CD work have also been training

---

17Hence, missionaries avoid becoming pastors or bringing in expatriate pastors. A popular "discipling" model is to model, assist, watch, and leave (M.A.W.L.). See Garrison 2004:186–189 & 250–251.

18Ibid.:180–181, 189–191 & 229–231. See also the "cascading model" of an Indian CMM (234–235). In a Cambodian CMM, they say "Never do anything by yourself; always bring a brother along with you so you can model and mentor as you go" (187).

among the poor contextually, using their local or popular communication media, like storytelling, poetry, and drama. This equips the poor to become "trainers of trainers" within their cultures and communities without having to catch up with modern education.

In CMM training, contextualization is imperative since biblical values and standards have to be applied to particular issues in specific contexts. There seems to be a simple interactive meeting training model that fits contextual TM best and can perhaps be used universally even among preliterates. It automatically trains effective disciple-makers out of every believer for CMM through its free mixture of activities according to the needs and giftings of the participants, as set by the leaders in close consultation with the members. Activities include prayer/worship, Bible reflection, fellowship (including a simple/potluck meal together always), community service, and missions support. Following the 1 Corinthians 14:26 pattern of meeting, all members have to come prepared to "disciple (or teach, encourage, confess sins to, serve, etc.) one another," as they participate in building their lives together.

For Bible reflection (*lectio divina*), the leader facilitates discussion by choosing an appropriate biblical text and just asking three questions, as in the Viral Simple Bible Study (VSBS) method mentioned above. This simple meeting format that emphasizes contextual application and obedience of the Word best fits TLD with its practical multiplier effect, and may be taught and modeled among the poor and illiterate. It has the other added value of our last TLD indicator: it is also participatory, hence empowering.

Participative

Lastly, to be empowering and replicable, the best TLD must also be participatory. It is only through discussion types of meetings that all participants are naturally trained to become leaders, especially servant-leaders for both CMM and CD. Since Paolo Freire's *Pedagogy of the Oppressed* (1970), most educators have come to realize that transformational education must be dialogic and therefore participatory through democratic processes (cf. Ringma 1996, 3–11). Otherwise it will fail to empower the people, particularly the poor (yet surely including the rich), to make decisions that truly will benefit them and fit their contexts.[19] People learn best through a series of question-and-answer experiences so that they can use their creative imagination to discover for themselves and find better ways to develop a better future. A dialogic I-thou (personal) relationship as partners and co-learners is prerequisite to developing an openness to others and to risk changing one's pre-understandings. This requires TLD advocates to be open-minded mentors and co-learners in community with their students (Ringma 1996, 7–9).

In emphasizing participatory processes, TLD will also be "liberative," which means that students will naturally be trained to take a "prophetic critical" stance. This is based on the theology of the reality of sin and the necessity of repentance (Greek: *metanoia*): everything, except God and his Word which are absolute, is to be relativized. Nothing on earth (not even any form of Christianity) should be absolutized, given the tendency of humans and their societies to fall into sin.[20] Hence, TLD should develop critical awareness which raises new social consciousness. In a situation of sin, poverty, and injustice, the consciousness of people is submerged in a reality simply adjusting itself to natural and/or supernatural forces. Liberation happens only when they become aware that they are active subjects of their history and culture, through an educational process that seeks to produce a critical mind, especially in light of the gospel.

In CMM, even in contexts used to rote learning, critical thinking can be introduced and promoted naturally though collective exercises in real-life case studies by listening to one another's views as they reflect on God's Word together in an atmosphere of mutual respect. In areas where religious intolerance, discrimination, and even persecution prevail, TM leaders need to model the use of participative strategies that uphold human dignity and freedom. This may include skills on how to resolve conflicts, how to build communities of love (starting even with just one "(wo)man of peace"), and how to develop sustainable socioeconomic programs that fit the local market and global realities. And evangelizing in the contexts of religious pluralism requires humility, especially since most of us will bear witness from the margins of societies dominated by a non-Christian religious majority. We need to learn to invite with-

---

19On a theology of "people empowerment," see Ringma 1992: 101–197.

20On the Protestant critical stance, see Mendoza 1999.

out arrogance, and propose without trying to impose. We must allow the strength of the other's arguments and admit the limits of our own knowledge. All knowledge and truth belong to God, and God has not revealed everything, and we do not understand all that he has revealed.

Further, TLD must aim at critical discernment which results not just in personal transformation, but also in societal transformation. This also means taking the side of the poor. The rich benefit from the status quo, thus are normally conservative if not reactionary. It is the poor who are pressed by survival needs to seek transformation. Sadly, most of our training structures have an elitist outlook: that their education will trickle down to the grassroots. Thereby they fail to reflect on how their theological and missionary education can be relevant and beneficial (in short, transformational) for the poor.[21] Only when our churches, seminaries, and Christian institutions become truly the "churches (and organizations) of the poor" can we start to truly train TM workers for the UPGs who are mostly poor.[22]

Perhaps the ultimate test is whether our TLD is ready to critique and transform ecclesiastical structures: What kind of churches are we going to plant and multiply in Asia? Are we going to perpetuate the non-liberative Christendom system which has on the whole kept the poor remaining poor and the laity disempowered to do transformation in the world? Are we ready to teach our students how to transform our churches into networks of small groups (Roman Catholic "Basic Ecclesial Communities" (BEC) and Protestant house churches)[23]? In these networks, each Christian grows spiritually in their respective cells (each serving as a small missional training center), each Christian can lead his/her own disciple-making groups (DG), preferably one in his/her place of residence (during the weekend) and another in his/her place of work/study (on a weekday),[24] and each DG discerns who

21 Failing to be pro-poor, our schools have produced leaders who are at best reformist, becoming bureaucrats or even entrepreneurs who are unable to critique our defective cultures (i.e., colonial, paternalistic, patronage-based) so as to develop alternative transformative structures that liberate.

22 On the methodological ingredients for TLD, cf. Craig 1996:37–52. On some social agenda items for empowering TLD, see Carr 1994:45–67.

23 Note that though the NT churches had their problems, they were able to impact their communities and the Empire within a generation, even if they were truly "churches of the poor and oppressed," not unlike what's happening in China, India, and some other developing nations today.

24 Modern life has added this new dimension of an 8–5 world, thus the need for "office groups," to locate the church in the streets, offices, and boardrooms of the nations.

are the TM leaders worth supporting to become clergy, some to serve as coordinators (or pastors) of local networks of cells, while others as missionaries to start disciple-making networks elsewhere in the world.

Are we ready to adopt this integral, participatory, and liberative philosophy of education for TLD? May we dare to come up with radical answers to both truth and structural questions, resulting in individual and societal change. Then the next issue is whether we have the moral courage to apply the implications of the answers that we discover. TLD should help liberate us from fear, so we can obey God's call, no matter how radical, in light of our Christian conscience and commitments, particularly for the rapid and effective evangelization of people of other faiths, particularly those in the Buddhist world.

CONCLUSION

So what kind of training programs should we develop to achieve the above TLD paradigm, perhaps with the best use of the least possible resources? May I suggest that it should be in the form of (nonformal) disciple-maker training programs rather than more academic degree programs? We should be setting up small disciple-maker training centers (as small as each house church) that develop the effective leaders that we envision—without pulling them out of the marketplace and their residences, and without the need for much external funding. The key concept is to disciple an expanding core group of leaders, who will work inter- or cross-disciplinarily to impact key structures (lay leaders) among the unreached (cf. Wanak 1994, 69–97). Seminaries should become major training centers to develop servant-leaders who can transform their church networks into such TLD or disciple-making centers.

These centers shall recruit and develop teams of faculty who can mentor others and develop resources for TM, through nonformal short-term seminars which may offer certificates of participation. These would best be monitored and nurtured in (decentralized) fellowship structures, each being self-governing, self-sustaining, self-expanding, and self-theologizing, yet interlinked with other disciplines through some coordinating centers.

This training paradigm calls us to follow the way of the cross. Our human instinct and desire is to follow the tempting way of the world, to form power structures to promote, project, and propagate our ideals, even our way of the cross ideals. But this runs counter to (actually contradicts) the way of Jesus and the apostles.[25]

To be consistent with this educational paradigm, we may have to constantly remain a "mustard seed conspiracy"[26] which develop soft structures to use the humblest and simplest possible means in the most loving (read: empowering) and the least domineering (read: powerful) way possible to bring out the best from the bottom up (i.e., democratically) and not from the top down (i.e., autocratically), serving alongside with (not for) the people. It seems that the Quakers were the most consistent in following this "mustard seed" strategy. They provided the leadership in social movements for slavery's abolition, women's rights, temperance, peace, and American Indian rights; and presently in some major transnational social movement organizations (Greenpeace, Oxfam, Amnesty International, etc.). And they were able to propagate effectively without major structures except their meeting halls, and just with seminars among ordinary people led by small teams of committed disciples. How I wish that they had laid an equal emphasis on CMM also.

This contrasts with the past elitist (read: colonial or imperialist) models of Western missions which set out to transform (read: civilize) societies with Christian colleges and universities (which have fast become secularized, and rightly so). After pouring so much Christian resources, their impact (especially in the mission field) has been minimal—having won some youth (rarely the nationalistic ones), they succeeded in turning their families, clans, and even whole peoples against Christianity. This aggressive approach is being replicated today by many evangelical groups which are trying to set up mega-churches with their mega-projects, like Christian cathedrals, Christian universities, Christian tri-media, Christian hospitals, even Christian sports centers, especially to propagate their largely Westernized interpretation of

---

25The most developed TLD program was that of Paul renting a hall for public dialogues in Ephesus, which contributed to the total evangelization of Asia Minor within three years. Cf. Acts 19:1–10; 20:17–35.

26Evangelical seminary graduates should be familiar with the writings of E. Trueblood, T. Sine, W. Stringfellow, D. Kraybill, J. Ellul, H. Yoder, Os Guinness, etc.

Scriptures. Yet the more fervently they do these, the more marginalized they become, creating a subculture that is irrelevant and unintelligible to the unreached. We've also discovered that worldliness (unspiritual spirituality) is very much present and alive even in these "holy" churches and Christian institutions.

So it seems best to pause a while from going into more sophisticated training programs and expensive educational projects that will force us to develop faculties and build facilities (especially libraries), which are already available in the well-endowed state and private universities, and in Catholic and Protestant schools in some Asian countries. This will require not just a lot of overhead and talents to develop and maintain, but also demand a lot of unnecessary duplication which the existing universities are already providing. Our methodology must fit our mission to reach the unreached, and give enlightened and effective witness in our pluralistic world today.

For those who are still convinced that we can do TLD by establishing more Christian schools and universities, I hope we can invest and work together with a common vision of establishing one Christian university for every country or every 3,000,000 population in Asia, like in Thailand. To be integral or transformational, Christian academic institutions should have at least the following four characteristics: 1) vision: political economy of solidarity (shalom); 2) curriculum: social engagement with the community; (3) competency: skill in community organizing; and (4) pedagogy: learning through contextual dialogue, as elaborated in my article on "Transformational Education" (Lim 2010a).

Yet, I believe that there are two more cost-effective and strategic ways forward. One is to strengthen campus ministries (and initiate new ones) to reach the future intelligentsia who are studying in the universities and colleges today. Related to this is the development of Graduate Studies Scholarship Funds that will encourage and support evangelical college graduates to pursue higher education in secular universities, especially so that they will become the leaders in the academe, government, and businesses of their respective nations in the near future.

Secondly, another priority strategy is to mobilize the present righteous elite in our churches by encouraging our professionals and businesspeople to establish their own ministries to reach their peers in their respective professions and businesses, as has been raised in recent years as tentmaker movements, workplace (or marketplace) ministries, diaspora missions (especially international students ministries), community-based youth and children ministries (by reaching the 4/14 Window), and business as mission (BAM). I am glad that all these were highlighted in the third Lausanne International Congress in Capetown in October 2010 (cf. "The Capetown Commitment," Part II, Sec. III-IV), and a tenth of its 4,000 delegates represented government, business, academe, media, and medicine. We badly need to prioritize these in our TLD for the effective evangelization of all nations, especially the Buddhist world.

Now that we have the strategies for TLD that will effect rapid and effective evangelization of UPGs, the problem remaining is their implementation. It may seem too radical for most of our churches and even many schools and missions today. It requires a major paradigm shift: not just in our vision and objective (to multiply house churches rather than build mega-churches), but also in our evangelistic strategy (to simply do disciple-making for CMM, not just plant a church) and in our development strategy (to reach entire peoples holistically and not just win a few individuals at a time for CD). This may be our best chance to positively fast-track the effective evangelization and transformation of entire people groups in our generation. With our limited human and financial resources, involving so much prayer, effort, and sacrifice, let's do God's mission in God's way to biblically and strategically get the world truly reached and transformed.

The call is to just go back to biblical basics and strategic simplicity for TM through TLD. The Filipino mission movement seeks to mobilize a million tentmakers to do this type of mission and TLD by 2020 (cf. Lim 2010; Claro 2007). China's house churches are trying to send 100,000 such missionaries with this mission and TLD paradigm in their Back to Jerusalem movement ("like ants, worms and termites," cf. Hattaway 2003). Several house church networks in China, India, Japan, Indonesia, and the Philippines that I know of are going ahead with TLD. And this is what ASDECS and our training staff (through our simple formal/graduate and nonformal training programs) are committed to doing for the evangelization of Asia and beyond. The harvest of Asia and its peoples has been ripe and plentiful for a long time already. May the global church be trained to share the gospel with the whole world, especially Asia and the Buddhist world. May multitudes of effective disciple-makers be raised for TM/JM and through TLD, so that "the end will come" soon (cf. Matt 24:14). *Maranatha!*

References

Allen, Roland. 1962. *Missionary methods: St. Paul's or ours?* Grand Rapids: Eerdmans.

_____. 1962a. *The spontaneous expansion of the church.* Grand Rapids: Eerdmans.

Andres, Tomas. 1988. *Community development: A manual.* Quezon City: New Day Publishers.

Bobo, Kimberly. 1986. *Lives matter: A handbook for Christian organizing.* Kansas City, MO: Sheed & Ward.

Boff, Leonardo. 1986. *Ecclesiogenesis.* London: Collins; Maryknoll, NY: Orbis.

Carr, Neville. 1994. "Evaluating theological education: Ten Biblical criteria." In *Directions in Theological Education,* ed. L. Wanak, 45–67. Manila: PABATS.

Claro, Robert. 2007. *A higher purpose for your overseas job,* rev. ed. Makati City: CrossOver Books by CSM.

Coleman, Robert. 1964. *The master plan of evangelism.* Old Tappan, NJ: Revell.

Comiskey, Joel. 1999. *Groups of 12.* Houston: Touch Publications.

Craig, Jenny. 1996. The relevance of a liberation theology hermeneutic for Filipino Theology. *Phronesis* 3:1 (1996): 37–52.

De Neui, Paul, ed. 2010. *Communicating Christ in Asian cities: Urban issues in Buddhist contexts.* Pasadena, CA: William Carey Library.

Donovan, Vincent. 1978. *Christianity rediscovered.* London: SCM.

Eims, Leroy. 1981. *The lost art of disciple making.* Colorado Springs: NavPress.

Elliston, Edgar, ed. 1989. *Christian relief and development.* Waco: Word.

Freire, Paulo. 1971. *Pedagogy of the oppressed.* New York: Seabury Press.

Garrison, David. 1999. *Church planting movements.* International Mission Board of the Southern Baptist Convention.

_____. 2004. *Church planting movements.* Midlothian, VA: WIGTake Resources.

Gauran, Johani. 1991. *The witnessing kit.* Makati City: Church Strengthening Ministry.

Gnanakan, Ken. 2007. *Learning in an integrated environment.* Bangalore: Theological Book Trust.

Hattaway, Paul, et al. 2003. *Back to Jerusalem.* Carlisle: Piquant.

ION/LCWE (International Orality Network & Lausanne Committee for World Evangelization). 2010. *Orality breakouts: Using heart language to transform hearts.* Hong Kong: ION/LCWE.

Johnson, Todd, David Barrett, and Peter Crossing, eds. 2010. Christianity 2010: A view from the new *Atlas of Global Christianity. International Bulletin of Missionary Research* 34.1: 29-36.

Koyama, Kosuke. 1999. *Waterbuffalo theology (25th Anniv. Ed.).* New York: Orbis.

Lim, David. 1992. *Transforming communities.* Manila: OMF Literature.

_____. 2003. Towards a radical contextualization paradigm in evangelizing Buddhists. In *Sharing Jesus in the Buddhist World,* ed. David Lim and Steve Spaulding, 71-94. Pasadena: William Carey Library.

_____. 2004. Mobilizing churches for evangelism and missions. *Journal of Asian Mission* 6:1 (March): 43-57.

_____. 2008. Catalyzing "Insider Movements" among the unreached. *Journal of Asian Mission* 10.1-2 (March-September 2008): 125-145.

_____. 2010. Filipino urban missions in the Buddhist world. In *Communicating Christ in Asian Cities: Urban Issues in Buddhist Contexts,* ed. Paul De Neui, 201–223. Pasadena, CA: William Carey Library.

_____. 2010a. "Transformational education: Academic mission to marginalized peoples." In *Christian Higher Education & Globalization in Asia/Oceania: Realities & Challenges,* ed. Dinakarlal. Sioux City, Iowa: IAPCHE.

_____. 2011. Towards closure: Imperial or incarnational missions? *Asian Missions Advance:* 33 (October): 20–22.

Linthicum, Robert. 1991. *Empowering the poor.* Monrovia: MARC.

Mendoza, Ernesto. 1999. *Radical and evangelical: Portrait of a Filipino Christian.* Quezon City: New Day Publishers.

Montgomery, Jim. 2001. *I'm gonna let it shine!* Pasadena: William Carey Library.

Myers, Bryant. 1999. *Walking with the poor.* Maryknoll: Orbis.

Neighbor, Ralph Jr. 1990. *Where do we go from here?* Houston: Touch Publications.

Petersen, Jim. 1992. *Church without walls.* Colorado Springs: NavPress.

Ringma, Charles. 1992. *Catch the wind.* Manila: OMF Lit.

_____. 1996. Adult Christian education and theological hermeneutics. *Phronesis* 3:1: 3–11.

Samuel, Vinay, and Chris Sugden. 1999. *Mission as transformation.* Oxford: Regnum.

Simson, Wolfgang. 2001. *Houses that change the world.* Carlisle: Paternoster.

Sluka, M., and T. Budiardjo. 1995. "A church emerging in rural Cambodia." In *Serving with the poor in Asia,* eds. T. Yamamori, B. Myers, and D. Conner, 47–78. Monrovia: MARC.

Smith, Steve, with Ying Kai. 2011. *T4T: A discipleship rerevolution.* Monument, CO: WIGTake Resources.

Snyder, Howard. 1975. *The problem of wineskins.* Downers Grove: IVP.

Stephens, George. 1995. "Living a new reality in Kandy, Sri Lanka." In *Serving with the poor in Asia,* eds. T. Yamamori, B. Myers, and D. Conner, 103–115. Monrovia: MARC.

Suderman, Robert. 1999. *Calloused hands, courageous souls: Holistic spirituality of development and mission.* Monrovia: MARC.

Travis, John. 1998. Must all Muslims leave Islam to follow Jesus? *Evangelical Missions Quarterly* 34.4: 411–415.

_____. 2000. Messianic Muslim followers of Isa: A closer look at C5 believers and Congregations. *International Journal of Frontier Missions* 17.1: 53–59.

Wanak, Lee. 1994. "Church and school in symbiotic relationship: Toward a theology of specialized institutions." In *Directions in Theological Education,* 69–97. Manila: PABATS.

Yamamori, T., B. Myers, and D. Conner, eds. 1995. *Serving with the poor in Asia.* Monrovia: MARC.

_____, _____, and K. Luscombe, eds. 1998. *Serving with the urban poor.* Monrovia: MARC.

Zdero, Rad. 2004. *The global house church movement.* Pasadena: William Carey Library.

APPENDIX 1:
EFFECTIVE DISCIPLE-MAKING MADE SIMPLE

The Philippine house church and mission mobilization movements seek to effectively catalyze Jesus Movements (JM) across the nations through *disciple-making* (= leadership development). Our Lord Jesus trained his twelve apostles to do this "master plan for world evangelization" in and through the Jewish diaspora, and they did it (Luke 9–10)! The Apostle Paul did it, and in seven years he testified that he had no more people (Jews and Gentiles) to evangelize in the northern Mediterranean area (Rom 15:18–20, cf. Acts 19:1–10).

Effective disciple-making consists of seven simple steps, all of which can be done in six to ten months by beginners, and less than a month by experts.

1. *Make a second home.* When disciple-makers arrive in any new place, they should seek the help of a "person of peace" and quietly settle down in such a way that the people they will invite later will feel comfortable to visit their new home. This includes: loving the people, learning the language, appreciating the culture and religion, and following their cultural customs as much as possible (1 Cor 9:19–23). They should never criticize their host culture (especially politics and religion) in front of them, even in private.

2. *Make friends.* The disciplers must aim to make two to six "best friends" (usually related to the "person of peace"). They must be approachable and sociable. They must be good conversationalists by being good listeners. They must spend much time with their new friends, making most of their interests their own, too. As much as possible, they must give gifts on special occasions, be hospitable, and invite their friends to eat, cook, or even sleep overnight at their place. Above all, they should help their friends in their time of need.

3. *Make friends with leaders.* They must try to make one or two leaders to be their friends, too. Upon arrival, they should visit key leaders and give them a gift or at least offer to help in community affairs. They must do their jobs as well as possible, and give extra free service sometimes. They should participate in community activities, volunteer as members or officers in working or planning committees, and share any suggestion for improvement with their leader-friends, and proceed only with their approval.

4. *Make converts.* When opportunities arise (and there will be plenty), the disciplers should be ready to share Jesus with these friends (1 Pet 3:15). According to their needs or concerns, they can share their testimonies with them: how Jesus works in their lives. Then they can share about the life and teachings of Jesus that are relevant for them

(each one may need a different emphasis). Once they are sure that the friends truly want to follow Jesus as their leader, helper, forgiver, and/or guide, they can invite them to be baptized; and when they freely consent, they can baptize them in private. The key is to be sure that the friends have changed their allegiance from idols (religious or material) to Jesus. If trained, they can opt to wait until the time is ripe for the converts' whole families or whole community to be converted and baptized.

5. *Make disciples.* They then must disciple the two to six converts in one-on-one and small group discipling relationships. The more time they spend together right after their conversions, the better. There is no need to use any materials; they just urge the new believers to read the Bible in the language(s) they understand, and discuss their questions and insights with them. They must trust the Holy Spirit to speak to them through the Word, and they will have the wisdom to guide them to learn from the Bible (cf. Acts 20:28–32). For "*Bible sharing*" sessions, they just choose a short passage and ask, "What lesson or insight do you get out of this text?" and "How do we apply what we have learned?" The goal is to bring each one to spiritual maturity in Christlikeness (Col 1:28–29), which is to live a life of obedience to God—a life full of agape love/grace (out of sinful self-centeredness to sacrificial service for others, especially the poor, cf. Matt 22:37–39; 25:31–46; Gal 6:1-10).

6. *Make disciple-makers.* As they are discipling their new converts, they should encourage the latter to make their own converts and disciples from among their own friends, relatives, and neighbors—a few individuals or groups at a time. Their disciples can start discipling their own disciples by just following what they have been doing with them. The new disciplers just have to be a couple of steps ahead of their disciples. They should lead their own group and not bring their disciples to the discipler's group. It's best that they do not even visit their disciples' groups. After all, their disciples will be growing spiritually faster as they learn to relate with Jesus and his Word directly, and as they lead their own group in our *life-based* (not material-based) interactive mutual learning model of discipling.

7. *Make a planned exit.* To disciple is to Model, Assist, Watch, and Leave (M.A.W.L.). This is actually step 1: to plan to exit as soon as possible, so that our disciples "graduate" to be our equals—disciple-makers and servant-leaders in their own right. The discipler's role is just to be a mentor, guide, or coach for a while, and then stop meeting them regularly and tell them, "Greater works you will do without me," just like what Jesus told his disciples when he was about to leave them (John 14:12). They must not be surprised when their disciples (especially the leader types) do better (contextual) witness and multiplication than they have done. Of course, they can keep in touch with them, as Paul did with his disciples. Then God can send them to another unreached area, so that they can repeat the same process there.

APPENDIX 2:
BIBLICAL BASIS OF JESUS MOVEMENTS

Actually, Jesus' mission paradigm was "Jesus Movements" (JM, or "Insider Movements"). His church multiplication movement (CMM) was radically contextualized—Jews multiplying disciples among Jews without creating another organized religious system parallel or counter to the synagogue (of early Judaism). He did not intend to found a new religion (though his simple spiritual transformation became a complex religious institution later on). He even had converts in Nicodemus and Joseph of Arimathea, and perhaps through them, Gamaliel, who were entrenched in the Sanhedrin (the highest Jewish sociopolitical structure of his time).

The early Christians followed the same pattern, too. They reached out to their compatriots as Jews to Jews within the Temple and synagogue structures of Jewish society, and just met "from house to house," evangelizing and discipling a few households at a time. Within a few years of such IM, they had literally turned the Roman Empire upside down (Acts 17:6 KJV). They did not create a clergy class, nor construct (or even rent) a religious building nor hold regular religious services, except to break bread weekly in their homes. It was the teaching and practice of the Apostle Paul (perhaps the best model of a cross-cultural missionary) not to plant a growing "local church," but an indigenous disciple-making movement in house churches that were formed by converts who did not have to be dislocated from their homes and communities (cf. 1 Cor 7:17–24; 9:19–23; 2 Tim 2:2). With just seven years of three missionary journeys, he claimed that he had no more region to evangelize "from Jerusalem to Illyricum" (Rom 15:18–20)!

This New Testament practice is not different from that of Old Testament Israel, which shows God's design and structure for a reached, discipled, or transformed people:

1. There were no local altars, shrines, or temples in each village or town.

2. There were no weekly Sabbath worship services. Synagogues came later in 200 BC as multipurpose community centers among diaspora Jews. In Jesus' time, synagogues served as schools for the boys, wards for the sick, motels for visiting Jews, etc., which the Pharisees used to teach their interpretations of the Torah.

3. There were no weekly nor monthly collection of tithes and offerings. These were collected only three times per year, during the three annual festivals (Ex 23:14–19; Deut 16:16, etc.). First Corinthians 16:1–4 shows weekly collections in the early church were mainly for immediate survival needs, especially of widows and orphans (cf. Acts 6:1; Jas 1:27); Paul did not receive any objection from them when he suggested that he would bring their entire collection with him as "emergency aid" to the famine-stricken believers in Jerusalem.

4. There were no "full-time" clergy; the levitical priests were provided not just with cities, but also with pasturelands (Josh 21). They were not exempt from being stewards of God's resources; thus they were shepherds and cowboys to provide livestock products for their neighbors and nation (cf. 2 Thess 3:6–10). This was how the priests learned to be expert butchers for animal sacrifices in the Temple.

5. · The OT Jews were required to celebrate communally as a people in the national Temple (note: God's original design was a portable

and transportable Tabernacle) only three times a year: Passover
(= Holy Week), Pentecost (= church anniversary of each community), and Tabernacles (= Christmas or Harvest festival) (Deut 16:16).

6. The actual teaching and obedience of God's "way of righteousness"
   (cf. Mic 6:6–8) and the commemoration of the Passover meal were
   in the homes (Deut 6:1–11; Ex 12:43–49).

Therefore, biblical Christianity should be structured as a network of
simple churches (usually called "house churches"). It is not "*churchless*
Christianity" nor "*religionless* Christianity," but "*simple* Christianity."
Its mission is to reproduce simple groups of Christ-worshipers without
elaborate religiosity. It should fully express the Reformation doctrine of
the "priesthood of all believers" (not just the priesthood of the ordained).
God's plan for his people is that all will be priests, prophets, and kings
(= servant leaders), like the Messiah/Christ Jesus.

Thus the mission statement of the Philippine house church movement is: "to multiply God's church throughout the world, one household at a time." This seeks to fulfill God's covenants with Abraham
that through him every family on earth will be blessed (Gen 12:3; cf.
Gal 3:14, 29), and with Israel that she will be a kingdom of priests (Ex
19:6; cf. 1 Pet 2:9–10).

6

Leadership Development among Neo-Buddhist Disciples

J. N. MANOKARAN

Within the social framework of Hindu India, one large group remains oppressed at the bottom and outside the system of caste. This group is known as the Dalit, literally meaning "broken people." Confined to society's most dehumanizing roles, they are trapped, unable to change profession, deprived of both horizontal and vertical social mobility. Human Rights Watch reports, "Some 160 million people in India live a precarious existence, shunned by much of society because of their rank as 'untouchables' " (Narula 1999).

On October 14, 1956, a charismatic lawyer by the name of B. R. Ambedkar led a group of several thousand Dalit, and other dissatisfied low-caste Hindus, in a symbolic mass conversion out of Hinduism to embrace Buddhism. Buddhism was born in India but over the centuries lost its place of dominance to Hinduism. By the nineteenth century Buddhism had almost completely disappeared from its country of origin. Ambedkar started what is generally termed the "neo-Buddhist movement" in India. This mass conversion was primarily a social and political decision rather than a spiritual one. Though it was a highly visible and defiant act against the caste hegemony, it ultimately did not alter the life of neo-Buddhists dramatically. The new religious status provided a socially approved identity for the former Dalits involved, yet political power remained elusive, economic opportunities beyond their grasp, and the deepest concerns of their spiritual quest ignored.

A truly empowering movement among Dalit-background neo-Buddhists addresses more than political and even economic issues. While many Dalits followed Ambedkar and consecutive movements into Buddhism in order to throw off the chains of Hinduism, there were a few who made the decision to become Christians. Today the challenge is to develop leadership from within this Christward movement among neo-Buddhist disciples. The reader will note that the terms *neo-Buddhist* and *Dalit* are used interchangeably in this chapter. It is the author's opinion that since the majority of neo-Buddhists in India come from a Dalit background, the principles discussed here apply to both.

GROWTH OF CHRISTIANS AMONG NEO-BUDDHISTS

It is not uncommon for various members of large extended Dalit families to follow different religions. Some may have become neo-Buddhists, others may continue their attempts toward Hinduism, and still others may become Christian. The social pressure found among the higher castes ensures that within the families of the top levels of society, this phenomenon will almost never be found. But for Dalit, religious diversity is another attempt at survival.

According to Hindu belief, continual encounters with day-to-day difficulties and struggles are interpreted as acts of invisible spiritual, usually evil, forces. Buddhism in India does not address the existence of these formidable forces, nor does it equip its followers to deal with them. In cases where this has become problematic, neo-Buddhists turn to their Christian relatives for help. Dalit are seeking power to cope and respond when it is found. When times of spiritual crisis come, family members who have experienced Christ's power share how Jesus the Messiah has triumphed over Satan and the demonic angels. When these relatives realize that the Buddhism they embraced is unable to help them in this area of life, they turn to explore the Christian faith which has helped their relatives. In conversation with family, they find freedom from evil spiritual influences in their lives through Christ's intervention. Because of this type of spiritual encounter, church planting among neo-Buddhists has been fairly successful. It is estimated that there are over 100,000 disciples from neo-Buddhist backgrounds in the state of Maharashtra alone, planted primarily through the connections of family networks (Mohod 2011).

CHALLENGES OF LEADERSHIP DEVELOPMENT AMONG NEO-BUDDHISTS

Pastor Vijay Mohod of Maharashtra estimates that there are one hundred pastors from neo-Buddhist backgrounds in his state and only five to ten percent have three years of theological training. Twenty percent have one or two years of training, twenty percent have six months of training, and the rest do not have any training at all (ibid.). Neo-Buddhists are like sheep without a shepherd. They have numerous spiritual, social, psychological, mental, physical, and material needs. Leadership development in this cultural context is a serious challenge.

Due to their history of subjugation and betrayal, the Dalit have a deeply ingrained inferiority complex. It is part of their lifestyle and psyche. Even if a Dalit has earned an education or has somehow attained economic independence, his or her social status is always under question. The performance or achievements of the Dalit are mocked, minimized, and undermined by the Hindu majority. Many times individual Dalit are publicly humiliated. This long history of social oppression has become a cultural weakness contributing to the instability of the social structure of India. History has shown that any country with a large percentage of its population living under subjugation will in time suffer an internal collapse.

Neo-Buddhism has failed to help the Dalit escape their karma or the inequality that enslaves them in the Hindu social system. They may have aspirations and desires, yet may never have the fortitude or opportunity to express or pursue them publicly. They need care, counsel, and constant encouragement to move forward. Initially this was provided by outsiders. Today indigenous leaders are rising up from within their number who are able to extend this same kind of mutual encouragement to their peers. Developing leadership for the body of Christ among new disciples from Dalit and neo-Buddhist backgrounds requires discernment, divine wisdom, commitment, and a huge investment of time and energy.

Some Christian disciples from neo-Buddhist backgrounds have had the opportunity to attain a good education, but the majority have not.

To equip people to lead who have no reading or writing skills requires special expertise. Christian leadership training among neo-Buddhists usually starts with well-educated missionaries from outside the Dalit culture who often lack experience equipping preliterate people to become Christian leaders. Missionaries should continue to encourage literacy at all levels as well as acquisition of practical life skills and the pursuit of formal education when possible. At the same time Christian missionaries, church planters, and educators should become familiar with other methodologies of training that are more easily applicable and replicable among people in oral cultures such as the Dalit.

Developing leadership among the new Christian community from neo-Buddhism is context specific. Unless the neo-Buddhist background believers remain sensitive to Dalit contextual needs, they will not emerge as effective leaders. All leadership development involves discernment between following the Word and following the patterns of the world. "Worldly conceptions of greatness and leadership cannot be carried over into His Spiritual kingdom. In that kingdom there is a complete reversal of earth's values" (Sanders 1967, 13). Generally speaking, neo-Buddhist background believers have only experienced the type of leadership that expresses power in ways that control and exploit others. There is a need for neo-Buddhist background Christian leaders to experience and then replicate biblical models of servant leadership, even if this means rejecting popular (and often foreign-funded) forms of power-oriented Christian training. In addition to this, leadership development among neo-Buddhist background believers must be contextualized to the Dalit social, economic, and political contexts.

Dalit Social Context

As was mentioned, caste hierarchy keeps all Dalit, including neo-Buddhists and Christians, under severe social oppression. They are expected to provide services as per their outcaste duty or socially prescribed dharma. This dharma is not a personal path to righteousness but is merely an imposed system of obligations and social duties allotted to them as one of the outcaste groups. Any threat to the maintenance and obedience to this system has huge implications for the whole of society.

By fulfilling dharmic duty, all who participate in it hope for a better future birth within the Hindu caste hierarchy in the cycle of birth and reincarnation. The Dalit, however, remain outside of the possibility of accruing a better future life until they are first born within the caste system. Their only possibility is to remain faithfully in their subservient roles and hope for a better future life. Even after conversion, Dalit background neo-Buddhists (and some Christians) often fall back on the Hindu-based social requirements expected of them as Dalit in order to fit in.

Leaders of new Christian communities of Dalit or neo-Buddhist background believers must be trained to enable their members to become a supportive close-knit social unit. These leaders must be proactive in preparing their members for the life of sacrifice chosen when becoming public Christ followers. Leaders must share their own stories and experiences and be transparent about the cost of this life-changing decision. Real Christian unity will enable the believers, as a group and as individuals, to counter the constant social oppression which comes from the larger society. Loving, caring, and sharing with one another enable all to face external threats with serenity, solidarity, and common sense.

Today neo-Buddhist background believers are facing increasing persecution not only from Hindu sources but now from other neo-Buddhists as well. On October 2, 2011, a Sunday worship service led by Pastor Amit Aryan was attacked in the Maharashtra city of Aurangabad (2011a). This was the first time a group of neo-Buddhists attacked a Christian worship service of Christian neo-Buddhist background believers in India. It is predictable that more persecution will continue toward those who persist in challenging the social power structures until an effective change has truly occurred.

Dalit Economic Context

To say the Dalit are exploited economically is an understatement. This exploitation continues even after they have become neo-Buddhists or Christians. With no access to capital, assets, or land ownership, it is impossible for them to qualify for improvement loans for any economic activity from formal sources such as banks or the government. As a result, they have to depend on private lenders who charge interest at exorbitantly high rates. Until they repay their loans, they are forced to provide their goods and services at the low rates fixed for them by the loan sharks. This results in multigenerational cycles of perpetual poverty.

Because they are below the lowest rung of the social ladder, economic ascension for Dalit and neo-Buddhists is unfeasible. An Indian neo-Buddhist, for example, may operate an excellent restaurant business with wonderful delicacies. However, if people from the higher castes learn of the original outcaste ethnicity of the owner, they will boycott the shop and encourage others to do the same. As much as they would want to, Dalit background customers may not have the economic means to patronize such a business. The business will fail without regular patronizing customers.

Congregations of neo-Buddhist and Dalit background believers require strong leaders who understand the desperate need for economic survival among the Dalit. They must recognize the reality of the complex historic dynamics of their culture and be able to find creative solutions to raise their economic as well as social standing. Some examples of ways that Christian leaders have helped neo-Buddhist background congregations develop economic independence include the organization of self-help groups, the creation of small businesses sustained by the community itself, and starting micro-enterprise projects.

Leaders must also prepare their congregations to face the suspicion that any successes from these efforts will inevitably raise. A pastor in the city of Aurangabad analyzes the reason for persecution of Dalit Christians thus:

> The families which believed and started coming to Sunday worship regularly received terrific financial breakthrough. And as a result, a housemaid purchased a car, installed an air conditioner at her home in a slum area and many others received blessings in different forms. This brought unnecessary misunderstandings. So the leaders who are hungry for money started thinking, that the Church is providing money to those who change their religion. Many of our church members are new converts from Buddhist background, who work as housemaids, etc. and have

very limited source of income. But because the work of Holy Spirit in their lives, they were blessed with material resources. And the community leaders took it otherwise accusing us, you are being supported from missionaries abroad. Amazingly, I personally have not received a single cent from abroad till now, forget the new believers. (Aryan, October 12, 2011)

Dalit Political Context

Dalits are considered "vote banks" in the Indian democracy. Neo-Buddhists also generally support the Dalits in politics since they can function as a group and can be influenced by local leaders. "In Indian elections people are classified by their caste or their religion. Politicians, journalists, and psephologists all talk of 'vote banks' of Dalits or former untouchables, OBC or Other Backward Castes, and the upper Castes" (Tully 2011, 57). Political parties cultivate area leaders from these communities and provide those individuals with perks and positions of power, demanding loyal votes in return. This creates political leaders supposedly elected to represent the concerns of the people to the political party and the government but who, in fact, become promoters of particular political agendas instead. Thus, instead of becoming saviors, these recruited Dalit-background leaders join the class of oppressors in exploiting their very own people. In this political climate it is the small group of missionaries and church planters who have the opportunity to become true leaders and prophets giving a voice to the voiceless.

Potential leaders from among the Dalit are particularly vulnerable to temptation and frequently fall victim to political exploitation. Novice Dalit leaders who lack the opportunities open to others may be desperate enough to seek personal promotion at the cost of joining those who oppress their own constituency. They then become part of perpetuating the same evils of an unjust social system they were originally called to address. The Christian community from the neo-Buddhist background must remain faithful to its task of raising up leaders who value political justice above corruption. It must remain willing to speak out whenever possible, even when it comes at a price. This will require a great deal of support. Pastors and missionaries should be able to mentor Dalit-background politicians, whenever possible, by giving them a vision of equality, justice, and righteousness, along with economic prosperity.

KEY COMPONENTS OF LEADERSHIP TRAINING

Leadership development in any context is not an automatic process. It is an intentional process. Some churches and Christian organizations seem to operate out of the belief that leadership development simply happens by itself. Many Christians feel that the Holy Spirit provides and equips new leaders so nothing further need be done to facilitate the process of leadership selection and development. However, although the seed is planted, it needs to be watered regularly and carefully nurtured. Leaders may be called by the Spirit, but no leader is called alone. The body of Christ has been given responsibilities by God for the selection, training, and ongoing support of its leaders.

Creating leaders is a deliberate act. In order to multiply new leadership the established structures should prepare appropriate contexts from which new leaders may emerge. This does not happen by default but by strategy. Strategy can be risky, but there is biblical precedent. The Apostle Paul modeled this by sharing responsibilities, designating new authorities, and deploying the younger generation in ministry. The strong support network created by Paul sustained a safe and expanding environment for emerging leaders by which they could face their inevitable challenges confidently (Manokaran 2007a, 202).

Leaders should pray and plan for new recruits who would own the vision for ministry and become greater leaders than themselves. Think of the example of the Russian nesting doll. The same type of toy is made in five sizes. The smallest can be packed in the next larger one and so on until all can be packed inside the largest one. If leaders recruit people of lesser caliber than they are, their organizations will become nothing more than a collection of dwarfs or Lilliputian pygmies (ibid., 50).

Development of new leaders happens when established leaders communicate easily understood intentional strategies with passion and clarity to others. Sanjay Diwe says, "I attended a seminar on 'Leadership Excellence' conducted by Manokaran and got a vision to develop leaders.

Within two years I developed leaders and my church also grew. Vision changed my mission and ministry" (2011). If established leaders communicate a vision for recruiting and training their own replacements, it will happen. If they do not, the cycle will flounder.

God provides leaders with wisdom and discernment to choose the right kind of people to be trained as future leaders. Paul exhorted Timothy to choose reliable people who would teach others for leadership (2 Tim 2:2). "The spirit of teachability is a humble spirit. It is noteworthy in many women and men of God down through church history" (Lundy 2011, 174). When disciples are keen learners, there is a great potential to develop leaders.

There are three important components in a strategy for recruiting and training new leaders that must be included in any vision for the future. These three key components of the developmental training of leaders are in the areas of knowledge, character, and skill.

Development of Knowledge in Leadership Training

Knowledge includes sound knowledge of the Bible, and basic knowledge about the history of the nation, the culture, current social issues, and salient features of neo-Buddhism. Training in biblical subjects must not merely be "head" knowledge but must be oriented toward practical application.

One example of this is in regard to the doctrine of the sovereign rule of God and its application (or lack thereof) in all aspects of life. There is a widespread practice in India, prevalent among neo-Buddhists as well, that carefully notes auspicious times and inauspicious times every day before making decisions and planning out events. Auspicious times are chosen to start any new venture, to conduct weddings, to schedule a housewarming ceremony, to start a business, or to begin a journey. Auspicious times are considered favorable and good. In contrast, inauspicious times are considered to be dominated by cosmic evil forces and no good thing can be started or attempted at those times. Even in today's modern technological age, many children are delivered by unnecessary caesarean section because of a felt need to give birth during an auspicious time. Unfortunately, many Indian Christians still practice a strong allegiance to the dictates of auspicious times. They do not apply the doctrine of the sovereign rule of God to their day-to-day lives. Instead of scriptural application, there is more often only an uncritical acceptance of cultural practices.

Most formal biblical and theological training emphasizes cognitive knowledge, while character building and cultural contextualization skills may not have priority. There is a need to integrate knowledge growth with character formation and skill development. Institutional training is inadequate; it must be accompanied by apprenticeship and mentoring.

Development of Character in Leadership Training

Character formation is essential for Christian leadership. Leaders with head knowledge and even ministerial skill, but who lack noble character, are like a body without a soul. People cannot accept a message given by a substandard messenger. A bald man cannot sell medicine to cure baldness. "If the blind lead the blind, both will fall into a pit" (Matt 15:14). In the same way, character development is essential in training leaders for work among neo-Buddhists. Basic spiritual disciplines should be imbibed as personal habits. "Spiritual disciplines prepare our minds and hearts for obedience, like a rehearsal. Musicians train so that when their key moment arrives, they will perform as they desire" (Spencer 2010, 37).

In the Dalit culture of honor and shame people tend to lead dual lives. A poor man borrows money to marry off his daughter with a grand wedding ceremony in full knowledge that such an elaborate function will make him a debtor for several years. In his worldview, one day of honor is worth a long life suffering impoverishment. This is the context for believers from the neo-Buddhist culture. There is a private life and a public life, but each may be radically different from the other. Unfortunately, many Dalit-background Christian leaders follow the pattern of secular leaders in their context and continue to follow this worldview living two-faced lives of public and private. In public ministry they are respected and are compassionate in their relationships. However, they may indulge in physical abuse of their wives. There is a need for inner transformation that would help them lead a holy life and not a hypocritical life. "In Jesus' vision of the faithful life, the inside and the outside both matter. As disciples, we are called to be consistent, to have our 'outside' good actions come from corresponding 'inside' motivations" (ibid., 71).

Development of Skills in Leadership Training

Leaders working among neo-Buddhists need two sets of skills: ministry skills and leadership skills. There are many general skills that are "musts" for a leader, while there are specialization skills that may be required only in certain contexts. The list of skills varies according to the social, economic, and educational level of the people among whom the leader is called to serve. There are simple skills for ministry with children, like using puppets. More complex skills are required for pastoral ministry, especially in the context of poverty. There are skills required in dealing with domestic violence, alcohol addiction, and demon possession.

Skills can be attained by short training or learning by observing what others are doing. However, to work among neo-Buddhists there is a need for skills in training entrepreneurship, social transformation, and micro-enterprise development. Project identification, project development, and management skills are also needed for effective leaders.

MODELS OF LEADERSHIP TRAINING

There are three basic models for training new Christian leaders among neo-Buddhists. It has been debated which one is the best. Today some training efforts have adopted all three models and try to integrate them.

Formal Training

Formal training is a structured form of education that generally emphasizes academic knowledge. Here the aspiring leader is usually required to stay in a distant residential setting for a period of time and undergo a structured curriculum. There is an academic evaluation of personal progress with some degree of character development and skill training.

Courses range from three months to a few years. At the present time, however, there is no specific curriculum for new disciples from the neo-Buddhist community. Unfortunately, there is not even a well-developed curriculum specific to the Indian context. Most of the curriculum used is a mirror image of Western seminaries and Bible colleges.

In formal training the delivery, forms, and concepts are difficult for neo-Buddhists to understand as a majority of them do not have a college education. Indian writers should be encouraged to write curriculum appropriate for disciples from the neo-Buddhist (and other) backgrounds using Indian case studies, metaphors, and images. There are a few potential Indian Christian leaders who can write, and they need to be encouraged to do more. There is a need to conduct writers' workshops to develop their skills and get their training materials into publication.

Nonformal Training

Nonformal training is a more appropriate model for leadership development among new disciples within the neo-Buddhist community. Residential training is not favored as it uproots a person from his or her context. Also, it is expensive in terms of time and resources, including finances. Nonformal training is usually delivered on-site in various formats like modular courses. In the modular course one subject is chosen and offered for three days. Another mode of delivery is to have evening classes, maybe three or four days a week. A dozen courses over a period of two or three years are offered in packages of three days each. This is user friendly, contextual, affordable, and flexible, and a wide variety of leaders can attend. Also, topics of study are chosen that are relevant and have practical application.

Distance education is another option. With modern technology, lessons can be delivered via email and contact classes can be conducted on a regular basis. However, distance education is feasible only in the urban areas where people are educated and can afford the computers and equipment necessary for accessing the Internet. Among new Christians only the elite, educated, and economically powerful can access this option at present. Furthermore, distance education is more individualistic, while the other two options are community oriented.

Informal Training

The third model of training and developing leaders can be termed informal training. In this form there is no structured syllabus; however, structured pieces of lessons may be used. This form is more experiential learning rather than learning from concepts, ideas, or books. Pastors know gifted individuals. Mentoring them regularly is one way of developing leaders through informal training. On-the-job training can be termed apprenticeship. Choosing leaders as Paul did to be teamed up for ministry is a valid method. Paul trained leaders like Timothy and Silas by taking them along with him on missionary journeys. George Verwer writes: "Training can start with the young. I am committed to the task of training young people for leadership right where they happen to be, while at the same time presenting them with a truth of a world vision" (Verwer 2010, 15). "Mentoring is an effective form of 'on-field' training, but it seems to be frequently overlooked as a valid method for training" (Harrison 1997, 268). Being an apprentice with a senior leader can help a novice learn ministry skills. Paul trained several young people by mentoring. Mentoring is biblical and a valid Christian strategy (Thomas 199, 12–15). "Missions may fail when the leaders leave all the mentoring to be done in the Bible Colleges by a few teachers who themselves need a lot of mentoring" (Rajendran 199, 21). Mentoring occurs best in the context of ministry or on the mission field, not in the classroom.

"Community Bible Study International (CBSI) is an in-depth, systematic study of God's Word led by trained nationals who are both in the local class and are the small group leaders. CBSI is set in an informal context where every person who attends is Comfortable, Confident in the Word and Cared for" (Vroegop 2011). Pastor Suresh Nagpur said: "We used Community Bible Study International material in Hindi to develop our leaders. That has helped our sixteen leaders to form a good devotional life. Such informal training would help us to build leaders" (Godbole 2011). Informal training sometimes takes a long time to bring effective results. "Perseverance waits for God's timing to vindicate, to give growth, to justify all the time and energy invested in others" (Lundy 2011, 227). There has been investment by leaders who are outsiders in the emerging leaders in informal training among disciples of neo-Buddhist background. Yakub Wadagale, Vinay Gaikwad, and Anil Ghodke are a few of the leaders who have mentored new leaders in Aurangabad region in this way.

Modeling, mentoring, and monitoring were the components that were part of the strategy of Paul for training. He was a model for the youngsters who followed his footsteps in the ministry. His life was a model for youngsters to imitate in the areas of vision, passion, hard work, and strategy (Manokaran 2007a, 199).

Apprenticeship and personal mentoring are good informal methods of developing leaders among neo-Buddhists. "A great deal of Timothy's training was received on the job, as he travelled with Paul—a unique privilege for so young a man" (Sanders 1983, 168). Sometimes it is difficult for youngsters to cope with the demands of senior leaders. Young leaders who are not willing to pay the price fall off. John Mark was not able to match the expectations of Paul, which led to a division between Paul and Barnabas (Acts 15:36–39). Yet, that is one of the best ways for a young leader to develop. "Learning to work under a senior person is a desirable part of the early training of a leader" (Prior 1997, 144).

Informal training also provides opportunity for leaders to discover the natural talents and spiritual gifts of potential leaders. Vijay Mohod, a neo-Buddhist background disciple, came to attend a fifteen-day training in Pune that this author coordinated. He did not have the fees to pay for the training. Discerning the potential, he was admitted for the training and his life was transformed. He gained new vision and a sense of direction.

Most talents and gifts are discovered or spotted by others. "Discernment of spiritual gifts is essential for allotting the right job for the right person" (Manokaran 2007a, 153). Pastors who wish to develop leaders should pray for discernment to spot the right people for the right job. "Discerning spiritual gifts is a vital factor in making people decisions" (ibid., 153). Leadership development with the discernment from the Holy Spirit would produce "right-fit" leaders for effective ministry.

APPROPRIATE TRAINING TOOLS FOR LEADERSHIP DEVELOPMENT

Training of new disciples among neo-Buddhists requires a unique set of training tools. Basic discipleship as a training tool (or manual) is critical to understanding prayer, the word of God, witnessing, fellowship, worship, the local church, the sacraments, and daily spiritual life. Buddhist prayer is monotonous repetition or rotation of wheels. However, the new believers should learn and practice prayer as a dynamic conversation with God. These training materials should introduce the uniqueness of Christian faith and practice in contrast to neo-Buddhism.

Stewardship

The next training tool is stewardship of time, talents, treasure, relationships, and all aspects of life. These would help a person to be a good steward in the society. A leader has to be a steward of all God-given resources. The leader has to model to the new believers how they could optimally, wisely, and strategically use these resources to bring glory to God. Such training helps new believers excel in whatever they do. The new disciples do all things in the community as they would do it unto the Lord—creating a new work ethic.

Vision-Building

Another training tool would be leadership that provides training in creating group vision and ministry purpose. Visionary leadership development can take the community of believers into a new realm of life spiritually, socially, economically, mentally, and morally. In order for this to occur, leaders should have a long-term vision, broad-mindedness, an appetite for learning, courage to bring about change, and the ability to steer progressively toward the goal. Unlike other leaders in the political, social, and religious realms of neo-Buddhist society, Christian leaders must demonstrate dedication to the vision through modeling servant-hood and Christlikeness in their leadership roles. The Christians from the neo-Buddhist background who were persecuted in October 2011 in Aurangabad have planned to invite the people who persecuted them for a Christmas celebration in which they will wash the feet of those who harassed them. This will be a powerful demonstration of servanthood in the community.

Networking

Networking of existing churches and leaders is needed for developing leaders for the future of the church and church planting movements. Networking helps ministries share resources, experiences, expertise, and tools for optimum effectiveness. Since neo-Buddhist background churches are new and emerging, it is not possible for each mission, ministry, or local church to develop their own training institutes to develop leaders. Their own local experiences are not enough to provide adequate training to produce mature leaders. There is a need for sharing such experiences and expertise, a willingness to work together in developing leaders for the kingdom of God.

Networking churches with a majority of disciples from neo-Buddhist backgrounds with churches having no neo-Buddhist background believers is possible in Indian cities such as Nagpur, Aurangabad, Amravati, and Akola. By networking, they can host events and programs as a united Christian witness to people around them in the city. Such attempts have already been made in these cities.

CHALLENGES AHEAD

The need for leadership development among the disciples of Jesus Christ from the neo-Buddhist background is a challenging task. The historical, cultural, and contemporary context created by the political, religious, and economic environments shapes these people into a unique group with traits of inferiority, lack of motivation, a corporate sense of inadequacy, and a lack of future orientation. The Indian church has to mobilize resources and initiate mentoring to develop dynamic leadership among this community.

Holistic Vision

The vision of the Dalit is political freedom and an aspiration of equality in the social, economic, and political spheres. They desire to be their own masters. For most, however, this seems to be nothing more than a mirage. Just as it is about to be reached it becomes elusive once again. Under the law of Indian democracy, political and social aspirations of Dalits are guaranteed; nevertheless they are ignored in day-to-day life. The reasons are many, including the lack of awareness among these people. Without understanding their legal rights, they allow others to exploit and oppress them. The new Christian community needs leaders who educate, create awareness, and collectively inherit their rights.

Dalits also need spiritual democracy. Leaders from among the Christian community should be able to guarantee that this occurs. In Hinduism, the top spiritual leadership is reserved only for those from the Brahmin caste; only that caste group can become high priests in the most holy temples of India. Other castes are deprived of that spiritual right. However, within the church, a Christian from the Dalit community could aspire to the highest possible position such as pastor, seminary principal, bishop, or even pope. Leadership development includes creating numerous leaders from among this community who would benefit the larger kingdom of God in India, and globally.

Vision helps people move forward, harbor hope in adverse situations, and create methods to reach one's destination. The new Christian community among neo-Buddhists needs visionary leaders who can integrate social and spiritual concerns in their outreach ministry.

Holistic Training

The impact of sin was holistic in nature. When Adam and Eve committed sin, their whole lives were affected. They lost their spiritual relationship with God. Adam's relationship with work became toil; even the environment was not friendly. Relationships were no longer transparent and healthy. The humans were exiled from the familiar surroundings of Eden. Conversely, the gospel has to impact a person who believes in the Lord Jesus Christ holistically. However, evangelical church planters fail to understand the holistic impact of the gospel and restrain the good news to spiritual boundaries. Pastor Sanjay Diwe says, "There are some super rich individuals and families among the neo-Buddhists. Some of them run educational institutions, have power and prestige and enjoy political offices. However, these leaders do not care for the development of fellow Neo-Buddhists who are poor and deprived" (2011).

There are, however, some models of hope that are used to train leaders among other people groups in holistic ways. These models have proven to be successful and effective in helping train pastors in various parts of India (Manokaran 2007b). Some of these models include Trainers of Pastors International Coalition (TOPIC), CARE Counseling Institute, Global Modular Studies, Bible Training Centre for Pastors, Training Network, summer schools run by a few seminaries, and short-term courses. Some of these models have been adopted and are being used to develop leaders among the new church planting movement among neo-Buddhists.

In the coming days, there is a great expectation for a Christward people movement among neo-Buddhists, especially in the western part of India. However, the Indian church seems to be overwhelmed by multiple challenges. Bible colleges and other training institutions have not created relevant, contextual curricula for developing leaders for such people movements. There is hope in the small local efforts by concerned outsiders who wish to see a great harvest among neo-Buddhists. They are praying and encouraging young people to take up this challenge among the new Christian disciples from neo-Buddhist and Dalit backgrounds. It is heartening to see such humble beginnings expand. These are just small drops, but we are expecting showers of blessings. The challenge is great but exciting, and with the help of our Lord and obedience to the guidance of Holy Spirit, this task can be accomplished.

References

Ambedkar, B. R. 2002. Annihilation of caste. http://wcar.alrc.net/mainfile2.php/Documents/76/ (accessed August 4, 2011).

Aryan, Pastor Amit. 2011a. Email prayer letter sent out on October 3.

Aryan, Pastor Amit. 2011b. Email dated October 12.

Diwe, Pastor Sanjay. Interview conducted at Amravati (Maharashtra) on August 20, 2011.

Godbole, Pastor Suresh. Interview conducted in Nagpur on August 22, 2011.

Harrison, Myron S. 1997. *Too valuable to lose*. Pasadena: William Carey Library.

Ilaiah, Kancha. 2009. *Post-Hindu India: A discourse on Dalit Bahujan socio-spiritual and scientific revolution*. New Delhi: Sage Publications Pvt. Ltd.

Lundy, J. David. 2011. *Servant leadership for slow learners*. Hyderabad: Authentic.

Manokaran, J. N. 2007a. *Christ & missional leaders*. Chennai: Mission Educational Books.

Manokaran, J. N. 2007b, July. Re-thinking of pastoral leaders? http://www.lausanneworldpulse.com/themedarticles.php/710/?pg=3 (accessed October 17, 2011).

Mohod, Pastor Vijay. Interview conducted in Nagpur on May 24, 2011.

Narula, Smita. 1999. Broken People: Caste Violence Against India's "Untouchables." http://www.unhcr.org/refworld/country,, HRW,,IND,4562d8cf2,3ae6a83f0,0.html (accessed October 17, 2011).

Prior, Kenneth. 1990. *Perils of leadership*. Mumbai: Gospel Literature Service.

Sanders, J. Oswald. 1967. *Spiritual leadership*. Chicago: Moody Press.

Sanders, J. Oswald. 1983. *Paul the leader: A vision for Christian leadership today*. Bromley: STL Books.

Spencer, Gregory. 2010. *Awakening the quieter virtues*. Downers Grove: IVP.

Tully, Mark. 2011. *Non stop India*. New Delhi: Allen Lane.

Thomas, Chacko. 1999. Need of the hour: Mentoring for missions: A practical and Biblical outlook. *Indian Missions*: July–September.

Verwer, George. 2010. *Grace awakened leadership*. Hyderabad: Authentic.

Vroegop, Frank. International Director of CBSI. Email dated December 20, 2011.

7

Understanding and Strategizing Christian Leadership Development for the Thai Buddhist Context

CHANSAMONE SAIYASAK

The goal of Christian missions in Thailand is to develop Christian leaders so as to bring Christ's redemption and kingdom reign to the people living in the Thai Buddhist context. The successful outcome of these evangelization efforts depends significantly on the development of indigenous leaders who are the most effective agents of religious change in their local contexts. Because of the observable direct correlation between leadership development and effective Christian evangelization, the importance of indigenous leadership development cannot be overestimated. It is therefore imperative to precisely determine the perceptions of good and acceptable leadership according to the local context where evangelization is to take place. In this paper, the context is the Buddhist communities of northeast Thailand (also known as Isaan).[1]

The expected qualities and the selection process of leadership as perceived and practiced by contemporary northeastern Thai people need to be identified. The aspects of leadership development that would "inspire willing obedience" in these people to become followers of Christ should be analyzed and developed (Adair 2005, 39). Thus, this paper will discuss the importance of context and the relevant Thai concepts of leadership applicable to Christian ministry. It will attempt to assess

---

1 Editor's note: Isan, sometimes appearing in English as Isaan, is the Pali word for northeast. This name was given to the northeast region of what was later renamed Thailand by Rama V of Siam to unify the country and identify it as part of the Siamese kingdom. At the same time the northwest region of the country was named Payap, meaning northwest.

the Thai Buddhist perception of leadership from the perspective of both Christian and non-Christian leaders, and to make missiological implications for indigenous leadership development for Buddhist contexts.

THE IMPORTANCE OF CONTEXT FOR THAI CHRISTIAN LEADERSHIP DEVELOPMENT

Effective Christian leadership development is context specific. Each local context in need of God's redemption and kingdom reign presents unique characteristics, beliefs, and values. The context determines the nature and character of development. Leadership training and development endeavors that do not take into account contextual particulars could fail and/or experience setbacks.

Paramount to the effectual, contextual development of leadership is the need to ascertain the leadership qualities or character traits perceived as essential or compulsory in an acceptable and effective leader in that particular setting. Laura C. Leviton states: "First and foremost, it is imperative to grasp that 'leadership always takes place in context'" (2006, x). So, what are the requirements for leadership that would result in effective ministry in the northeast Thai Buddhist context? I have been grappling with this question for some time in order to focus on effective indigenous leadership development for my ministry. Since my specific context is the northeast region of Thailand, the starting point for my inquiry was the Thai people themselves residing in this particular Buddhist environment.

RELEVANT THAI CONCEPTS OF LEADERSHIP APPLICABLE TO CHRISTIAN MINISTRY

The Thai culture tends, in general, to create respect for leaders as father figures. The leader who occupies the top position can make decisions that are even life-changing for those lower in the social structure. Thanasankit and Corbitt hold that Thai leaders are obligated to act as "fathers" (2000, 7). The social structure of the northeast region of Thailand is similar to the rest of the country inasmuch as it exhibits classic characteristics of an affiliative society as described by Weerayudh Wichiarajote:

Affiliative societies emphasize the paternal leaders. A younger person has to be obedient and fearfully respect the leader. As long as the leader is in the leading position, his followers also have power, but as soon as the leader retires or loses position his followers also lose it. (1982, 13)

Besides viewing leaders as father figures, the Thai also regard leaders as patrons. Australian anthropologist Graham Fordham, who conducted his field research in Thailand, describes it thus:

The patron, from a position of economic security, offers tangible goods such as economic aid and protection. In return, the client, from a position of economic insecurity, offers more intangible goods. These include loyalty, a commitment to increasing the good name of his patron, information and political support. ... Also, there may be several hierarchal levels of patron-client relations. Patrons at lower levels are themselves clients of higher level patrons who, in turn, are clients of still higher level patrons. (1991, 9)

Leadership Legitimacy

Northeastern Thai Buddhists stress the importance of leadership legitimacy. Not just anyone can become a leader or hold a prominent leadership position, including a religious one. There are certain beliefs and standards that justify leadership positions and roles among Buddhists of northeast Thailand. Thai anthropologist Kusuma Chavinit argues:

The Isan [northeastern Thai] society views the community leaders to belong to the line of the *tan* spirit whom the Isan believe created the world. From the influence of Buddhism, the Isan society perceives the community leaders to possess significant amount of merit. The right to govern derives from his lineage from the *tan* spirit and his power to govern from his merit. His position and influence as a community leader should be respected and obeyed (trans. from the Thai by the writer). (1988, 294)

Apart from the traditional belief in the *tan* spirit and the Buddhistic belief in the power of merit that lend legitimacy to a person's leadership, the outcome of his or her leadership also confirms and/or justifies that leadership. Chavinit further described:

> The model of the leadership in northeast Thailand can be traced back to the toad king whom the northeastern Thai believe to have ruled with prosperity and peace in the northern Thai region in the ancient past. Besides the meritorious action of the community that justifies and endows him with the power to govern the villagers, it is also believed to produce a prosperous and peaceful community absent from any misfortune or calamity (trans. from the Thai by the writer). (ibid.)

If a person's leadership is characterized by calamities or absence of peace, he or she might lose legitimacy to be a leader. Calamities or absence of peace are believed to be an indication of the absence of support from the spirit world and/or the absence of merit.

Additionally, there are personal leadership traits that cannot be overlooked. A northeastern Thai normally assumes a leadership role in society after he has gained economic independence and respect among his group. American anthropologist Charles F. Keyes, who conducted extensive research in northeast Thailand, describes:

> Between the ages of 20 and 40 a man should devote himself to create a new family and providing for its needs. By forty, a man has usually obtained full economic independence from his parents-in-law and has established a reasonably sound position with the group of heads of kin groups. Between the ages of 40 and 60 many men play a leadership role in community matters. (1967, 22)

Because these factors, namely age, economic independence, and respectable position within one's kinship group, are important determinants for establishing qualification for being considered for a leadership role in the community, most Thai Buddhists of the northeastern region of Thailand are extremely cautious about these matters. While a person's age cannot be controlled, his economic status and position within his kinship group can and must be earned. Thus, before a potential leader can earn leadership respect by society, he must first earn it within his kinship group, indicating his position also by his age and economic means.

Leadership Authority

According to the Thai Buddhist value system, leaders occupy a position of authority. No one underneath him may challenge his authority or decisions made by him (Mole 1973, 11). Traditionally, in Thailand the authority over conversion from one faith to another resided in the power of the ruler of the kingdom. Authority to judge religious matters was also entrusted to the highest ruler of the realm and not to ordinary citizens (Saiyasak 2007, 21).

In the northeastern region of Thailand, the ancient Isaan laws specified the authority to judge matters in the realm of a village be given to the elders of the village community. Even at the present time, most conflicts are solved by the elders of the village and not the court system (Somjitsripunya 1987, 233). Since the village elders are entrusted as keepers of local traditions and customs, their leadership authority over religious, cultural, and social matters cannot be disputed. Somchai Rakwijit agrees: "The groups of people villagers strongly disapproved of are those who do not respect villager elders, are arrogant, speak badly, are trouble-makers, are irresponsible to their own family, and are uncooperative in community affairs" (1971, 56).

Leadership Hierarchy

The Thai worldview includes a social hierarchy influenced by Buddhism; however, that hierarchy is not perceived as permanent. Individuals can later change their position in the hierarchy by appropriating moral and ritual actions (Kirsch 1975, 182). Because of the hierarchy, a Thai person regards himself as "above or below but seldom precisely equal to those around him" (Smith 1968, 218). Thus, individuals are believed to be fundamentally unequal. American sociologist Lucien M. Hanks concludes:

> Each Thai regards every other person in the social order as higher or lower than himself. The elder, more literate, richer persons tend to be higher due to greater virtue or 'merit,' as the Buddhist *bun* is usually translated. Based on these differences in social standing, a hierarchy arises where each person pays deference to all who stand above and is deferred to by all below. At the top is the king, and at the bottom some lone person who survives miserably in the dark jungle. (1975, 198)

With the top-down hierarchal leadership structure, decision-making power is generally deferred to the person occupying the highest position in the hierarchy in matters related to the whole group. In changing or converting to another religious faith, the family heads, kin group elders, and community elders play a significant role in the individual's decision making.

Leadership Relationship

Leadership does not exist in absence of relationships. In the Thai Buddhist context, leadership grew out of reciprocal relationships, translated into Thai as *bunkhun*. The *bunkhun* relationship exists when the leader, on one side, obligingly provides and protects the followers, and the followers, on the other side, declare to give obedience, respect, and deference; to show gratitude; and to perform their duties for the good of the leader.

In the Buddhist context of northeast Thailand, when there is an absence of leadership, the followers initiate the process of recognizing a leader. The followers would approach a potential leader and request that he or she become their leader—which means to provide and protect others. As he or she agrees, the followers then declare their allegiance to the new leader. The followers would then relate to the leader in obedience, respect, deference, gratitude, and duty performance. Both parties in the relationship are bound to carry out their obligation or declaration as long as the other side carries out his or hers. William J. Klausner agrees, "There was also an element of acceptance of the privilege of rank and status and the obligation to show respect, deference to and diffidence towards those on the higher rungs of the social ladder whether it was in terms of rank, seniority, wealth or power" (1991, 4).

A person can be relinquished from performing obligation in the relationship only when the other party has defaulted in carrying out his or her obligation or declaration. In such a case, the party defaulting in the relationship is declared a morally bad person unless he or she publicly seeks restitution. The followers may quietly withdraw from performing the obligations to the relationship and cease to follow their leader only if the leader ceases to provide and protect. It is shameful if the followers withdraw from the relationship first. American anthropologist Robert L. Mole, who has extensively researched Thai values and behavior patterns, notes,

> There is always deference, courtesy and proper status respect formally expressed toward those in authority over the individual. ... However if the authority figure does not honor the accepted reciprocal relationships, the oppressed individual may simply quietly cease to follow higher directions. (1973, 69)

Regarding the reciprocal relationship, an American anthropologist Herbert P. Phillips, who conducted extensive research in Central Thailand, explains:

> The entire authority system is based upon the individual's willingness to consider himself a dependent subordinate to somebody else. But his dependency is phrased in terms of the reciprocal relationship existing between the subordinate and his superior. He remains dependent only as long as the superior satisfies his individual needs. (1963, 306)

Leadership Behavior

While the top leadership figures are expected to make decisions and act on behalf of their followers, certain behaviors are also expected of them. Mole notes that "leaders are likewise expected to act calmly, in a self assured manner as they exercise their authority" (Mole 1973, 73). Thai anthropologist Supon Somjitsripunya observes that the northeastern Thai Buddhist villagers expect their village elders, who are natural leaders in the village community, to maintain "morals or moral standards, have experience in governing people, and sustain the Isan ancestor's traditional customs (known in the Isan as *chareetprapaynee*) from the ancient past" (1987, 268).

In addition to the personal and moral character traits, the leaders are expected to possess traditional/cultural knowledge and competency (another aspect of *chareetprapaynee*). In the Buddhist context of Northeast Thailand, accepted behaviors of a leader should conform to keeping the *chareetprapaynee*. Anyone found breaking the *chareetprapaynee* is viewed as behaving outside of societal norms. Consequently, the society would likely dispel him or her and impose certain measures of sanction against the violator. Rakwijit observes that "the Isan perceive an 'evil' man as one who lacks respect for the village tradition and customs" (1971, 73).

THAI CHRISTIAN AND NON-CHRISTIAN PERCEPTIONS OF CHRISTIAN LEADERSHIP

In 2011, eighty Thai church pastors and Christian leaders from the predominantly Buddhist context of northeast Thailand were surveyed as to their perceptions of Christian leadership. Shortly afterward, the perception of more than thirty Buddhist teachers and leaders toward Christian leadership were also surveyed. The results of the surveys appear in the table below.

Important attributes of a Christian leader in the NE Thai Buddhist Context	Buddhist Teachers/ Leaders	Christian Pastors/ Leaders
Character (honesty, humility, etc.)	17.1%	17.8%
Knowledge of cultural/religious customs	13.8%	5.3%
Able to represent group to authorities	13.8%	14.2%
Ability to lead locally	13.2%	10.9%
Knowledge of the Bible and theology	11.8%	14.2%
Charismatic/zealous leadership style	8.6%	14.7%
Serves others well	6.6%	8.4%
Maturity	5.5%	4.3%
Diploma or degree from Bible school	4.6%	5.8%
Ability to lead globally	3.9%	4.6%
How leaders who can influence others to Christ in their local communities are chosen/elected	**Buddhist Teachers/ Leaders**	**Christian Pastors/ Leaders**
Members choose leaders without endorsement by higher authorities	9.7%	18.6%
Members choose leaders who must be endorsed by higher authorities	32.3%	21.4%
Higher authorities choose leaders regardless of acceptance by followers	0.0%	4.3%
Higher authorities choose leaders who also need to be accepted by members	58.1%	55.7%

Table 1

Comparison Analysis of the Attributes and Selection Approaches of a Christian Leader in the Northeast Thai Buddhist Context

Attributes of a Christian Leader in the Buddhist Context

When Thai Christian and Buddhist leaders were asked separately what qualifies a person as an effective leader, the top response from both groups was "character" (17.1 and 17.8 percent respectively). For Christian respondents the second highest attribute was "charismatic or zealous leadership style" (14.7 percent), whereas for Buddhist respondents the second highest attributes were tied between "knowledge of local religious, cultural and customary practices" and "ability to represent the group to higher authorities and outsiders" (both 13.8 percent).

The third most important attribute for leadership selected by Buddhists was the "ability to lead locally" (13.4 percent). However, for Christians third was tied between "knowledge of the Bible and theology" and "ability to represent the group to higher authorities and outsiders" (14.2 percent). Lastly, the fourth most important attribute for leadership selected by Buddhists was "knowledge of the Bible and theology" (11.9 percent), whereas for Christians it was "ability to lead locally" (10.9 percent).

Several important observations can be made from this comparison of important qualifications for leadership from Thai Christian and Buddhist perspectives. The first observation is that the second most important qualification for leadership by Buddhists was "knowledge of local religious, cultural and customary practices," yet this attribute did not even make the list for the Christians. Second observation: the second most important qualification for leadership in the Christian perspective was "charismatic or zealous leadership style," yet this did not make the Buddhist list. Third observation: formal education in Bible and theological degrees was next to the bottom of the list for Buddhists and sixth in importance by Christians. Final observation: personal character topped the list for leadership qualifications for both Buddhists and Christians. However, the Buddhist understanding of character differs slightly from that of the Christian, as indicated by their differences in the second most important qualification.

An Analysis of the Differences in Perceptions

The differences between the Buddhist and Christian perceptions of leadership have several important meanings. First of all, both groups agree that the character of the leader is the most important qualification; however, as mentioned above, the interpretation of the meaning of character differs remarkably between Buddhists and Christians. The Thai word for character is *khunnattum* (คุณธรรม). This word is often translated into English as "moral principles," as it appears on the website of Mahamakut Buddhist University in Thailand (Mahamakut Buddhist University). The Thai derive their moral principles from the Buddhist religion and the traditional customary practices of their ancestors.

For the Buddhist, therefore, the character of a leader is defined not only in terms of personal virtues but also in relation to keeping the moral principles of Buddhism and the traditional teaching of the ancestors. For the Christian who no longer holds values relating to Buddhism and traditional customary practices, character is defined only as personal attributes. Inward attributes, such as humility and perseverance, and outward attributes, such as charisma and zeal, are most desirable. Thai concepts of leadership legitimacy as previously discussed stress the important role of traditional cultural knowledge and competency as well as the Buddhist belief in merit in lending credence to leadership legitimacy.

In the Buddhist context, it appears that legitimacy to leadership should be undergirded in a type of leadership character that is derived from a moral and religious foundation. It could be interpreted that a Christian leader should have character that is derived from the moral and religious teaching of Christianity, whereas a leader whose followers are Buddhists should have character that is derived from the moral and religious teaching of Buddhism. In either situation, moral and religious manifestations are expected in the personal character of the leaders.

Second, the differences regarding the second most important qualification between Buddhists and Christians indicate a significant divergence in understanding of leadership legitimacy and authority as well as acceptance of that leadership. In leadership legitimacy, Buddhists expect local acceptance and competency of any person aspiring to leadership in that location or realm. To gain acceptance, the potential leader is expected not only to have qualified leadership characteristics, but also to demonstrate competency in his or her knowledge of the local religious and cultural matters as well as ability to lead people to live harmoniously in the context. That potential leader is also expected to demonstrate that he or she has the acceptance and support of the group (see earlier discussion in the *Leadership Legitimacy* section). Without legitimacy, the exercise of his or her leadership authority will be in question and thus, potentially, it may fail.

Another reason that local credibility is important for the leader is because all leadership is context or local specific. Leadership is a relationship between the leader and followers, taking place in a specific local context. Thus, local acceptance as well as local knowledge and competency are considered essential requirements for a leader.

In contrast to Thai Buddhists, Thai Christians placed "charismatic or zealous leadership style" as the second most important qualification for acceptable leadership without giving any consideration for local knowledge and competency. For leadership qualification, outward attributes such as charisma and enthusiasm occupy an important place for the Thai Christian context, but they are not attributes acknowledged by Buddhists. Contemporary Thai Christian leaders have mostly had this leadership value passed down from predecessors who are either Western missionaries or those influenced by Western Christianity. For this reason, Christian leaders may be lacking legitimacy and authority to be leaders in the eyes of Buddhists. While they may be effective in their small group of Christian believers, they are not accepted in predominately Buddhist communities in Thailand. They therefore remain ineffective in reaching the people living in the Thai Buddhist context.

Third, less emphasis is placed on formal Bible and theological education as a qualification for leadership for both Buddhists and Christians, although Christians consider this attribute of slightly higher importance. The reasons that formal degrees are not stressed can be seen from several factors. Firstly, local leadership, in particular religious [Buddhist] leadership, is not established or legitimized through a formal educational process. Secondly, traditional knowledge and religious authority is normally not passed down through formal education but rather primarily through mentorship. At the local level, all village elders became recognized leaders primarily because they had knowledge and competency of cultural and customary procedures. (Again, refer to the section on *Leadership Legitimacy* above.) Nevertheless, formal education is important for official or government-recognized leadership.

LEADERSHIP SELECTION APPROACHES FOR THE THAI BUDDHIST CONTEXT

With regard to the selection of Christian leaders, the majority of both groups supported the top-down approach for leadership selection (Buddhist, 58 percent; Christian, 60 percent). One group (Buddhist, 58.1 percent; Christian, 55.7 percent) favored higher authorities selecting leaders with followers' acceptance. A small minority of Christian respondents (4.3 percent) agreed that higher authorities should select leaders without followers' acceptance, but none of the Buddhists agreed with this.

The rest of the respondents (Buddhist, 41.9 percent; Christian, 40.0 percent) approved of the bottom-up approach. On one hand, there are those (Buddhist, 32.3 percent; Christian, 21.4 percent) who favored followers selecting leaders with higher authorities' endorsement. On the other hand, there are those (Buddhist, 9.7 percent; Christian, 18.6 percent) who favored followers selecting leaders without higher authorities' endorsement. About two out of ten Christians (twice as many as Buddhists) expressed that leadership selection should involve only followers and not higher authorities. Overall, the Thai—Buddhist and Christian—who are living in the Buddhist context of Northeast Thailand seem to favor leadership selection by appointment of high authorities.

The pattern of leadership selection indicated by the survey confirms the Thai concepts of leadership as discussed in the beginning of this paper. Leadership legitimacy, leadership authority, leadership hierarchy, leadership decision making, leadership relationship, and leadership behavior all seem to support the top leaders making the leadership selection decision and gaining support from followers. As indicated by the survey, Buddhists do not favor the exercise of absolute authority;

none of the Buddhists agreed that higher authorities should appoint leaders without followers' acceptance. Because of the Thai concepts of leadership relationship and leadership behavior, Thai people believe that leaders will act in order to provide and protect the followers as well as to act with moral character. To act otherwise is to risk losing leadership legitimacy and authority and may result in a lowering of the leader's position in the leadership hierarchy.

Another striking observation is that twice the number of Christians over Buddhists favored followers selecting leaders without the endorsement of higher authorities. This suggests that Christians give less importance to existing official leadership or those leaders' involvement or endorsements. However, for Buddhists, the legitimacy of the activities must have official authorities' previous approval. Failing to understanding this significant difference in point of view could lead to a conflict between Christian leaders and the existing official leadership structure.

Although the Thai Buddhist perception of leadership gives weight to knowledge and competence, the findings indicate that Buddhists maintain personal character as the highest attribute of any leadership qualification. Those in higher authority, with the acceptance of their followers, are bestowed with the authority to appoint leaders.

MISSIOLOGICAL IMPLICATIONS

After examining relevant Thai concepts of leadership and assessing perceptions of the Christian leadership of the Thai, five important missiological implications have surfaced. Although more implications can be drawn, these five are significant for developing leaders for Buddhist contexts.

Developing a Deep Understanding of Thai Leadership Concepts and Dynamics

The results of the assessment of the perceptions of Christian leadership indicate that Christians lack deep understanding of how leadership structure and decision making in the Thai Buddhist context works.

This is confirmed by survey results that "knowledge of local religions, cultural and customary practices" did not make the list of leadership qualifications for the Christians. It is possible that due to dominant Westernized Christian influence in most Christian leadership training that current Christian leaders place less importance on local hierarchal leadership dynamics. Western leadership is essentially non-hierarchal in structure and highly performance-oriented. To promote effective indigenous leadership, the focus of leadership development must include these important contextual leadership concepts and dynamics.

Centering on Character Development

Our survey indicates that character tops the qualification list for a Christian leader. The importance of character is highlighted by well-respected leadership scholars. Warren Bennis describes leadership as "character in action" (2007, 143–44). Jacque S. Benninga and Edward A. Wynneboth maintain, "People with good character habitually display good behavior, and these people are known by their behavior" (1998, 442).

Since both Buddhists and Christians agree that character is the most important qualification of a leader, it would be of great importance that indigenous leadership develops potential local leaders along the line of character so that they become agents of religious change in their local contexts. Character development of leaders suitable for the Buddhist context needs to reflect Thai concepts of leadership. The leader needs to establish leadership legitimacy along the line of the Thai concepts of leadership prior to allowing him or her to exercise authority. As much as possible, contextualization in keeping with the Thai concepts of leadership needs to be done when a leader exercises authority or carries out his or her leadership role.

In light of the importance of character in the credibility and acceptability of the leader, it is vital that character development be an integral part of the strategy for indigenous leadership development for leaders working in the Buddhist context. The effectiveness and success of any leadership undertaking should be measured by its ability to establish respectable and acceptable leadership character within a specific context where those leadership roles are being carried out.

Building on Reciprocal Relationships

In developing indigenous leaders, building on a reciprocal (*bunkhun*) relationship is foundational to effective ministry in Buddhist contexts of Asia, particularly in northeast Thailand. In a Thai Buddhist context, when a Christian accepts a leadership role, he or she is a senior party to a reciprocal relationship. The relationship exists only when the leader and follower fulfill their roles. The follower will continue to remain faithful and loyal as long as the leader continues to provide and protect.

Reciprocal relationship provides a natural bridge for a Buddhist to change his religious faith. According to the Thai concept of leadership relationship as discussed in the first part of this paper, the subordinate party in the reciprocal relationship is expected to show obedience, honor, respect, and gratitude to the superior party. A subordinate changing his faith to that of his superior's faith would be socially allowed as long as the reciprocal relationship is well established publicly.

Thus, to increase effectiveness in advancing God's kingdom in the Buddhist contexts, an important priority should be given to building and maintaining ongoing reciprocal relationships. Relationship development in line with Thai concepts of leadership should then be reflected in the continuous planning and implementation of every indigenous leadership training program.

Developing Cultural Knowledge and Competency

The survey reveals the critical importance of cultural knowledge and competency. When a leader ignores these cultural intricacies, setbacks for the work of evangelization are certain. When Christianity entered the northeastern region of Thailand, some Roman Catholic missionaries ignored a highly regarded Isaan value, that is, to display public respect and deference to those in authority. The missionaries disrespected the Sakon Nakon's governor by slapping the face and kicking the foot of one of the officials sent by the governor.

In the past, Christian and Missionary Alliance missionaries had selected culturally ignorant young men over elderly men to be trained for

Christian leadership (no women). They regarded the elders as ignorant, uneducated, and incompetent, and they were not allowed to receive Bible training. After completing their Bible degrees, the young men, who lacked knowledge and competence in local cultural traditions and customs, wielded their power and leadership position over the elderly men. However, because the wider Buddhist community of northeast Thailand has always accepted, appointed, and recognized seniority over youth for positions of leadership, the role of the young Christian men was not publicly recognized.

Northeast Thai Buddhist society highly esteems hierarchy and power with the Thai king being at the top of the social hierarchy, whereas most Western missionaries place importance on equality and strength. As a result, the Buddhist society of Northeast Thailand views Christianity as a Western lifestyle that disrespects authority figures and ignores local culture, tradition, and customs. Rakwijit explains, "The Isan perceive an 'evil' man as one who lacks respect for the village tradition and customs" (1971, 73). Today, Western missionaries are not received as respectable local leaders among Thai Buddhists due to their lack of cultural knowledge and competency. Thus, a strategy to advance the gospel in Buddhist contexts should incorporate developing indigenous leaders who are knowledgeable and competent in local culture, tradition, and customs.

Establishing Locally Accepted and Competent Leaders

In the survey, Buddhists ranked "ability to lead locally" third for leadership qualification, showing the tremendous significance placed on local credibility and acceptance. This coincides with the Thai concept that a legitimate leader must demonstrate his or her economic independence and respect among his or her group prior to being advanced to a leadership role. In view of the emphasis on local competency, it is imperative that indigenous leadership development be designed to produce leaders who are acceptable to the people they seek to lead.

CONCLUSION

The effectiveness of developing indigenous leaders who serve as agents of religious change in their own local contexts significantly affects the successful outcome of the evangelization efforts of people living in the Thai Buddhist contexts. However, forming a strategy for indigenous leadership development effectual for achieving the evangelizing of the Thai Buddhists requires a thorough understanding of the Thai concepts of leadership as well as what the Thai perceive as acceptable Christian leadership.

Understanding dynamics of Thai leadership concepts such as leadership legitimacy, authority, hierarchy, relationships, and behavior are essential to structuring Christian leadership development that are contextual to the Thai Buddhist context. In addition, assessing Thai perceptions of acceptable Christian leadership have provided the framework to apply these concepts to Christian leadership development.

Having understood the dynamics of Thai leadership concepts and approaches as well as having grasped the Thai perception of acceptable Christian leadership, important missiological implications have been drawn for strategizing Christian leadership development for the Thai Buddhist context. The writer believes that a sound Christian leadership strategy that focuses on developing a deep understanding of Thai leadership concepts and dynamics, centering on character development, building on reciprocal relationships, developing cultural knowledge and competency, and establishing locally accepted and competent leaders will increase effectiveness in reaching people for Christ living in the Thai Buddhist context.

References

Adair, John Eric. 2005. *How to grow leaders*. London: Kogan Page Limited.

Chavinit, Kusuma.1988. Sasana chow ban nai wanakam nitan puen ban isan (folk religion in Isan folk tales) (in Thai). Master's thesis, Srinakharinwirot University.

Hanks, Lucien M. 1975. The Thai social order as entourage and circle. In *Change and Persistence in Thai Society*, ed. William Skinner and A. Thomas Kirsch, 197–218. Ithaca and London: Cornell University Press.

Keyes, Charles F. 1967. Baan Noong Tyyn: a central Isan village. In *Thai Villages*, ed. Clark Cunningham, 1–30. Seattle: University of Washington.

Kirsch, A. Thomas. 1975. Economy, polity and religion in Thailand. In *Change and Persistence in Thai society*, ed. G. William Skinner and A. Thomas Kirsch. Ithaca: Cornell University Press.

Klausner, William J. 1991. In remembrance of things past: Thai society thirty-five years ago. Paper presented at the Symposium on Cultural Change in Asia/U.S., July 12–16, in Bangkok, Thailand.

Leviton, Laura C. 2006. Foreword to *The handbook of leadership development evaluation*, edited by Kelly M. Hannum, Jennifer W. Martineau, and Claire Reinelt, x-xii. San Francisco, CA: Jossey-Bass.

Mahamakut Buddhist University. Moral principles, ethics, and morality for character development. http://www.dhamma. mbu.ac.th/th/index.php?option=com_content&task=view &id=57&Itemid=60.

Mole, Robert L. 1973. *Thai values and behavior patterns*. Rutland, VT: Charles E. Tuttle Company.

Phillips, Herbert P. 1963. Thai peasant personality: A case study of Bang Chan villagers. PhD diss., Cornell University.

Rakwijit, Somchai. 1971. Village leadership in Northeast Thailand. Research report no. 71–011. Bangkok: Joint Thai-U.S. Military Research and Development Center.

Saiyasak, Chansamone. 2007. A study of the belief systems and decision making of the Isan people of Northeast Thailand with a view towards making use of these insights in Christian evangelism. PhD diss., Leuven, Belgium. Evangelische Theologische Faculteit.

Smith, Harvey H., et al. 1968. Social values. *Area Handbook for Thailand*, 217–23. Washington: U.S. Government Printing Office.

Somjitsripunya, Supon. 1987. Lokkatat chow ban pak tawan auk sieng nua chak nung seu karm (a worldview of rural society from short palm-leaf manuscripts in northeastern Thailand). Master's thesis, Srinakharinwirot University.

8

Training Indigenous Leaders in Thai Buddhist Contexts

ALEX G. SMITH

Each of the world's people groups has a particular uniqueness which indigenous insiders know best. This chapter describes a process of selecting indigenous leaders and training them for evangelism and church planting from my experience as a missionary in a Buddhist setting in central Thailand. I unapologetically use the term "indigenous" because it represents an insider or emic perspective rather than simply local, which could be the case when missionaries or other outsiders live and lead locally. Indigenous leaders are those who arise out of a particular people, a specific context, and a unique culture. New models of nonformal training of indigenous leaders require sensitivity to local cultural dynamics, ameliorated through biblical parameters. It can be anticipated that new models will often be at odds with traditional forms of theological education. For this reason prayer and reliance on the Holy Spirit must saturate the whole process. In this chapter I suggest that the demanding work to determine better models for training indigenous leaders is worth the effort in the long run.

RELIGIOUS AND CULTURAL INSIGHTS

Undertaking serious research into a particular people's culture, religious context, and social structure helps determine the appropriate processes for selection and training of indigenous leaders. Too frequently this hard work is ignored in favor of an easier importation of outside, usually Western, models of leadership selection and training. Much can be gained from understanding leadership selection processes found in the society at large. For the context of Thailand, cultural elements found in folk Buddhism greatly impact the recognition and function of indigenous leaders within local communities. One determining factor is the influence of accumulated karma and merit, unrelated to what may be considered normal morality or spirituality. Leaving it to fate (in Thai, *taam bun taam kam*) is a frequently encountered attitude. Buddhists have a concept that karma from past lives affects one's life, status, position, wealth, and well-being in the present existence. The Thai saying *phu dip phu dee* is literally "from raw person to good person." This means getting position and riches through good luck. It indicates this effect of karma in one who obtains status and means and thereby could be considered a potential leader. By chance or fortune some gain a better life than others, being raised from lowly to high status. This is not a statement of good in terms of the personal morality of the leader, but of karma that has thrust him or her into power, position, status, and affluence. Chakrit Noranitipadungkarn's research on Thai secular leadership determined

that wealth and position are the essential features which characterize the Thai elite. Without one or both of these, a person will not be regarded as a member of the elite. Wealth comprehends both money and valuable properties. ... Positions may be in public or private organizations, part-time or full-time. (1970, 23)

The potent combined influences of power, prosperity, and position are basic to Thai business and political leadership, irrespective of moral or ethical standards of the person. Understanding this worldview is important. It should not be posed as the expected mark of a Christian leader, though sadly this does occur. Unmasking and discussing this common cultural value as a Thai Christian community is an important process in selecting leaders following kingdom values.

Furthermore, sharp insight is required to discern the incongruous disparities and consequent confusion that results from Buddhist worldviews in comparison with biblical ones. When humans do not acknowledge or recognize the Creator God, spiritual distortion can arise. Any accountability to a higher authority is minimized or even negated, making "self" the determiner of justice, ethics, values, holiness, and morality. Within Buddhism the absence of a Creator God impacts to a certain degree how leaders are selected and how they are (or are not) held accountable. This variant standard of values may adversely affect the selection of Thai church leadership. The characteristics of true biblical leadership need to be taught and applied contextually, not so much from an etic perspective of the outsider's culture as from an emic view within Scripture. Again, this is a process in which the gospel will encounter values and the community must be in discussion regarding decisions that are made. As a concerned outside foreign missionary, I wanted to stimulate indigenous church leaders to make decisions. Jacob Loewen's articles on missionary roles helped me in this, especially his suggestions to be a reflective mirror (1965, 168), a source of alternatives (1964, 246–248; 1965, 170–173), a catalyst (1964, 247–248), a stimulus for indigenous experimentation (1964, 249–254), and a friend of court (1964, 246–248; 1965, 205–208).

Another avenue of insight into indigenous leadership selection is found in a review of the training patterns used in the Buddhist *Sangha* and local Buddhist temple committees. In many cases, prospective monks and novices are sent to the temples from indigent families in the community, with the hope that by gaining merit they may advance from their lowly state to higher levels of leadership. The local village temple is the normal venue for short-term training of boys whose families cannot afford public education, and they become novice monks. The local temple is part of the community. Novices and monks are expected to live in the monastery. A course of training with a set curriculum guides their indoctrination. Monks learn by rote the Tripitaka scriptures, the meditative rituals, and related functions of service to the community. They participate in daily merit opportunities (*tak baat)* and funeral rites, along with assigned duties at the temple. Strong discipline and order are tightly practiced, while strict uniformity is expected. High value is placed on Buddhist education. This ongoing intensive training of indigenous leaders is given at the local temple, and is especially concentrated during Buddhist Lent (*Varsha*). Only selected permanent monks go on to higher levels of education, usually at Buddhist universities where a detailed set curriculum, enforced standards, and strict discipline are maintained. These are the expectations for training of qualified Buddhist leaders.

Monks and novices are not paid salaries. Nevertheless, they are supported from the local society. They obtain their daily food through voluntary offerings received each morning from the community's residents. The Buddhist laity voluntarily supports monks, novices, and the entire temple complex from their own resources. Along with food, the community provides appropriate Buddhist garments and personal items, monies, gifts, labor or materials for repairing edifices, and offerings for services rendered. Societal roles and paired relationships are strong. *Bhikku* mentors and their associated services to the community mutually match the opportunities monks provide for the Buddhist laity to accumulate merit by helping them. Thereby a reciprocal relationship of merit (*bun*) and good virtue (*khun*) is exchanged. Paired roles also include being master guides to the laity in meditation and forms of yoga. Once trained and ordained, the monks reside in the temples and serve the community. Some go as missionaries to other places and peoples, in indigenous settings or in foreign ones. The hierarchy of the *Sangha* with its aged authority and detailed organization maintains supervisory control and scrupulous discipline over the *bhikkus, nain* (novices), and *bhikkunis* (nuns), as well as over their temples and sectarian groups.

While Christianity is based upon grace, not merit, many principles and applications can be gleaned from the Buddhist model of leadership selection and training. Historically, missionaries and local pastors teach short-term Bible courses within concentrated time frames from a week to a month, not unlike *Varsha* lent. Often these are held in residential facilities. Some questions that challenged us were: Could the monk and temple model be adapted for training church leaders, or would it become confusing and unacceptable to churches? Would a separate facility be needed where men and women leaders would live in community, receive instruction, and serve the community? Would entry ceremonies comparable to those for monkhood be necessary? What about distinctive robes like monks and nuns wear? What symbolism and festivals might be adopted? How would this learning community be supported? Would believers continue giving sufficient resources for long-term sustainability of expanded training? Would a structured, disciplined life benefit participants and their churches? How would this fit principles of John Nevius and Roland Allen? Would there be reactions from Buddhists and the *Sangha*?

Reflecting on these questions I suggested our team follow a modified application rather than fully copying the Buddhist model. Practical needs also affected this for, in contrast to centralized concentrations of majority Buddhists, Christians were few in number and their small churches were strewn across the province. The mother church became the center for training leaders for the whole region. With family responsibilities lay leaders needed a program that allowed them to stay in their farming villages. They traveled to the central facility for two full days every few weeks over several years. This provided concentrated times of training and included a full night's stay each session. No special ceremonies, festivals, or robes were used for induction into training, but a special service to dedicate the leaders at the close of training was instituted. Leaders continued to serve their own churches and communities. The believers gave voluntarily to meet necessary expenses for the program. Trainees developed disciplined lives together, reflecting their dedication to serve. This modified program received no significant reaction from Buddhists, whereas fully duplicating the Buddhist pattern likely would have.

OBSERVATIONS ON THAI SOCIETAL LEADERSHIP

When developing leadership training for the indigenous church, missiologists should not ignore foundational social structures. In my research of rural Thailand from 1971 to 1974, I looked for principles and qualities for existing societal leadership in Thai Buddhist culture. Many scholars supported Embree's concept of Thai society as a "loosely structured social system" of "individualistic behaviourism of the people" (Evers 1969, 3f). Yet social structure also relied much on kinship relationships and friendship networks. I found that the social environment was built on multiplied patron-client relationships, frequently including family members.

Phillips affirms, "The family is functionally the most significant social unit in the village" (1965, 37). The nuclear family is dominant, but extended lines are also important for cooperative and reciprocal work, loans, and help in emergencies. In the village live many other relatives (*phi nong*) through blood or marriage connections.

Mole notes, "Social status is always of concern when two or more Thai are associated with each other" (1973, 89). A Thai individual has few equals. Everyone else is seen in relation to oneself as older or younger. Superiority is differentiated by age, position, or birth. The patron-client structure with "its superior-subordinate distinctions in both formal and informal relations" permeates the social structure (Mole 1973, 62).

Despite the prevalence of these paired relationships, the Thai have a strong disposition to independent individualism, probably developed from their self-centered religious core, influenced by Buddhism. A low tolerance for discord and interpersonal conflict causes easy separation between parties, including married couples, usually by avoiding instead of facing problems and finding solutions. This stems from the face-saving shame culture of the majority, making them gentle, good-humored, polite, helpful, courteous, agreeable, and often flattering. Thai seek to make positive impressions on others and are hesitant to tell bad news. They can be polite without getting involved. Lightheartedness is a technique used to avoid face-to-face conflict. Both the family and employer-employee paired relationships are quite fluid. An employee might leave with little or no notice when the relationship is no longer profitable to him or her. Generally women are given a high, if not equal, status with males. They usually hold the family purse—this despite being relegated to secondary social positions behind husbands and elders (Smith 1974, 3). With such a complex array of relationships in society, one wonders what patterns of leadership structure are valid or relevant for the church.

Furthermore, Blanchard recognizes that in the midst of this social lateral matrix stand two vertical structures—the Buddhist *Sangha* and the political government, both of which "are built in pyramid form and encompass the whole country. Even these hierarchies mean little to most Thai; for them Buddhism means the local temple, and government means the village elders" (1958, 8). Four structures direct "the social world of the individual—family, village, temple, and nation" (ibid., 9). The Buddhist temple symbolizes religion as "a dominant force in Thai life" (ibid., 11). The Thai have a common saying showing their identity revolves around "the nation, the religion, and the king" (*Chaat Sassana Phramahakasat*). This order is deliberate. The unity of the Thai nation is governed by the dominant religion—Buddhism. Even their highly respected king is required to be a Buddhist.

Generally, class distinctions are reflected in the ruling class of the educated elite and the lower class of peasantry. Wilson divides the ruling class into "a three tiered pyramid." At the top is the minority that dominates the ruling class, comprised of the head political leaders and a few close to the throne. The second level is the general military officers, high grade civil servants, prominent parliamentarians, royalty, and businesspeople. Third is the political public largely in the bureaucracy, schoolteachers, professional people, journalists, and commercial white-collar executives (1962, 60–61).

The lower class may similarly be divided into at least two levels. The upper includes the money lenders, the middle men agents, and the unlettered merchants usually found in the provincial and district towns. A minority of wealthy farmers and some who own extensive lands could be included. The bulky balance of the population, mostly peasant farmers with small properties or hired fields, forms the large base of the second level. The structure of the Buddhist *Sangha* with its ruling hierarchy at the top, its abbots, administrators, and leading monks next, and a host of junior monks, nuns, and novices below, is an obvious pyramidal structure.

My analysis of research from many scholars discerned that three influences in Thai leadership compete with and complement each other simultaneously—administrative pyramids for control and management, reciprocal paired patron-client relationships for functional personal interaction, and individual independence typifying the Thai pride of being free. Thai means free. Powerfully, paired relationships permeate the whole and provide the glue that holds society together. Even the political system fosters these reciprocal relationships.

Neher notes that Thai politics are conducted within the bureaucracy with little pressure from extra-bureaucratic structures such as interest groups, religious parties, or legislatures. Citizens' needs in undifferentiated societies such as Thailand are often satisfied through the clientele system. The limited number and paucity of political resources have strengthened the system of patron-client ties (1974, 93).

> Patron-client relationships help shape the society into a national whole. They are not separate and isolated relationships, but connecting parts of a whole system of groupings. A patron becomes a client to a group higher in the hierarchy. Theoretically, it is possible to chart a chain of patron-client bonds from the peasant farmer to the highest reaches of the power elite. (ibid., 73)

Akin Rabibhadana, a student of Thai society, claims that the Early Bangkok Period (1782–1873) reflected superior-inferior dyads as an important principle of Thai behavior. Not only was Thai society stratified and differentiated, but it was also integrated through a series of client-patron relationships throughout the society (1969, 72). Neher confirms that this pattern was still perpetuated in the 1970s and that these relationships were more personal than institutional (1974, 74).

In the preface of Neher's book, Chayachoke Chulasiriwongs writes:

> To Western eyes, the overlapping relationships and the employment of personal influence (as shown in the patron-client system) in various branches of the Thai bureaucracy are probably factors contributing to the slow-down of its development. These problems are certainly familiar to the Thai intelligentsia, and especially the ruling class. However, they are, in effect, being mobilized to the latter's own advantage, and the methods employed are age-old socio-political facts indispensable to the Thai way of life. (1974, v)

This pattern persists in leadership and affects dominant patron-client relationships in the twenty-first century. Recent popularized "Peoples' Power," through the movements of Yellow-shirts and Red-shirts, became cohesive forces of clients of political strongmen who have mobilized the populace as allies through this paired relationship model.

Neher's study claims that headmen initiate plans and implement village projects. (Village headmen pose an appropriate model for Thai local pastors and church leaders.) Neher analyzes the case of Headman Peng, who

> owes his reputation and influence to several factors: his unique personal qualities, his extensive list of clients, the resources he controls, his official authority role, and his subordinate relationships with powerful patrons. Villagers consider that, within the limits of his role, the headman's actions are authoritative. In this case, however, it is difficult to distinguish between the villagers' attitude towards the office and the man, since he so nearly personifies the ideal headman in most of their minds. (1974, 53)

Power, prosperity, and position, in conjunction with charismatic personality, visible ability, effective practice, and proven results, produce a recipe for success in Thai secular leadership. Undergirding all are the dominant patron-client patterns throughout Thai society. Through them information is disseminated, resources allocated, and people organized from top to bottom, even across the bureaucratic structure (ibid., 73). Wealth and position provide power to endorse these relationships as middle men between patrons higher up the ladder and dependent clients below.

From these case studies some positive qualities for the indigenous Christian leaders can be affirmed. First, relationships are the key to leadership influence on others. Church leaders must build relationships strenuously within their fellowships and with those in the community. Second, paired patron-client structures provide the potential power and the key value for selecting mentors in their roles as influencers rather than controllers, especially in training and church leadership roles. If every believer was a mentor to one or more members in the church, imagine what an important influence and power for change that would be. Third, this dyad pattern is truly valid for use in the spiritual realm. Pastors and Christian leaders are primarily responsible to God above on the one hand and responsible for the spiritual, compassionate care of their clientele around or below on the other, including those within the church and those outside in the macro society. Being accountable in both directions is necessary, healthy, and wise. The selection and training of indigenous church leaders should take these dynamics into account.

Discerning the cultural kinds and the societal roles of indigenous leaders is important. Leadership's functional styles may be either positional or functional, figurehead or executive, influencers or decision makers, controlling dictators or mentors with apprentices (clones of their masters). Some specific communities depend on lengthy open public discussion on issues, followed by the summation of a gifted discerner who then voices the consensus of the discussion to which the groups inevitably agree. Differences in leadership styles may be noted between those in urban contexts and those in rural settings. But relational qualities are fundamental to selecting effective Thai church leaders.

A perennial need is preparing to pass on the baton to newer, younger leaders. The mentor role is vital here. Apprenticing suitable prospects to function in future leadership is wise. One principle stands out for missionaries—establishing indigenous leaders from the start is superior to having to transfer control from outside to indigenous management later. Long dependence on foreign leaders causes serious weaknesses in producing indigenous church planting movements. Too often slow turnover to indigenous direction in so-called indigenized churches are screens for continuing foreign management under local leaders, who have been trained predominately in Western ways and are often still supported from Western sources. They may look indigenous, but are often still dependent. Who holds the purse often calls the tune. Freeing church leaders to be self-governing, self-supporting, and self-propagating accelerates church multiplication.

BIBLICAL EVALUATIONS ON GOD'S SERVANTS

Since much biblical data already exists on the qualifications of leaders in the church, I will not overly describe these. Instead, an analysis of local or indigenous methods of mentoring as seen throughout the Bible will be explored. Is there an emphasis on the mentor role of training in Scripture? While there are many different types of leadership training in the Bible, mentoring is one that has a strong relational emphasis and is one to be modeled particularly in the Thai Buddhist context.

Scriptural definitions of leadership always center first upon God as the supreme commander. God's servant leaders within Israel, the church, or the community operate in dependence under God's guidance, wisdom, and direction. In the selection and training of spiritual and secular leaders, the Old Testament primarily identifies prophets, princes, and priests.

Prophets functioned as God's spokespersons transmitting God's word to the people. The serving role of prophet had a kind of paired mentor-apprenticeship method of training. References to Elijah coaching Elisha are numerous (1 Kgs 19:19–21; 2 Kgs 2). Prophets often had a servant living with and working under them, for example, Gehazi under Elisha (2 Kgs 5). The sons of the prophets seemed to congregate and live together (with their wives), often having a notable prophet who functioned as a mentor, trainer, and teacher to them (2 Kgs 4:1; 6:1–4). Maybe this was an informal "school of the prophets," though that term is not used specifically. Certainly this was different than the institutional schools and seminaries of today. The curriculum was not so much academic knowledge as practical know-how and spiritual exercises. In both the familiar family style training of the priests and in the training of indigenous prophets, the mentor-coach model was commonly the main means for teaching.

Princes serve as managers of the earthly kingdoms, usually prepared under wise elder mentors. Priests serve as the mediators between the people and God, and sometimes vice versa. Usually priests were born into that role, exclusively through the line of Aaron. They were trained under an apprentice style, officiated at all sacrifices, and had other duties. They owned no land, but lived normal family lives. Their inheritance was the Lord. According to Numbers 18, priests "were supported by the tithes, first fruits, firstlings, and the various sacrifices" (Harrison 1960, 419).

In the New Testament, the development of indigenous leaders is quite evident. Jesus' way of training leaders was to call them to follow him, frequently travel and live together, and allow them to experience ministry alongside him. For three years they were with Jesus, hearing the teaching, witnessing (and performing) miracles, observing his prayer life, and learning how to respond to critics. Generally these apprentices still maintained reasonable family and work lives. By the time of Pentecost when they received the Holy Spirit, the apostles were already fully trained and ready to join in God's kingdom activity to the ends of the earth.

Paul the Apostle had been highly trained under Gamaliel, a respected teacher among the Pharisees (Acts 5:34; 22:3). Again a mentor and coach model was employed. It was Barnabas who brought the new convert Saul (later Paul) to work alongside him at Antioch. When others feared and hesitated to do so, Barnabas recognized Paul's abilities and went to Tarsus to bring him back so he could encourage and mentor this prospective new leader for the Kingdom. On his various missionary journeys Paul likewise took different mentorees along to coach and train them for ministry. A long list of individuals serving under his mentorship could be compiled. Paul's pattern to coach and set up elders in every city and church is also well known. Most of his epistles were written as a follow-up form of mentoring.

Once when D. E. Hoste of the China Inland Mission was asked how to discern if someone was a leader, he simply replied that he would look behind to see who was following him. Leadership at its most fundamental level is influencing others. One of the greatest examples of this is not from the stature of greatness, position, or power, but from humility and servanthood. A Jewish girl became a captive of Syria and the slave of the wife of the captain of the Syrian army, Naaman, who had leprosy. The captive girl told her mistress about God's prophet in Samaria who would cure her master. The wife told Naaman, who told the Syrian king. The king sent Naaman with a letter to the king of Israel requesting him to cure the commander. The distraught Israelite king's fear became known to Elisha, who told the king to send Naaman to him so he would know there was a prophet in Israel (2 Kgs 5:1f). Naaman was eventually healed through this chain of events. Because of her simple witness and faith, that unnamed Jewish maid became a leader, influencing others. Encouraging the development of this kind of indigenous influencers is the most potent means of increasing active and effective leadership. Everyone has a sphere of influence they can exercise, but that power remains mostly untapped.

CASE STUDY:
PRACTICAL RESEARCH AND EXPERIMENTAL MODEL

As a new missionary I, with my family, was assigned to work with Thai rural people. Over the next decade or so a modest movement of several hundred new followers of Christ and more than thirty small fellowships arose. This soon sparked my research for an effective indigenous leaders' training program for Central Thailand. Analyzing my survey of questionnaires on the profile of potential indigenous leaders for the growing fellowships, I identified some key qualities acceptable for local church leadership. The research design included surveys of existing pastoral leaders and functioning church elders throughout Central Thailand, as well as the rural member converts in our province. Most of those interviewed were personally known to me. The majority had an education of only the fourth grade level or less.

In June 1971, a preliminary program to develop lay pastors and church leaders in the province was started. It continued for many years. This program included two kinds of church groups: the older established ones in the eastern part comprised mostly of leprosy families and their relatives, and the newer groups in the west which arose from a pioneer movement in previously unevangelized districts. Only a few of these new folk were infected with that dread leprous disease.

The results of my research surveys revealed that the members' dominant concern for the ideal pastoral leader was the spiritual qualifications and skills that facilitated the ministries. Among other qualities, the responses overwhelmingly suggested that leaders needed to exercise the pastoral gifts of counseling, teaching, preaching, problem solving, evangelizing, administration, prayer, and other work of the church. Determination to use these gifts and live an exemplary life in spite of problems and discouragement was expected (Smith 1974, 13 and 17).

The normal biblical expectations for apostles, pastors, evangelists, and teachers were affirmed. A demand for leaders to be mature adults was emphasized. Preferred age was in late-twenties or older. Significantly in the secular world, the 1972 Thailand Constitution required a minimum age of thirty-five for membership in the elected legislative assembly (*Bangkok Post* 1972). My survey indicated that both male or female and married or unmarried were acceptable for church leadership, though many preferred married elders. Education was not an issue, except for literacy sufficient to read Scriptures. In contrast to Thai political leaders, wealth was not seen as essential, but true spiritual experience was. Having monies or lands was not viewed negatively, but the avoidance of covetousness, greed, and selfish pleasure was strongly enjoined. However, good social standing in the community was a top priority, particularly having a good name, good character, and appropriate manners and behavior (Smith 1974, 12–14).

Three other preferences in the findings were emphasized: First, leaders primarily were to come from the local community rather than from afar. The most effective local servant leaders and elders came from "among you," the local church context (1 Pet 5:1). Local leaders knew their people and the latest gossip in the community, whereas foreigners and even Thai leaders from outside regions were not in the inner circles of local knowledge and confidence. Second, older proven and mature leaders for the church were preferred to youth. This is contrary to the established pattern of normal theological training in the West, which depends primarily on youth graduating from high school for entrance to Bible colleges, before later ministry. The churches and their elders usually saw these youth as immature and inexperienced. Over time, however, some were able to gain the confidence of the church members and prove their developing abilities as leaders. Third, unpaid lay leaders seemed to be preferred to paid clergy for the church. Later, some of the latter category was likely to be needed, especially at training and supervisory levels as the churches multiplied outwardly. Two appropriate cultural observations on finance were noted. The locally elected village headmen were not paid for their services, but were economically independent, except for a small allowance to help defray the cost of hospitality required of them because of their position. Furthermore, since most churches had small numbers of members, they would be hard pressed to support their own pastors fully (Smith 1974, 16). Historically, before 1903 among the Lao churches in North Thailand, A. J. Brown declared, "Most of the native helpers ... are paid by the Christians themselves" (1903, 280). Hugh Taylor affirms that up to that time "no Laos Christian community had thought of having a pastor. The elders and natural leaders in each village had ministered to the group, and without pay" (1934, 160).

Prior to launching the lay pastor program, I struggled through ways to minimize the social disruption of these farming families. To optimize training for the indigenous leaders in their localities required a serious look at practical considerations.

First was a deep concern for how to maintain normality as much as possible in this agrarian situation. This required practical solutions to cater for the farmer-leaders' responsibilities while providing for their families. In this regard, the writings of missiologist John Nevius affected our thinking. During the 1880s in China and Korea, Nevius had advocated keeping pastors local and financially independent, rather than sending them off to some institution, far away from fields and family. From Paul's injunction to the Corinthians (1 Cor 7:20–24), Nevius suggested "most emphatically that Christianity should not disturb the social relations of its adherents, but requires them to be content with their lot, and to illustrate the gospel in the spheres of life in which they are called" (1958, 19). His pattern recommended unpaid church workers staying with their families and local occupations, over against leaving and obtaining church stipends elsewhere.

Second, rather than utilizing distant residential education, a phased plan of ongoing local training over longer periods with a graded approach was devised. This fit local needs and did not significantly disturb family relations, nor did it disrupt the churches.

Third, practical matters concerning the village leaders' travel into the training sessions revealed that buses traveled into the city of the mother church in the morning and returned to the villages in the evenings. The mother church offered their facilities for the overnight stay and provided food for the trainees. Hospitality is a high Thai value. The final solution was to have training periods of two full days with one night at the church, allowing trainees to arrive early, receive concentrated training, and return home conveniently. The sessions were held every three weeks, giving them plenty of fuel for preaching over the next three weeks. Through this arrangement the disadvantages of traditional extraction into external residential institutions were overcome. Within a couple of years we learned that, in South American Pentecostal circles, hundreds of unpaid lay leaders multiplied and shepherded churches in a similar manner. This affirmed the value of our approach for local training, with an emphasis on unpaid indigenous leaders, and hope for a greater harvest in the future.

CURRICULUM APPROPRIATE FOR INDIGENOUS LEADERS

I struggled with the implications arising from my research, which antici-pated an adequate solution to the expectations of the churches already noted above. This indicated a need to rethink curriculum for training, under these conditions. I recognized that the best training curriculum required careful honing to fit the indigenous situation, the cultural context, and the social structure, while taking scriptural principles and guidelines into account.

A vital necessity still in the twenty-first century is to create relevant training models throughout much of the majority world. In 2011, Caldwell and Wan called for "a radical reworking of existing training programs" which have been largely "based on old curriculum models from the 19th century with emphasis primarily on classic disciplines of Bible, theology and church history" (2011, 1–2).

That echoes my concern expressed to theological educators in Thailand in 1978: "This realistic problem is at the center of the world's crisis in education today, which revolves around curriculum" (Smith 1978, 1). Three problems I observed then in Thai fellowships included a low level of biblical knowledge for the majority of members, an inad-equate mature leadership in two-thirds of the local congregations, and an insufficient number of qualified people coming out of the training institutions.

I recommended further research in four areas of the training: selection of acceptable trainees, curriculum, the training process, and methodology. Goals were to "develop willing skilful workers" (ibid., 2), training them to function in the gifted roles of Ephesians 4:11–12, and to discover "sociologically accepted roles and functions for church leadership" (ibid., 2). An adequate curriculum was needed to train leaders to be functional—what they were to do and be rather than just to accumulate knowledge. Curriculum should be oriented to specific skills required for practical pastoral and ministry duties related to church and community, and be compatible "with the cultural environment and indigenous acceptability." It needed to utilize methods that "make the student think, work, research, solve problems, and find solutions to practical issues." This avoided "the baby bird with the mouth wide open or the beggar with his hand out" mentality (ibid., 2). The use of "parables, symbols, analogy, Old Testament festivals, agricultural ceremonies, cultural stories, and functional substitutes" was emphasized. A contextual circular logic approach rather than a Western style straight-line linear logic one was encouraged in discussion, preaching, and witness (ibid., 2–3).

Such a curriculum would take into consideration "thinking patterns, felt needs, worldviews and religious beliefs" of the Thai rural Buddhist society. It would focus on developing strategies for group or people movements and family evangelism as seen in Scripture and human history. Furthermore, "Curriculum must be indigenously related to the Thai communicative process, including educational and mass media inputs. Note that the Thai have indigenized or acculturated borrowed forms from the West. These are transformed subtly to make them truly Thai" (ibid., 3). Communicators need to define scriptural terms clearly, and illustrate them in ways that the Thai will comprehend the true biblical meanings. This is the true heart of communication and the key to effective evangelization.

The average syllabus and curriculum of most Bible schools and seminaries in Thailand and much of the East reveals that the majority mostly copied curriculum of institutions in the West. Little adaptation to the local needs of the cultural and religious context was included. Imported Western catalogs of subjects were (and still are) counterproductive to ministry in the social milieu of Eastern worldviews. These only reinforced the foreign look and Western conceptualization of Christianity, alienating it from the Thai masses.

In the early 1970s I instigated a local institute in rural Thailand, the Lay Pastor Training School, rather than following the popular approach of sending high school or college youth to Bible schools in large cities.

I developed a dynamic curriculum around practical issues covering the three dimensions of the functioning church: upward—worshiping God; inward—mutual caring for believers; and outward—ministry to the outside community (Smith 1977, 17–27). This basic curriculum initially included four broad categories: first, Bible knowledge, interpretation, exposition, obedience, and teaching; second, pastoral and counseling skills; third, evangelistic practices to multiply churches; and fourth, leadership matters including goal setting, delegation of work, accountability, problem solving, analytical evaluation, and practical administration. I also attempted to adapt contextual methods suited to various stages of development of the churches. The use of indigenous style drama-dance, hymnology, and other Thai cultural forms was strongly encouraged. A number of the leaders had been Buddhist monks, and their input helped bridge gaps of cultural confusion and religious interpretation (Smith 1974, 16). From the start I invited two mature local Thai leaders with previous Bible school training to be part of the teaching staff along with me and another missionary.

I recognized three levels of related training—oral culture, nonformal learning, and formal education. Because of the low educational levels of the participants, the Lay Pastor Training School combined nonformal and oral components. This model utilized multimedia methods. The tools were simple and easy to use. Regular lesson assignments for homework included a combination of reading sections from a basic Thai commentary on Bible books, listening to a Thai dramatization of the story on cassettes, filling out work sheets which were corrected and returned to the trainees, and memorizing biblical texts and tools. Concentrated exposure in training sessions followed for two consecutive days every three weeks. These sessions included group discussions after lectures or demonstrations. We also had the trainees immediately teach back the lesson on the spot before all the leaders. This helped them get experience in public speaking before groups and crowds. Sometimes the group deliberately acted toward the lone preacher like most Buddhists might. In the evenings movies, filmstrips, or slide presentations reinforcing the materials of the day were shown, followed by communal interaction as the leaders stayed overnight at the facility. Previously missionaries did much of the teaching in the churches, but with the start of this Lay Pastor Training School, the Thai leaders immediately became the teachers and preachers in their fellowships from then on. During this phase missionaries quietly sat in the congregation, listening, praying, and encouraging the evolving indigenous leaders.

The process of recognizing and ordaining local indigenous leaders had three phases. Initially their recommendation to the training program came through their own local congregations, along with their voluntary sacrificial willingness to attend consistently. Next was their faithful participation in the intensive training sessions, as well as practical service as apprentices in their local fellowship contexts over the next few years. Lastly was their official ordination after acceptance by the consensus of the combined leaders and their trainers. In this Central Thai model at the end of the first round of training, seventeen local church indigenous leaders were ordained and commissioned publicly. By then, three church districts with quarterly fellowships of celebration were already operating. Three additional regional or area supervising pastors were ordained and set apart, including the two Thai trainers who had proven their responsibility for mentoring local leaders in their districts. Thus two levels of functional leadership arose: local pastors and area pastors. This milestone was reached in June 1974, three years after the commencement of that lay pastor institute with its modified local oriented practical curriculum.

A constant upgrading of indigenous leadership training to address needs for the future was essential to sustainability, vitality, growth, and maturity of the training program. The continued development of existing servant leaders would be enhanced by mobile external extension programs held locally. This was our vision for the indigenous lay pastors' growth through the projected itinerating Home Bible Seminary. This approach was anticipated and planned for the future. Trainer-teachers would travel to meet with small groups or individuals to help them in their continuing extension studies, along with assisting them with problems and difficulties faced in ministry. This was instituted within a decade after the first students graduated. Beyond this was the vision for training a new level of replacement leaders for continued extension and growth. This contributed to long-term sustainability of the churches and vitality in evangelistic outreach, rather than stagnation and the slow death of the movement of church multiplication.

EVALUATION

Some surprising lessons were learned from applying the Lay Pastor Training School experiment. First, it took considerable psychological preparation of both the indigenous leaders and the missionary team before they were ready to give wholehearted agreement to it. The foreigners thought the local folk could not handle the responsibility well enough. The Thai felt they would need to continue to depend on missionaries as before. Once the program got under way the missionary team began to recognize its value as leaders' abilities and ministry skills improved. The Thai leaders also soon became excited about what they were learning and doing locally as a result of the training sessions.

Second, a new unexpected dynamic arose in training sessions between the older believers and the newer converts. The evangelistic zeal of the young challenged the older ones. They were surprised by the vitality and expertise of the young witnesses. On the other hand, the older Christians brought theological correction and stability to the group, rising to the occasion when the newer converts, because of their lack of spiritual knowledge and maturity, at times shared unbiblical ideas with the group. This interaction proved to be both enlightening and stimulating. It provided a self-correcting mechanism.

Third, when the program started, the change to indigenous teachers was begun immediately. At first some were inept and lacked depth. But I held the line not to supplant the indigenous leaders with foreign missionaries. I assured the lay pastors of our confidence in them. As time passed, most of them became quite efficient teachers, good evangelists, respected pastors, and some even adept Bible expositors.

Fourth, these leaders with various backgrounds, experiences, statuses, and occupations were drawn and molded together with high motivation, consistent commitment, and deep spiritual unity. Though it was difficult for some, they stayed with the training program and carried out their responsibilities faithfully month after month.

Fifth, the dynamics of the mentor-apprentice model facilitated local training, practical service, and local recognition. I frequently took one or two elders with me as I went to visit new converts or to evangelize a new family or village. Other missionaries and mature Thai did likewise. These coaching opportunities contributed to the growth of the indigenous leaders, but also provided me with valuable lessons as I observed and listened to them. Through these experiences a reciprocal synergy of learning occurred.

Sixth, as unpaid servants of the cross, the indigenous church leaders continued to have a fair level of normal regularity in their lives and in their home localities. This local training program was less disruptive for their families, work, income, personal relationships, and local monitoring of what was happening. They were also more readily aware of community needs, problems, crises, gossip, and hurts and were able to respond pastorally to the people because they were available locally.

Finally, the program took a lot of energy. The preparation of new materials, fresh lessons, and training tools demanded much time, particularly for me. The financial cost was minimal as the churches helped with their leaders' travel, the mother church provided and prepared the food, and no stipends or funds were handed out to the trainees. My expenses for the spirit duplicator, training materials, and media products were minimal.

Seeing indigenous leaders working effectively in Christ's church, helping the members grow, and efficiently reaching out to the families in their communities was a reward in itself. Indigenous leaders are priority for Christ's growing kingdom.

CONCLUSION

What happened to this experimental program of selecting and training unpaid lay pastors from the early 1970s? After I left in1974, it continued on strongly, still functioning locally in the Thai language into the early 1990s. Most of the unpaid pastors remained faithful shepherds and teachers to their local flocks until old age. They aptly stimulated evangelism and outreach to families, and reproduced new fellowships. Some lay pastors died, but newer ones replaced them. In 1983 a group of the trainers and lay pastors visited me in Bangkok, asking advice on developing a new generation of lay pastors, since they were getting older. I encouraged them to renew the program. New leaders were added regularly to the lay pastor training. This remained the strength of the movement. Years later, two of the Thai trainers and area pastors honorably retired, as did some lay pastors.

Some factors negatively affected the program. A couple of leaders moved away to other areas. In one case, economic realities forced an entire congregation to migrate to another province to find work. In that new place they started a new fellowship. One of the area pastors accepted employment with a foreign Christian aid agency. We had invited him into the program because he met the qualifications and lived on the border of the province next to us. He was the only one not raised through the program! One Korean missionary recruited another of our lay leaders and paid him to be pastor in a pioneer work in the province south of our area. A denomination outside of the region came in and took over two of the churches with their lay pastors. One of the groups died out within a couple of years and the worker left. The second was visited by our other lay pastors and reconciled with the provincial fellowship, regaining its lay pastor. Significantly, some lay pastors from our area were recognized as key leaders in the national Thai associations of churches.

The biggest problem was pressure from some missionaries and the national church associations, influenced by other denominations, to appoint and ordain salaried, seminary trained pastors. Some of our churches succumbed to this pressure and desired that their pastors be recognized in ways equivalent to Western churches. In the late 1980s, one such paid leader from the dominant Western pattern came from the outside, robes and all, to pastor the provincial mother church. By the early 1990s, the Home Bible Seminary program we had already projected was instituted. This valued effort seems to have gradually affected a slow demise of the lay pastors training program. It focused on upgrading existing leaders, trained under the Lay Pastor Training School, but it reverted to an academic curriculum similar to Western seminaries, without the practical courses for local contextual ministry. While there may be a place for both patterns, the future of growth still lies in training many unpaid indigenous lay pastors for reproduction of indigenous ministry.

Considerable crises exist in current church leadership, particularly in the majority world. Truly indigenous leaders are scarce and desperately needed. The existing church and churches yet to be born cry out for direction, relevance, and significant impact in the modern world of cultural plurality. The pressures to remain insignificant under the status quo of Western influenced leaders, foreign patterns of training, and often imperial institutional bias seem overwhelming. A revolutionary approach that produces a multitude of efficient indigenous workers is needed. While not ignoring the value and impact of existing theological institutions in Asia, a radical reexamination of basic premises in training methods and curriculum is long overdue. Fresh approaches with new experimentation and creative thinking that will multiply indigenous leaders for the twenty-first century must take priority.

References

Bangkok Post. 1972. December 16: Vol. XXVI, No. 348.

Blanchard, Wendell. 1958. *Thailand , its people, its society, its culture*. New Haven: HRAF Press.

Brown, Arthur Judson. 1903. The remarkable movement towards self-support in Siam and Laos. *Missionary Review of the World*. April–May: 273–280.

Caldwell, Larry W., and Enoch Wan. 2011. "Riots in the city: Replacing 19th century urban training models with relevant "urbanized" training models for the 21st century." Paper presented at EMS annual meeting, September 20–October 1. Bellevue, WA.

Embree, J. F. 1950. Thailand: A loosely structured social system. *American Anthropologist*. 52(2): 181–193.

Evers, Hans-Dieter, ed. 1969. *Loosely structured social systems: Thailand in comparative perspectives*. New Haven: Yale University, Southeast Asia Studies.

Harrison, Everett F. 1960. *Baker's dictionary of theology*. Grand Rapids: Baker Book House.

Loewen, Jacob A. 1964. Reciprocity in identification. *Practical Anthropology.* 11(4), July–August.

_____. 1964. The Church: indigenous and ecumenical. *Practical Anthropology.* 11(6), November–December.

_____. 1965. Field, term & timing in missionary method. *Practical Anthropology.* 12(1), January–February.

_____. 1965. Missionaries and anthropologists cooperate in research. *Practical Anthropology.* 12(4), July–August.

_____. 1968. Relevant roles for overseas workers. *International Review of Missions.* 57(226), April.

Mole, Robert L. 1973. *Thai values and behavior patterns.* Tokyo: Charles E. Tuttle Co.

Neher, Clark D. 1974. *The dynamics of politics and administration in rural Thailand.* Athens, OH: Ohio University Center for International Studies, Southeast Asia Program.

Nevius, John L. 1958. *The planting and development of missionary churches.* Philadelphia: The Reformed and Presbyterian Publishing Company.

Noranitipadungkarn, Chakrit. 1970. *Elites, power structure and politics in Thai communities.* Bangkok: Research Center, The National Institute of Development Administration.

Patterson, George. 1976. The obedience oriented curriculum. *Theological Education Today.* 6(4), November.

Phillips, Herbert P. 1965. *Thai peasant personality.* Berkeley: University of California Press.

Rabibhadana, Akin, 1969. *The organization of Thai society in the early Bangkok period 1782–1873.* Ithaca, NY: Cornell University Department of Asian Studies, Southeast Asia Program.

Smith, Alex G. 1974. Research report: Leadership profile for Thai lay pastors. An unpublished research project (1971–1974) of 18 pages submitted to International Institute of Christian Communication, Nairobi, Kenya, Africa.

_____. 1977. *Strategy to multiply rural churches: A central Thailand case study.* Bangkok, Thailand: OMF Publishers.

_____. 1978. Curriculum suitable to Thai churches. A paper presented at the initial meeting of the Thailand Theological Educators Fellowship held at Wattana Academy, Bangkok, Thailand , September 2.

Taylor, Hugh. 1934. Missionary biography. A 389-page typescript on missionary work in Siam (1888–1934). Chiangmai: Thailand Theological Seminary Library.

Wilson, David A. 1962. *Politics in Thailand.* Ithaca, NY: Cornell University Press.

9

The Buddhist Monk's Leadership Role as Parish Priest and Its Impact on Christianity in Sri Lanka

G. P. V. SOMARATNA

Religious leaders are trusted and respected in communities throughout the world. They maintain morale, pass on hope, and encourage others to contribute to the well-being and advancement of the community. They offer a process of social influence in service of a group's aspirations. It is a relational role that attempts to hold fast to the ethical standards of the religion. Leadership as a personal quality refers to a value that is foundational in influencing others and pursuing collective achievement (Scorgie 2011, 572). Contrary to the popular belief in the other-worldliness of the Theravāda Buddhist *Sangha*, in practice in Sri Lanka one can see monks' heavy involvement in what may be called "a parish priestly role." There are some similarities between the leadership characteristics of a Buddhist monk in contemporary rural Sri Lanka and those of a Roman Catholic priest.

HERITAGE OF CATHOLIC PRIESTHOOD IN SRI LANKA

Catholic priests began to work among the Sinhala Buddhist community from the second half of the sixteenth century and gained converts from them. During the next three to four centuries they had a pervasive influence in Sri Lanka's society even beyond the Catholic community.

Catholic priests have the authority or power to administer religious rites. The most significant liturgical acts reserved to priests in this tradition are the administration of the sacraments, including the celebration of the Holy Mass or Divine Liturgy. The sacraments of holy matrimony, anointing of the sick, and confirmation or chrismation are also administered by priests.

The close association of the Catholic priests with the laity has been a challenge to the *bhikkhus* (Buddhist monks) who previously had very little social involvement with the laity other than merit-making ceremonies. However, the Catholic priest's role among parishioners has been an inspiration to Buddhist monks to come out of their reclusiveness and become public figures. The merit-making functions came into the open and were no longer confined to the temple compounds. Monks came closer to the laity—even to the extent of disregarding some *Vinaya* rules. For example, the rules stipulating that another male be present when a monk and a woman would otherwise be alone together is now disregarded, as monks are in professional cadres and mixed educational institutions. Although the *Vinaya* specifies a prohibition on accepting and handling gold and silver, monks have resorted to the use of and indeed control over funds, bank notes, and credit cards.

Buddhists have long admired religious rites such as weddings, funerals, and baptisms offered by the Catholic priest. The popularity of the role of the Catholic priest in these events has made some Buddhist monks take up a similar parish priestly role in the activities associated with their temples. They have offered several social services and have gotten involved in the hitherto neglected life cycle events of the faithful who come under them.

A priest is a person authorized to perform the sacred rites of a religion, especially as a mediatory agent between humans and deities. Priests have the authority or power to administer religious rites—in particular, rites of sacrifice to, and propitiation of, a deity or deities. Priests must have frequent contact with those they serve and have a functional role in the society.

However, strictly speaking, the Buddhist order consists not of priests but of monks and nuns. One may see the difference between monks and priests in early Christian monastic development. A Buddhist monk joins the order not to function as a priest but to devote his time to seek his own salvation. On the other hand a priest is one whose training and commitment enable him to perform religious services for others. Theoretically monks tend to seek seclusion and have no functional religious role. The role of social worker does not form a part of the training of the *Sangha*.

DEVELOPMENT OF THE PRIESTLY ROLE OF SRI LANKAN MONKS

Buddhist monks in Sri Lanka are primarily of the Theravāda school, which emphasizes renunciation and noninvolvement in worldly affairs. Although the theoretical position remains thus, Buddhist monks from the time of the Buddha had to interact with the society and take part in social activities in a limited way. According to Walpola Rahula Thera, who is accepted as the popular opinion-maker regarding the role of monks, Buddhist teachings are based on service to others (Rahula 2003, 1).

At the original stages the monks did not settle in one place but wandered from village to village preaching the *Dharma*. They taught simple moral ideas conducive to the material well-being and happiness of the people, as the villagers were poor and illiterate and therefore not able to grasp the philosophical teachings of Buddhism. However, these situations are no longer applicable to comparatively well-informed Buddhist masses in Sri Lanka today. The Buddhist *Sangha* has to keep pace with the changes in the society in which they live.

The Buddha considered that close collaboration between bhikkhu and laity was necessary for the smooth life of the Buddhist community (Bechart 1991, 11). The *bhikkhu* was protected from need by the laity, who in turn received good doctrine from the monks (*Itivuttaka* 1889, 111). Strict training and discipline are required in the process of becoming a monk. The teachings given in this regard by the Buddha are known in the ancient texts as the *Vinayapitaka,* which contains lengthy details on the training rules, prohibitions, allowances, and regulations governing a *bhikkhu's* life. A good *bhikkhu* strives to train himself without committing any offenses in relation to the 227 training rules of the Patimokkha which he has undertaken to observe at the time of his acceptance as a *bhikkhu*. It is often said that the laymen keep five precepts, while the *bhikkhu's* load is 227. This is only a part of the truth since the *bhikkhu*, besides the fundamental rules in the *Patimokkha*, has to abide by numerous other restrictions, which are found scattered throughout the *Vinaya* collection.

Monks are the pillars of the faith community, spreading Buddhist teachings and also serving as living examples for the lay believers to follow. Furthermore, by serving as a field of merit, they give laymen the opportunity to gain merit by supporting the community of *Sangha* with donations of food and resources. It is believed that their disciplined life in the monastic order also contributes toward the monks' pursuit of liberation from the cycle of rebirth, which is known as *nirvāna*. Since the religious activities and interests of the laity are associated with meritorious deeds, the *Sangha* have come to be considered an indispensable institution for the religious activities of the lay people (Malalgoda 1976, 17).

Being a part of the Triple Gems, Buddhist monks in Sri Lanka are held in respect as leaders of the community. Robert Percival, a colonial chaplain in the first decade of the nineteenth century, stated,

> The priests of Buddou are in Ceylon superior to all others. They are called trinanxes and are held in high estimation at the court of Candy. ... In such venerations are the trinanxes held that their persons are accounted sacred; and the king of Candy, absolute as he is, has no power to take away their lives or anywise punish them even for conspiring against his own life. (Percival 1975, 142–143)

Their lifestyle is molded to support their spiritual practice, to live a simple and meditative life, and devote their life to attain *nirvāna,* which is the goal of all Buddhists. However, not everyone, including monks, is immediately interested in *nirvāna*. In addition to pursuing their own spiritual advancement, *bhikkhus* also stand in a position of leadership to the Buddhist community in which they live. The laity looks to them as an example and for guidance. They expect the *bhikkhu*, who is in a position of leadership, to maintain a high standard of faith and set a good example to them for their words and actions.

The ideal of separation from the world did not work smoothly even from the beginning of Buddhism. The *Mahavagga Pali* shows that the foundation of the Buddhist *Sangha* is not merely based on teacher-pupil relations but also on services in the area around the monastery (Sobita 1997, 127). *Bhikkhus* began to live in small shacks from the very early years in North India. These monks who dwelt in villages and towns had to have contact with the people in order to offer their services and to receive provision for their material needs from the laity. This led to the emergence of some parish priestly role even before the introduction of Buddhism to Sri Lanka. Over the years it developed further in Sri Lanka. As Buddhism began to spread to the interior villages, monks got more and more drawn into priestly functions such as teaching, counseling, visiting, and taking part in certain life cycle events, such as funerals (Geiger 1960; Ariyapala 1968).

Buddhism of the early period did not sanction rites, rituals, prayers, or ceremonial observances. The Buddhist ecclesiastical organization was originally a simple community. Monks turned out to be an important part of the Sinhala society, as they had developed some form of parish priestly role alongside the ideal of renunciation of worldly life, even before Buddhism was introduced to Sri Lanka.

IMPACT OF THE BUDDHIST PRIESTLY ROLE

The code of ethics for the monks—the *Vinaya*—acts as a demarcation to their leadership roles. On the other hand there are separate moral instructions for the laity. Taking refuge in the *Sangha* is a commitment to the moral ideal to which the laity aspires, even though one may not be able to achieve it. Although a layman may chant the three refuges and Five Precepts alone, the devotees believe that chanting with a *bhikkhu* is more efficacious. Devotional acts of Sinhalese Buddhism are centered around three objects. They are the *dagoba* (stupa for relics or burial), the Bo tree, and the Buddha statue. The Buddhist monk plays an important role in performing the rites associated with them. In addition, listening to the *Dharma* expounded by a *bhikkhu* is an act of immense meritorious value for Buddhist devotees.

For the Buddhist, the Buddha is the ideal of perfection. The Buddhist cult and rituals are based around his personality. This devotion has turned into a religion of the masses through the monastic system where the *Sangha* is assigned the responsibility of imparting the *Dharma* of the Buddha to the devotees. From the point of view of the Buddhist layperson, every good act creates good karma. The Buddhists invest much of their time and resources in order to acquire good karma. The meritorious acts associated with the *Sangha* are considered more valuable in the field of karma. Merit can be transferred to others who are either living or dead. The involvement of the monk in that process is regarded as significant. Every funeral oration performed by Buddhist monks ends with a stanza transferring merit to the living and dead relatives and other beings. Similarly the popular *bodhi puja* ritual is concluded by the usual transference of merit to the deities that protect the Buddha's Dispensation.

The Buddha did not appoint a person to succeed him or set up a particular order. As time went on, some form of organization evolved to deal with the practicalities of monastic life. The Buddhist monasteries do not assign particular duties to the resident monks. Originally no authority was conferred on anyone over their colleagues. The practice was to allow precedence of seniority calculated from the date of ordination. This order is followed even today when the *bhikkhus* go in procession to take part in a ceremony.

The special dress of an ordained Buddhist monk is a yellow robe. It originated from the idea of wearing low-cost clothing just sufficient to protect the body from weather and climate. According to the *Vinaya* code the robe should not be made from a single piece of cloth, but sewn together from several pieces. The saffron color, being the hue of a leaf about to fall from a tree, had cultural associations with death. However, the yellow robe of the monk is regarded as a symbol of respect and religious authority. Therefore, in Sri Lanka, even when a monk is caught in a crime, punishment is meted out only after removing the robe from his body because of the respect they have for the saffron robe. The robe is a symbol of religious respect.

PRIESTLY SERVICES PROVIDED BY BUDDHIST MONKS

The services of the Brahmin and that of the *shramana* (ascetic) have both been incorporated into Buddhist *Sangha*. This is supported through the institutions of popular Buddhism and canonical Buddhism. The latter division has never been clear. Therefore, the monks have attempted to take care of some of the services offered by the Brahmin while remaining ascetics, even to the extent of disregarding some *Vinaya* rules.

Among the services offered by monks to the society, teaching, preaching, and taking part in meritorious activities play a prominent role. The popular Buddhist practice of taking refuge in the Triple Gem (Buddha, *Dharma,* and *Sangha*) is believed to ensure safety and happiness in this life. The *Sangha*, being the only living reality among these three elements, has a special place in the popular mind.

Preaching and other forms of teaching are services which monks give the laity in return for their upkeep. The gift of the *Dharma* is regarded as the gift par excellence. However, the monks confer other benefits on the laity. Some of these functions have been inherited from the Brahminical foundations of Buddhism. Others are practices of popular religion. They coexist with one another. A significant part of Buddhist ethics therefore is that laity and monks reciprocate favors in this manner.

Laypeople give food to the monks with reverence and address them using the most respectful terms. Lay followers regard it as their duty to provide for the material needs of the *bhikkhu* (Gombrich and Bechart 1991, 48). They earn merit by doing so. The monks are regarded as "worthy of offering, worthy of hospitality, worthy of gifts, worthy of respect, the greatest field of merit in the world" (*Majjima Nkaya* III, 81; *Anguttara Nikaya* IV, 206).

Monks can visit lay households only when they are invited (*Majjima Nikaya* II, 380). On principle, these invitations are not given to a single monk. The *Vinaya* rule is that the invitation is to the community of *catu disa* (four directions). It is the community that decides who should represent the *Sangha* at social functions. When monks receive food in excess of their needs from the people, they are allowed to store it for times of difficulty (*Wijayaratna* 2003, 66). However, the items which the *Sangha* receive are regarded as *sanghika* (dedicated to the Buddhist order) and therefore cannot be returned to the laity. According to the canonical text, if the monks want to perform a social service, it should be directed through the laity.

Advisory Role

Because of the respect that monks have earned in their communities, the lay community accepts their advice and counsel. The cooperation of the monks of temples, both high-ranking and charismatic, is sought after and valued as they are still regarded as the people responsible for the development and well-being of the community. Because of this respect the lay community accepts their leadership even beyond the religious sphere. This is the reason that a political party of monks has been able to win some seats in the Sri Lankan Parliament. The superiority of the religious over the laity was taken for granted from the time of the ancient kings.

According to *Sigalovada Sutta*, where the duties of laity are described,

> In five ways should ascetics and Brahmans as the upper direction be respected: by kindly actions, speech, and thoughts, having an open door, and providing material needs. And, ascetics and Brahmans so respected reciprocate with compassion in six ways: by restraining you from wrongdoing, guiding you to good actions, thinking compassionately, telling you what you ought to know, clarifying what you already know, and showing you the path to heaven. (*Sigalovada Sutta 1990, 4*)

Parish Role

The Buddhist temple has been the center of social life in villages from ancient times. However, as a result of the encounter with Catholicism and Protestant institutions, the parish priestly role of the Buddhist monk has undergone improvements to encompass the needs of the laity, hitherto neglected. When the Catholic priests appeared on the scene beginning in the latter half of the sixteenth century, Buddhist monks were challenged by the social involvement of the new religious leaders. Consequently, we can see the gradual appearance of Buddhist monks in parish priestly activities imitating Catholic, and later Protestant, clergy.

Accordingly devotees have been encouraged to come to the temple when they have problems, to receive the counsel of a *bhikkhu*. For instance, pregnant mothers come and get the *Angulimala pirit* (ceremony) chanted for the security and health of the child (Piyadassi 1999, 128). When the child is born the *welapat kade* (astrological chart) is written by the monk in the temple. The child's name is obtained from the monk. The child is brought to the temple after three months. Cutting of the first portion of hair is done in the temple. When the child is given the first solid meal, a *dana* (alms) would be offered to the temple. When the child is taught to write letters for the first time, it is usually done in the temple by the chief monk or another monk assigned by him since they are regarded as the source of knowledge (EB VII, 545).

Teaching Role

Buddhist monks performed the role of teachers from the very beginning of the introduction of Buddhism to Sri Lanka in the third century BC. When Buddhism was a new religion, it had to be taught to a group of full-time learners in order to preserve the *Dharma* (*Mahavagga*). The laity had to be taught the basic precepts for good living. The responsibility to impart Buddhist teachings to the laity fell upon the *Sangha* who resided in various villages in the country. The temple had become the center of education prior to the arrival of Christian missionaries. Its education was based on the memorization of Buddhist texts.

Prior to any exposure to Western patterns, the learned monks kept historical records, explained the *Dharma* texts to people, and even composed astrological charts. The Buddhist temple was traditionally regarded as the center of learning. People looked up to monks for guidance. Monks have taken part in offering moral instruction, and in literary and cultural activities. Occasionally they have intervened in political events.

Ceremonial Role

There is a common belief in Sri Lanka that most of the afflictions that humans suffer are due to malefic, evil forces. Although there are many rituals in popular Buddhism which are supposed to placate the anger of demons, the only ritual sanctioned by the Buddha for this is the *pirit* ceremony (Kariyawasam 1995, 32). It is a very important ceremony in the domestic and social life of the Buddhists. Household social functions, festivals, and ceremonies are preceded by the chanting of *pirit* (De Silva 1974, 81). Such ceremonies range from simple rituals to the most elaborate functions (EB VII, 321–325).

The service of the Buddhist monks is important in the *pirit* chanting ceremony. It has become the practice of lay people to chant *pirit* sometimes daily. But the involvement of monks is treasured by all Buddhists. Their chanting is believed to have more power than that of the laity. For special occasions a pavilion is erected for this purpose. Some temples have halls with a permanent *pirit* pavilion. Before the ritual, monks are welcomed to the ceremony by offering a tray of betel leaves symbolizing respect to the *Sangha*. The feet of the monks are washed before they are led to the place where the ceremony is to be held (Rhys Davids 1899, 186–7; Kariyawasam 1995, 36).

The Buddhist scripture mentions *dana* (alms), *sila* (virtue), and *bhavana* (meditation) as three particularly meritorious works. *Dana* ceremony takes the form of an invitation to a monk by a layperson (Narada1988, 341). Monks preside over public merit-making ceremonies which are known as *pinkama* (meritorious work). Almost all the religious activities that have a ceremonial and a ritualistic significance are regarded as acts for the acquisition of merit (Kaiywasam 1995, 4).

Life Cycle Events

Life cycle events such as birth, puberty, and marriage are regarded as secular events. In the traditional Buddhist society the rituals relating to these events are solemnized by specialists in the popular religious systems by the *kapuwa* (indigenous Hindu priest), *kattadiya* (shaman), and astrologer. Thus, two aspects of Buddhism coexisted from the inception of Buddhism in Sri Lanka. Foreign visitors such as Robert Knox saw the clear demarcation of these two areas (Knox 1911, 204). A Christian missionary in the nineteenth century noted, "From their birth to their death, the Sinhalese are said to be Buddhists in heart. When a child is born they consult astrologers. Is it sick, they tie charms to its neck, hands and feet, does it eat rice for the first time, a heathen name is given" These popular religious performers never challenged the sphere of the Buddhist monk's role. Death, however, is a major event in which Buddhist monks have the monopoly of officiating the relevant rituals. This is because death is at the center of Buddhist religious awareness. The death ceremonies are ideal occasions to preach the *Dharma*, which emphasizes the three signs (*tilakkana*) known as *anicca* (impermanence), *dukkha* (sorrow), and *anatma* (no soul), forming the bedrock of Buddhism.

Marriage Ceremonies

Roman Catholic marriage is sacramental in character, with a priest performing the rites in a sacred church building. In this process, the Catholic priest plays a significant role. Prior to the arrival of Catholic priests in the sixteenth century, Buddhists did not have a formal marriage ceremony. This lacuna in the Buddhist lay life continued into the nineteenth century when it was settled with the introduction of the poruwa ceremony (Gombrich and Obeyesekere 1990, 262). "Christianization" of Buddhist social practices began in the late nineteenth century and later under the patronage of Henry Steel Olcott (1832–1907). His Buddhist Theosophical Society helped to baptize many Christian practices into the Buddhist system (Bond 1992, 49).

The marriage ceremony had to be "sacramentalized" by bringing it closer to Catholic practice in order to make the Buddhists feel respectable in their various social rituals, of which marriage was a central event. This was partly fulfilled by the poruwa ceremony, which was introduced in the 1860s with the leadership of Buddhist clergy. The new system gained popularity within a short period and became a powerful alternative to the Catholic wedding ceremony in a church setting. However, the monks could not directly be involved in the ceremony. Therefore, the rituals were reformed by a shaman priest. Unlike other religious leaders, Buddhist monks cannot take part in formal wedding proceedings. The monk is traditionally associated with sterility. His robe is a symbol of death and decay. The mere sight of a monk is regarded as inauspicious in secular contexts. The majority of Buddhists still find it strange for a monk to appear at a wedding. Therefore, wedding ceremonies have continued to be performed in secular premises.

This symbolically inauspicious character of the monk has so far prevented his involvement in this significant social and family event. Therefore, various nuances have been tried. In the recent past serious attempts have been made to secure the involvement of monks in Buddhist wedding ceremonies. When a marriage is arranged, the householders give alms to the *Sangha* so that all may go well. Monks are not invited to participate or officiate at weddings. However, the monks can offer blessings to couples. There is a gradual development to get Buddhist monks closely involved in marriage ceremonies. Couples have gone to the temple to request the monks to recite *pirit* for their protection. This does not conflict with the traditional views on fertility, which play an important part in Sinhala Buddhist weddings. There have been rare occasions where innovative monks have recited *pirit* at the wedding itself. Such innovations have made a calculated attempt to bring the *Sangha* in line with the role of a parish priest.

RECENT INNOVATIONS

The parish priestly role of the Buddhist monk culminates in new forms of Buddhist wedding ceremonies held within temple premises. Weddings in temples are a part of this process of "Christianization of Buddhism." In recent times, some young Buddhist couples have experimented, registering their weddings in temples and some of them in lobbies, for Buddhist monks vested in legal powers to register marriages, a power that the Christian priests possess. For example, recently a wedding took place in Gangaramaya, a famous Buddhist temple in Colombo (*Lanka Polity*, December 12, 2010). They invited the registrar of marriages to the temple to register the marriage while monks blessed the couple by chanting *pirit*.

There are also reports of monks performing Christian type weddings in their temple *bana maduwa* (preaching hall). Such practices have received reinforcement from Sinhala Buddhist monks residing in Christian countries. According to statistics there are over one million Sinhalese Buddhists living outside Sri Lanka. They have expressed the desire to have their weddings considered sacraments, similar to Christian church weddings. Buddhist wedding ceremonies performed in Sri Lanka, even after the introduction of the *poruwa* ceremony, lack Buddhist religious sacredness. In fact, the *poruwa* ceremonies performed either in hotels or in homes (secular environments), without the blessing of Buddhist *Sangha*, lack religious solemnity. Therefore, new experiments have been tried, keeping in mind the parish priestly role of the Buddhist monk. A wedding ceremony in Buddhist style has its own characteristic together with Christian elements such as blessing. The ceremony begins at an auspicious time, in the presence of well-wishers who are gathered in a Buddhist religious setting. The father escorts the bride to the congregation and stands before the Buddhist monk until the groom comes to stand beside her. Chanting of *pirit* and *jayamangala gatha* by way of ritual are a part of this process. *Pirit* thread is tied on the fingers of the couple by the presiding monk uniting them (Gombrich 1990, 267). The wedding ritual culminates with the monks receiving gifts from the bride and groom (Kennedy 1974, 13).

In another form of marriage ceremony in a Buddhist religious setting, the couple will give alms to the monks in order to make merit so that the groom and bride will be blessed in their married life. The groom and bride will light a lamp and offer incense in the front of the Buddha statue. This signals the beginning of the ceremony. There are occasions where the *poruwa* ceremony is held near the sacred *bodhi* tree of the temple. After these rituals, there will be a procession, led by the groom and the bride, to the shrine room. This is to symbolize that the groom and the bride have finally become one person. From now on, they will share happiness and sadness. This new style of weddings has brought the monk to play a central role in the process of officiating the marriage ceremony. This kind of experiment in elite society has the capacity to influence the rest of the society.

Extreme Unction

The Roman Catholic Church now uses the name "Anointing of the Sick" to emphasize that the sacrament of extreme unction is available, and indeed recommended, to all those suffering from any serious illness, and to dispel the common misconception that it is exclusively for those at or very near the point of death. The term "last rites" refers to administration to a dying person not only of the sacrament of Anointing of the Sick but also of Penance and Holy Communion. The last sacrament, when administered in such circumstances, is known as "Viaticum," which means "provision for the journey." Praying for the sick has been a part of the service of the parish priest irrespective of denominational differences and has remained so throughout the history of the church. This gives comfort to the sick as well as to the family.

A similar practice can be found in Theravāda Buddhism in Sri Lanka. Before a person dies, if all hope is given up, a special ceremony is held. The family members and relatives will go to the temple with offerings and conduct the monks to the house. *Pirit* is chanted and *bana* is preached to the sick person and to those assembled. In times of sickness *bhikkhus* are invited to chant *pirit* for the recovery of the patient (Kariyawasam 1995, 10).

For Buddhists, death is not the complete annihilation of a being. The particular life span ends, but the force within the being hitherto actuated it is not destroyed (Narada 1985, 261). Death does not spell either the entrance to eternal life or complete extinction. It is, rather, the portal to a new rebirth which will be followed by more growth and decay, until another death. They try to get good *cuti citta*, which is the last thought of a person at the moment of death (EB IV, 273–276). Monks may be invited to chant *pirit* in order to make the benefit more forceful. At the very moment of the end of the present life, the new life (*bhava*) begins. According to Buddhism this is the process of death and rebirth (ibid.).

In this pattern of service offered by the Buddhist monk, there exists some similarity between the parish priestly role of the Buddhist monk and that of the Christian minister.

Funerals

Among Buddhists, death is regarded as an occasion of major religious significance, both for the deceased and for the survivors. For the deceased it marks the moment when the transition begins to a new mode of existence within the round of rebirths. When death occurs all the karmic forces that the dead person accumulated during the course of a lifetime become activated and set about determining the next rebirth. For the relatives, death is a powerful reminder of the Buddha's teaching on impermanence (EB IV, 531–535). It also provides an opportunity to assist the deceased person on to the new existence. The Buddhist monk is an important person in the funeral rites. In fact, this is the only life cycle event in which monks have participated from early times. The "offering of cloth on behalf of the dead" (*mataka-vastra-puja*), "preaching for the benefit of the dead" (*mataka-bana*), and "offering in the name of the dead" (*mataka-dana*) are all *bhikkhu*-centered (Kariyawasam 1995, 45). However, it is necessary to mention that the involvement of the *Sangha* in a funeral ceremony, as it is practiced today, where the dead are buried with religious rites, owes its origin to Roman Catholic funeral practices in the church yard, where the parish priest played an important role.

Post Funeral

According to the Buddhist text—*Tirokuddha Peta* (EB VII 2003, 558)— the dead depend on the living for their sustenance. This transaction cannot be done directly. Various rituals have been devised to keep the dead supplied with their needs. The *pattidana* or the merits transferred through monks are regarded as efficacious. *Pattidana* transfers the merits they earned by the performance of religious rituals, such as making offerings of food, drink, flower, lamps, and so forth, to the *Buddha*, *Dharma*, and *Sangha*. This practice is especially seen at funerals and post funeral rituals when the departed one is offered the merit gained by gifting Buddhist monks their material needs.

The Roman Catholic practice of prayers for the dead (2 Maccabees 12:44) is somewhat close to Buddhist *pattidana*, although the premises

of the two religions are different. The Catholic belief is bound up insepa-
rably with the doctrine of purgatory and the doctrine of the communion
of the saints. These two practices have been used as bridges for those
who transfer allegiance from one faith to the other.

Some Roman Catholic practices also have been incorporated into
the modern Buddhist rituals in the process of post funeral customs.
One can notice monks participating in the *dana* offered on the seventh
day after death, which is followed by a *bana* preaching. These rituals
are repeated three months, one year, and three years after the death of
the person. These are among several Catholic practices incorporated
into the Buddhist system since the seventeenth century. Now these rites
and rituals have become part of the Buddhist heritage with additional
rituals drawn from the popular Buddhist background.

Other Rituals

There are several other rituals and events of social significance where the
services of monks run parallel to those of the Catholic priests. These are
new practices introduced following the example of the Catholic parish
priestly role. When a house is built monks have been invited to take a
leading part in various stages of building activities. Sometimes the invited
monk lays the cornerstone. He would chant *pirit* and bury security pots
in the four corners of the foundation. Similarly when the doorframes
are fitted and roof is constructed the monk's blessing is sought. Upon
occupation of the house, the owners have a *pirit* ceremony performed
by inviting a number of monks. Likewise when a child goes to school for
the first time, the parents hold a *bodhi puja* with the cooperation of the
monks. Some of these rituals of Christian origin, performed according
to auspicious times, make the act itself authentic to the Buddhist public.

THE FUTURE OF PRIESTLY ROLES IN
BUDDHIST SOCIETY

There are three separate *Sangha* organizations, known as *nikaya*, in Sri
Lanka. These three *nikayas* began to function at different times in the

course of the nineteenth century and were based on caste distinctions. The first to be established was the *Siam nikaya,* which confined its membership to the majority caste known as *Goyigama.* Subsequent to the arrival of the British, a new sect known as the *Amarapura nikaya* emerged in the Southwestern littoral and spread to other parts of the country. They were confined to non-Goyigama high castes. The third one, known as the *Ramanna nikaya,* appeared in 1864 encompassing all the castes, including those castes which were hitherto debarred from the *Sangha* establishment. All the Buddhist temples in the country are affiliated with one of these three *nikayas.*

The *nikayas,* being based on the traditional caste system, are bound to serve their own communities in villages and towns. The monks of these *nikayas* often get together for common purposes. However, their hierarchy and the services they offer are confined to their own castes. The *nikayas* have their own ecclesiastical organization with a constitution, a head, and advisory council. This body makes administrative appointments such as *Nayaka* and *Anu–nayaka* (De Silva 1974, 107). These ecclesiastical leaders are given certain spheres of administration according to territorial divisions and incumbencies. Their ecclesiastical organization with hierarchical gradations are far removed from the original institution of the *Sangha.* However, the modern practice is that a temple is under the jurisdiction of a central organization. The influence of the Catholic hierarchical structure is seen in this model. Therefore, the parish priestly role became an integral part of the system.

In this social relationship based on caste divisions there are duties that the lay person has to perform for the *bhikkhu,* and similarly the *bhikkhu* also has responsibilities regarding the well-being of the laity. The parish priestly role of the Buddhist monk is especially noticeable in these modern *nikayas* as they serve within their own communities. There is a fraternal bond between the monk of the temple and the villager who belongs to the same caste.

Politics and Charity

Social organization by way of the formation of modern societies has come about to meet contemporary social and political needs. The United

Bhikkhu Front, Patriotic *Bhikkhu* Front, *sasana* committees of the three *nikayas*, and *sasana* protection societies are a few examples (Sobitha 1997, 130). The *Sangha* gets involved in modern social activities by sometimes overstepping the boundaries laid down in the teaching of the Buddha. Institutions like homes for the aged, asylums for destitute children and orphanages, and Sunday schools have sprung up in imitation of Catholic and Christian institutions. The industrial schools run by the Catholic Church and some Protestant churches also have encouraged the monks to start similar institutions of their own. In addition to these institutions Buddhist monks act as advisors to various religious and secular institutions run by the Buddhist laity. Army chaplain, hospital visitor, and prison visitor are also new additions of the parish priestly role of the *Bhikkhu*.

Education of Monks

Even though there are no completely accurate statistics on the number of ordained Buddhist monks in Sri Lanka, estimates indicate that the total is around 30,000 in the country. Since the offering of state assistance to Buddhist temple schools in 1961, the quality and standards of education of the Sri Lankan *Sangha* have improved tremendously. This has been accentuated since the 1990s as a result of greater opportunities offered to Buddhist monks in the higher educational institutions. About twenty percent of monks, the bulk of whom are under twenty-five years of age, receive some form of higher education. There are two state-funded universities which function mainly for training Buddhist monks. Several other universities also provide training for monks in secular subjects.

Welfare assistance

Buddhist monks traditionally were contributors to society in a limited way. However, their roles have changed with the modern challenges and competitions from Christian and nongovernmental organizations. Recent disasters in Sri Lanka, particularly the tsunami in 2004, placed Sri Lankan Buddhist monks in the focus of the international community. They were offered large sums of funds to help the victims. Despite the prohibitions in the *Vinaya* rules, monks were faced with a situation in which they had to be in control of funds. Therefore Buddhist monks and nuns have helped in the running of free clinics, orphanages, homes for the aged and the sick, and other welfare organizations.

Buddhist monks in Sri Lanka took a leading role in this time of emergency and were able to rapidly mobilize their forces in order to help victims. Their temples became shelters for the victims and centers for relief work. *Bhikkhus* were involved in relief services, such as providing cooked food, water, clothes, medicine, and sanitation, as well as establishing welfare centers with the help of local and foreign well-wishers in their temples. However, most of these Buddhist monks have engaged in disaster management activities individually. They even demanded that Christian NGOs channel their assistance through the village temples. Whatever the methods they adopted, the Buddhist monks used the Catholic parish priestly role as their example.

USE OF CATHOLIC WORSHIP FORMS

The Catholic worship style has been attractive to Buddhists since the seventeenth century, when Roman Catholic missionaries were active under Portuguese rule. Abbé Dubois, a Catholic missionary in Mysore in the seventeenth century, stated that

> The catholic form which you Protestants call an idolatry in disguise: it has a pooja or sacrifice; it has procession, images, tirtan or holy water, fasts or feasts and prayers for the dead, invocation of saints, etc., all of which practices bear more or less resemblance to those in use among the Hindoos. (J. A. Dubois 1823, 18)

What Abbé Dubois says about the Hindus in Mysore may also be applied to Buddhists in Sri Lanka. The Sinhalese Buddhist king Vira Parakrama Narendra Sinha (1701–1739) praised the Catholics for the use of images in Catholic worship (Malalgoda 1974, 34).

There are similarities between Catholic priests and Buddhist monks both in their personal attributes and in the service they render. Buddhist monks actually have more similarities with the Catholic priests than with the Hindu Brahmin. The monks are celibate, dress differently from the laity, and live in dwellings set apart for them; they do not reside with laypeople even for one night. The Buddhist monk, like the Catholic priest, is respected in society.

However, there are areas where the Catholic priest is ahead of the Buddhist monk in involvement with social needs. Catholic priests can speak to women parishioners without inhibition, whereas the *Vinaya* rules limit the monks' speaking with female devotees to a few words. Monks are unable to drive cars, ride motorcycles, or take part in sports events.

Buddhist leaders who wished to get involved in social action have quoted *Ambalatthika-rahulovada Sutta,* where it is stated that it is the duty of bhikkhu to do that which is good to the society (Sobita 997, 125). The Venerable Walpola Rahula's The Heritage of the *Bhikkhu* is a vivid account of the monk's role as a servant to the needs of his community. This book, which is a classic work in understanding the essential role of service to one's community, provides a fascinating and practical doctrine for daily living and spiritual practice of the Buddhist clergy.

Originally there was considerable opposition to political and social involvement on the part of monks. Traditionalists have expressed that political and social activities would interfere with the piety of a *bhikkhu.* Walpola Rahula, who has had a great impact on the change of traditional behavior, has convinced them that "a *Bhikkhu* engaged in social work must necessarily possess nobler and more exalted virtues and qualities that a *Bhikkhu* living by himself and meditating in retirement in a forest" (Rahula 2003, 107).

As a result of this teaching, Buddhist monks have participated in rural construction and development work. The monks have argued that the construction work undertaken by the government had been carried out according to the wishes of the rich and powerful. Rahula encouraged monks to "embark on a genuine program of rural reconstruction to safeguard the legitimate rights and privileges of the destitute villagers and liberate them from the clutches of those powerful, rich landlords who keep them suppressed" (Rahula 2002, 109).

DEVIATION FROM THE TEACHINGS OF BUDDHA

In the *Brahmajala Sutta*, the Buddha has advised the monks to desist from senseless sciences such as astrology, magic, and the occult. But a respected Buddhist scholar of the fifteenth century, Totagamuwe Rahula, not only dabbled in these "sciences" but also actively engaged in political activities. Modern monks look up to him for justification of these and other occupations (Sobita 1997, 158). Monks have become involved in areas of service such as settling disputes, medical practice, army chaplaincy, trade union activity, political parties, work as politicians, and several other fields which were not regarded as the sphere of a *bhikkhu*. Traditional role restrictions sanctioned by the canonical texts are violated publicly. The Buddhist laity also has been unconcerned about developments of this sort which entail deviation from traditional norms, as long as they are able to benefit from the services of the *Sangha*.

One can notice several recent additions of Christian and Western practices. For example, the monks have started a midnight *pirit* ceremony to bless the New Year on the thirty-first of December. This is copying the midnight Mass of the Catholic Church and the watch night service of the Protestants. Buddhist priests have begun to visit houses of the devotees in their temple area following the parochial visits of the Christian ministers. We can note that the Buddhist leadership continuously made a valiant attempt to contextualize their religion to meet the modern challenges. On the other hand, Christianity, with 500 years of history in Sri Lanka, has failed to contextualize their religion within the Sri Lankan society. It has remained as a potted plant and has not taken root in the soil. This is especially depressing in view of the fact that the Christians spend so much money, energy, and other resources on the topics of enculturation, contextualization, and incarnation, and draw up numerous plans for achieving them.

PRIESTLY ROLE OF SRI LANKAN EVANGELICAL PASTORS

This study would not be complete if we disregarded the challenges coming from the parish priestly role played by the evangelical pastors to the position of leadership of Buddhist monks in several parts of the country. The New Testament pastor, whom the evangelicals take as their model of leadership, serves as elder, teacher, and shepherd. Evangelical pastors are not cast in the same traditional mold as Catholic priests or Buddhist monks.

On the other hand, the evangelical pastor is the most acceptable person in all ranks of society. Such social strata as the estate Tamil laborer, low caste Sinhalese, and outcaste Tamil villager, who did not receive the services of traditional religions, have been approached by them. They are especially prominent in the service of lower ranks of the society, often with the poorest of the poor. Evangelical pastors are viewed in one sense as lay leaders who are dedicated to the service of Christianity. One may observe the changes in lifestyle brought about by the conversions of subaltern communities as a result of the involvement of evangelical Christian pastors. These pastors have successfully covered the role of the Catholic priest as well as the Buddhist monk, however without much ritual associated with them.

CONCLUSION

Buddhist monks have continuously absorbed Christian practices without compromising their basic religious views. They made an attempt to survive in a competitive atmosphere by acquiring what would be beneficial to their survival. As we have noticed, the Buddhist monks were involved in some form of parish priestly role from the beginning. They, however, neglected some significant life cycle events. The only life cycle event that they originally took part in was the funeral, as it agreed with their basic doctrines of *anicca, dukkha, and anatma*.

When Catholic priests arrived in the sixteenth century with more attractive religious practices, many Buddhists were attracted to the

Catholic faith. Having realized the magnitude of the danger coming from this challenge, Buddhist monks gradually absorbed these practices and in the process they made them their own heritage. The *bhikkhu* maintains a bond of association similar to a Catholic parish priest, as family counselor, adviser, and religious guide in the Sinhala Buddhist society today. He performs various functions from birth to death and after. The presence of a *bhikkhu* on these occasions is believed to have a special significance. In the recent past, the leadership of Buddhist priests in performing social roles has been increased with adoption of Catholic, Protestant, and evangelical Christian traditions.

Most of these developments have been adopted in order to combat Christian influence which would lead to conversion of Buddhists to various Christian denominations. Yet amidst these challenges from the Buddhist monks, Christianity has been growing in Sri Lanka. Although most of the new conversions are attributed to miracles and some kind of tangible Christian experience, the real success of Christianity has been the introduction of a personal God with whom one can have a relationship. This personal relationship has pervaded all areas of service offered by Christian clergy.

Buddhist monks have been able to rival the Christians only as far as the merit making process allows. The idea of a personal Being who watches the deeds of man is absent in Buddhism. Therefore, the Buddhist monks who imitate the leadership of the Christian clergy have had only limited success in rivaling Christians.

References

Ariyapala, M. B. 1968. *Society in medieval Ceylon. Colombo: Department of Cultural Affairs.*

Bechert, Heinz, and Richard Francis Gombrich, eds. 1991. The world of Buddhism: Buddhist monks and nuns in society and culture. London: Thames & Hudson.

Bond, George D. 1992. *The Buddhist revival in Sri Lanka: Religious tradition, reinterpretation and response.* New Delhi: Motilal Banarsidass.

De Silva, Lynn A. 1974. *Buddhism: Beliefs and practices in Sri Lanka.* Colombo, Sri Lanka: Wesley Press.

Deegalle, Mahinda. 2006. *Popularizing Buddhism: Preaching as performance in Sri Lanka.* Albany, NY: State University of New York Press.

Dubois, A. J. A. 2007. *Hindu manners, customs and ceremonies.* New York: Cosimo.

Geiger, Wilhelm. 1960. *Culture of Ceylon in mediaeval times.* University of Göttingen.

Gombrich and Obeyesekere. 1990. *Buddhism transformed.* Delhi: Motilal Banarisdas.

Kariyawasam, A. G. S. 1995. *Buddhist ceremonies and rituals of Sri Lanka.* Kandy: Wheel Publication Society.

Knox, Robert. 1911. *An historical relation of the island of Ceylon.* London: James MacLehose & Sons.

Langer, Rita. 2007. *Buddhist rituals of death and rebirth: A study of contemporary Sri Lankan practice and its origins.* Abingdon: Routledge.

Lanka Polity. December 12, 2010.

Malalgoda, Kitisiri. 1976. *Buddhism in Sinhalese society 1750–1900: A study of religious revival and change.* Berkeley: University of California Press.

Morris, R., E. Hardy, and Rys Davids, eds. *Anguttara Nikaya*, Vol. I. 1885. London: Pali Text Society.

Percival, Peter. 1975. *An account of the Island of Ceylon: containing its history, geography, natural history, with the manners and customs of its various inhabitants, to which is added the journal of an embassy to the Court of Candy.* Dehiwela: Tisara Prakasakayo.

Rāhula, Walpola. 2002. *The heritage of the Bhikkhu: The Buddhist tradition of service.* Grove Press.

Scorgie, Glen G. 2011. *Dictionary of Christian spirituality.* Grand Rapids: Zondervan.

Sobita, Maduluwawe, Kamkurugoda Soratha, and Medis Rohandeera. 1997. *Bhikshuwa saha Lanka Samajaya* (Sinhala). Dehiwela: Systematic Printers.

Thanissaro *Bhikkhu*, trans. 2006–2011. *Ambalatthika-rahulovada Sutta: Instructions to Rahula at Mango Stone.* Recorded by the reader in Spring 2006 at Metta Forest Monastery, USA. Available at http://www.suttareadings.net/audio/index.html.

Thero, P. Pemaratana Nakaya, ed. 1999. *Sigalovada Sutta: the code of discipline for layman.*

Trenckner, V., R. Chalmers, and C. A. R. Davids, eds. 1925. Majjhima Nikaya, Vol. III. London: Pali Text Society.

Weeraratne, W. G., ed. *Encyclopaedia of Buddhism*, Vol. 4 (1998), Vol. 7 (2003). Colombo: Department of Cultural Affairs.

Wijayaratna, Mohan.1990. *Buddhist monastic life: According to the texts of the Theravada Tradition. Cambridge: Cambridge University Press.*

Windisch, E., ed. 1889. Itivuttaka. London: Pali Text Society.

Emerging Indigenous Leaders for Jesus Movements in the Myanmar Buddhist Context

PETER THEIN NYUNT

In order to become effective leaders, new Burmese Buddhist converts need to remain in their sociocultural religious contexts without compromising their new faith in Jesus. Deepening their relationship with Jesus in the midst of their Buddhist religious and cultural contexts is the discipleship process that enables them to become indigenous leaders to clearly communicate the gospel of Jesus with other Buddhists. Such movements, according to Rick Wood, are called indigenous movements, or Jesus Movements (2011, 4). In this chapter there are three major sections. First is contextual conversion, second is contextual congregation, and third is a case study of indigenous movements in the Rakhine Buddhist context in Myanmar (Burma). The missiological insights from this chapter may proliferate indigenous leadership principles from the Burmese sociocultural religious context and ignite Burmese Christians to rethink lessons from the Burmese church's historical experiences. These insights rooted in the Burmese context may or may not be similar to the principles in other Buddhist countries in Southeast Asia and beyond. However, I believe that they can help the disciple paint a more complete and comprehensive portrait of Jesus Movements within the Buddhist world.

INTRODUCTION

The Union of Myanmar is a country which has been deeply influenced by Theravāda Buddhism and its associated traditions. Burmese Buddhism presents a certain picture of its society as conforming to the *Dharma* teachings with implications that the development of the Burmese culture is religiously oriented (Lubeigt 2004, 244; Thittila 2000, 213; Soe 2005, 118–119). Buddhism has saturated social life, ideas, manners, and aspirations as the national identity. This interconnectedness of religion and national identity is inseparable. Meanwhile, churches in Myanmar have been adopting models of ministries manufactured in Western mission. As a result, the churches in Myanmar are just the replicas and potted plants of Western churches. Why might this be happening to the churches in Myanmar? This chapter will proceed to appraise the lack of equipping the indigenous leaders of Burmese churches past and present, and will develop contextual missiological insights for Jesus Movements. This may mean shaking our church model and mission strategy traditions to make a major paradigm shift in fulfilling the Great Commission in Myanmar.

A BRIEF EVALUATION OF CHRISTIAN MISSION IN MYANMAR: PAST AND PRESENT

Before addressing the critical issues of equipping indigenous Christians, it is appropriate to consider why Christian missions have failed to reach the majority of Burmese Buddhists. Ever since the arrival of the first American Baptist missionary couple, Adoniram and Ann Judson in 1813, the primary mission target was Burmese Buddhists. However, the harvest was reaped mainly from the minorities on the fringes of society, not from the Buddhist majority. In 1836, when there were only nineteen Burmese-Mon Christians in the entire country, 323 Karen were baptized in that year alone (Wa 1963, 128–129). While mission work among Burmese Buddhists was not as fruitful as it should have been, work among the hill-tribe animists was more fruitful. This is still true today.

From 1964 to 1966, the former socialist government expelled all foreign missionaries. Without indigenous leadership development, Christians in Burma (as it was named at that time) became sheep without shepherds scattered all over the country. Zau Latt points out,

In [the] post-missionary period, under the former Socialist Military Government, beginning with the 1960s, the Churches became limited both in resources and trained personnel to engage in active mission work among non-Christians. The Churches at that time were busy fighting for their survival, for they had suddenly become independent autonomous Churches from being mission fields of the American Baptist Mission. Lack of trained leaders was the hardest blow for the Churches. (2006, 86–87)

In his statement Latt does not mean that after the missionary period the church in Burma remained stagnant. His conclusions emphasize the result of what happened when missionaries failed to train indigenous leaders for Christian missions within their specific contexts.

In 1988, economic crisis resulted in general demonstrations and riots against the socialist government throughout the whole country. The military leader General Saw Maung seized control of the government and renamed it the State Law and Order Restoration Council. Subsequent leaders have changed the name of the government time after time, but the system of administration has remained centralized and authoritarian. Since 1988, government administrators have all been the same—all from military origin. Like the ancient despotic kings, the present government is promoting local indigenous forms of Buddhism as a means of unifying the country and to encourage nationalism. The church in Myanmar, however, is still predominantly Western-oriented with a dedicated allegiance to Western teachings and Western forms.

CONTEXTUAL CONVERSIONS IN JESUS MOVEMENTS

As communication always takes place in specific times and places, Christian communication to any particular people group must be contextual. Such a way of communication can be clearly seen in the incarnation of Jesus Christ (Gilliland 1989, 53). And, of course, the goal of Christian communication must also be contextual conversion. A contextual conversion is a genuine conversion where the converts receive a new identity as followers of Jesus, but where they are not converted out of the Buddhist context. It is a conversion where the converts remain in close contact with their own people so that they may express their new faith through Buddhist cultural forms. Let me identify three specific characteristics of a contextual conversion to Jesus from the Burmese Buddhist context.

Contextual Conversion within the Culture

A contextual conversion takes place within the culture. A scriptural example of this is found in the book of Acts before the Jerusalem council as recorded in Acts 15. Up until that time the early church commonly required Gentiles to "convert" to the Jewish culture/religion as a prerequisite for their conversion to Christ. In fact, changing culture/religion is not a prerequisite for, nor a guarantee of, salvation; conversion is a matter of the heart (Lim 2010, 33). That is why a contextual conversion, such as that which the Jerusalem council agreed upon at the recommendations of Paul and Peter, involves the convert being allowed and encouraged to express his or her new faith within his or her own culture. Hans Kasdorf states,

> The meeting point is that of reconciliation, the point when the person—regardless of his religious or cultural status—becomes a new person in Christ. This does not mean that he becomes *neos*, or new in point of time, but *kairos*, or new in point of quality. Thus when a person is converted to God, it does not mean that Christ Jesus makes all Jews into Gentiles or all Gentiles into Jews; He produces a new kind of person out of both, although they remain Gentiles and Jews. (1980, 87)

This shows that contextual conversion takes place with reference to points of contact already present in the culture of the convert. God has already provided points of contact for the gospel within every culture, and he uses these points of contact when leading people to conversion. This means that elements of God's truth may be found in religions outside of Christianity. As a result, new followers of Jesus do not need to abandon those truth elements to become Christians. For conversion, the key emphasis here is relationship with Jesus himself.

Contextual Conversion within Sociological Groups

People are social beings; a contextual conversion keeps the convert within his or her sociological group. In a contextual conversion, even the conversion of an individual, the church must always have in mind the larger sociological group to which the convert belongs. Donald McGavran explains the principle of conversion within the sociological group of the convert by pointing out that converts should

> remain thoroughly one with their own people in most matters. They should continue to eat what their people eat. They should not say, my people are vegetarians, but now that I have become a Christian I'm going to eat meat. After they become Christians they should be more rigidly vegetarian than they were before. In the matter of clothing, they should continue to look precisely like their kinsfolk. In the matter of marriage, most peoples are endogamous; they insist that "our people marry only our people." (1992, d-103)

As Jesus promised in Mark 8:34–37, conversion may involve exclusion and persecution from the convert's family and community. Even so, the convert should be encouraged and helped to remain within his or her own people group in order to witness to the family of the Christ who is in his or her heart.

Contextual Conversion through Encounter

A contextual conversion involves an encounter between the convert's old religion and worldview and his or her new faith in Jesus Christ. Kraft has pointed to three critical encounters between the old and new worldview.

> An allegiance or commitment encounter, leading to a new relationship with God, where allegiance to God takes precedence over all other loyalties. ... A truth encounter, leading to a right understanding about God and the relationship between God and humanity and between humans, in accordance with the biblical teaching. ... A power encounter, where the trust in God replaces the reliance on and/or the fear of other powers, leading to spiritual freedom. (1991b, 258–265)

These encounters, which lead to radical changes at the deep world-view level, are reflected in the behavior of the convert. Some aspects of the convert's life will therefore be changed, whereas others are incorporated into the new life (Myanmar Council of Churches 2002, 181–184).

For Jesus Movements to take place in the Burmese Buddhist context, conversion within the culture and within the sociological group of the convert and the encounter with the old religion of the convert are the three most significant aspects of a contextual conversion.

CONTEXTUAL CONGREGATIONS IN JESUS MOVEMENTS

People are often more impressed with statistics on conversion than with those on making disciples. In the Great Commission, the command is to make disciples. But "disciples do not stop with conversion; they keep moving on with Christ, always learning more of his grace and glory" (Coleman 2000, 255). After a person is converted, he or she begins the long but essential process of discipleship or Christian nurture. Thus, the next step following contextual conversion is to nurture converts in such a way that they become disciples who continually make new disciples in their own cultural context. For this to happen, like the early church in the book of Acts, the new converts have to be incorporated into a congregation in order to grow and mature in a contextual way (Cosgrove 1980, 21). Without forsaking their own cultures, converts need to feel at home and be equipped to cultivate reproductive fellowships through the word of God. Arn paraphrases the reproductive nature of the Great Commission this way:

The words of Christ in Matthew 28:19–20 communicate vividly Christ's understanding of a disciple. He saw a disciple as one who becomes a follower, who is taught, who is nurtured in the faith, who in turn goes out to make disciples, who are then taught and nurtured in the faith, who then in turn go out. (1982, 20)

It is a process of equipping converts to grow to maturity and to lead people to become recruiters or leaders. Jesus and Paul in the New Testament were interested primarily in developing these kinds of leaders. According to social science, "leadership is frequently defined as the process of influence" and in making disciples this sort of influence is most effective if disciples are made "within the immediate situation and in the overall community in which they live" (Van Rheenen 1996, 165; see also Wilson 1978, 60–61). There are four specific characteristics of contextual congregations appropriate for Jesus Movements in the Burmese Buddhist context.

Contextual Congregations within the Sociocultural Context

First of all, a contextual-local congregation should aim at helping its members to remain within their own culture and community, so that the congregation is not seen as a foreign element in the context. Instead of extracting its members from their culture and community, the contextual congregation should advocate a contextual conversion (McGavran 1955, 10–11). This congregation should be a fellowship of followers of Jesus who strive to continue to live in fellowship with their non-Christian relatives and neighbors. In attempting to be relevant in its context, a local congregation should never lose its unique Christian identity, which sets the church apart from any other institution. Being faithful to the biblical principles of the church, it will differ from its surroundings in the whole ethos of the Christian fellowship; however, it will never cease to be relevant for the surrounding community because it expresses its message, fellowship, and service in forms and structures that are familiar to the context and it addresses needs that are felt in the community.

Contextual Congregations within the Religio-Cultural Context

Secondly, a contextual congregation should endeavor to use the language of the converts and communication methods with which they are most familiar in services and other activities. One of the most important parts of the context is the language because much of a society's culture is stored in and transmitted through its language. Only when the word of God is communicated in the mother tongue of the members, and only when the members communicate with one another and with God through their own language, can a congregation be said to be contextual. Moreover, a contextual congregation should attempt to develop and use rituals, symbols, and worship forms which, while communicating the relevant biblical message effectively, address the needs of the members. For literate and nonliterate peoples alike, rituals are important for the life of the congregation in the Burmese religio-cultural context. That is why Hiebert states that "rituals, like sacred symbols, are languages for speaking of spiritual things" (Hiebert 1994, 167). In addition, Hiebert asserts that rituals are important to teach new Christians the meaning of the gospel in their new lives and to proclaim the gospel to non-Christians who gather to see what the Christians are doing (1997, 84–86).

Contextual Congregations as Place of Disciple-making

Disciples are made in small (not big) groups where a person looks to another person for instruction, counsel, training, and fellowship (Jenson 1981, 158). Jesus unfolded his teaching of truth in a relational context—discipleship. He chose twelve people to teach by example in the context of the day-in, day-out activities of living together and ministering to people in love and power. A contextual congregation insures that its method of education strengthens each member's faith as well as a sense of belonging to the local and universal church without alienating any from his or her original community or its values. This sort of approach to formal and informal education in the local congregation involves teaching of the knowledge of God and skills that are relevant to the members' actual Christian life in the congregation and to their social service and mission in their original community. If the teaching is not done contextually, the content and form of education may alienate the members from their own people within their own context and will not be relevant to the values of their culture (Hiebert 1997, 84–86). On the other hand, the converts being trained must be learners of biblical truth and visible followers of Jesus Christ, with the essential qualities of true disciples. That unbeatable combination makes a great impact on others in their community.

Contextual Congregations as a Place of Indigeneity

Last but not least, a contextual congregation should seek to employ indigenous organizational structures and leadership forms. Only when the patterns and styles used to govern the life of the fellowship are in harmony with those of the local culture may we speak of a contextual organization and leadership of the local congregation (Smalley 1992, 152–154). Moreover, the theology and ethics of the contextual local congregation should be developed by the members of the local con-gregations, as the congregations reflect on their life in their context in light of Scripture. Instead of taking a theology of a dominant Christian group developed in another context, contextual congregations will begin to develop their own understanding of the Christian faith and its implications for them.

CASE STUDY:
A STRATEGY FOR REACHING BUDDHISTS IN
RAKHINE STATE

The word *Rakhine* is traditionally derived from the word *rakshas,* which means the one who loves his or her race and keeps *Silas* (a Pali word meaning "precepts" in English). Rakhine State, formerly known as Ara-kan State, one of the seven states in today's Myanmar, is geographically situated in the western part of Myanmar and populated with about three million people. The majority are Rakhine who adhere to Theravāda Buddhism. Buddhism influenced the development of Rakhine culture centuries before Christianity was introduced. Christianity was first introduced into Rakhine state in the sixteenth century through Catholic missions. But until 2003, according to an oral report from the Rakhine Baptist Convention, the Christians in the whole state numbered approximately 10,000, including Catholics. Out of this number about twenty to thirty were from the Rakhine Buddhists and other small ethnic groups with animistic backgrounds.

From personal experience, I can attest to the fact that Buddhists in Rakhine state are very open to the gospel if the message is communicated appropriately in their specific context. In June 2003, my coworker Joshua Kyaw Soe and I, who both come from the Rakhine Buddhist background, started an indigenous movement called The Rakhine Missions Band for Christ (RMBC) to reach Rakhine people with the gospel and plant indigenous churches with new converts.

In Rakhine society, social solidarity is family-oriented. We have developed our own indigenous strategy which underscores the idea that the communication of the gospel is not a single event, but a series of communicational events that form a process or spiritual journey. The conversion process is depicted as having three dimensions: the dimension of awareness, the dimension of conversion, and the dimension of incorporation.

For the dimension of awareness, the first question we raise to Rakhine Buddhists is: What does it mean to you to be an authentic Buddhist? Over the course of time this preliminary acquaintance step will lead naturally into gospel communication with our Buddhist friends. Of course, we help them clearly see the liberator from samsara is Jesus, acquainting him or her with the truth of Jesus, which sets us free from the bondage of religion and sins. During this stage we communicate with them the foundational message of the gospel through the illustrations from 550 stories in Buddhism that God is the savior from the cycle of samsara through the mighty act of reconciliation in Jesus Christ. Humankind who is full of *akusala* (sin), however, must respond to him through keeping the Five Precepts of Jesus Christ: repenting their *akusala*, taking refuge in Jesus as the liberator from samsara, *shinbyu* in Christ (water baptism), participating in the Lord's Supper as the sign of faithfulness to Christ, and proclaiming Jesus to other Buddhists. The objective of this stage is to have converts (and their conversion process) remain within their cultural context. As communication is not an event but a process, conversion takes anywhere from weeks to months to even a year. When they are convinced that they need Jesus, we encourage potential converts to freely decide to enter into a relationship with Jesus in their specific context. Instead of separating the Buddhist converts from their community, we encourage them to remain within their cultural community, retaining their Buddhist identity while being faithful to Christ. Through being in this contextual conversion phase, the gospel has the potential to move rapidly from individuals to families to the community within these cultural contexts and to transform them from the inside.

Conversion to Christ involves a decision, but decision-making models vary from culture to culture. We strongly hold that Christian conversion should be in accord with the decision-making patterns of the convert's culture. For the dimension of incorporation into the body of Christ, discipleship takes place in the context of a small group. As the converts need to grow in their new faith, equipping them through the word of God meets their needs, as well as serving as a means to introduce new people to the Christian faith. In this phase, Buddhist converts are being trained by informal teaching rather than formal training. What is currently happening now within the Rakhine Buddhist society through the ministries of RMBC? There are over 900 Rakhine Buddhist converts remaining Buddhists, but faithful to Christ in six townships in Rakhine State.

RECOMMENDATIONS FOR THE CHURCH IN MYANMAR

As pointed out, churches in Myanmar have been employing Western-oriented mission strategies. How then can the churches develop Jesus Movements? The following recommendations should be considered very seriously.

First, contextual conversion within the Buddhist community is the goal. The missiological implication is to encourage Burmese Buddhist converts to remain connected to their households, their communities, and their other significant relationships. That is, churches should encourage converts to remain connected to their network of relationships, households, kin groups, and communities in as many ways as possible. As difficult as it may be, the convert's presence in his or her household, kin group, and community will build an essential channel through which the gospel can flow. This methodology will remove the perception that Christianity is a destroyer of relationships, families, households, and community solidarity. However, as converts remain connected to former surroundings, it is critical that churches provide the needed social and spiritual support for their newfound faith to be established. This is important so as to avoid the possibility of converts reverting to their former religion and way of life, under social pressure. The effectiveness of Christian missions among Buddhists will depend upon the extent to which the prevalent separating conversion pattern is replaced by a contextual conversion pattern. All mission approaches and methods should be tested against this criterion of contextual conversion.

Secondly, the church in Myanmar must establish house church fellowships. In order to reach the goal of translating contextual congregations into actual Buddhist convert house fellowships, churches need to develop a realistic and practical procedure for church planting. The initiative for the establishment of these house fellowships must come from Christian workers employed in missional activities in cooperation with those local Christians who are most directly involved in the conversion of Buddhist people. A house fellowship may start with as few as two or three Christians, for example, one or two Buddhist converts together with a mature Christian. Questions about when, where, and how often the house fellowship should gather will have to be considered, just as will questions about liturgy. The goal, however, should be to train one of the converts to become the leader of the fellowship as soon as possible.

Last but not least, indigenous churches and missions are recommended. Evaluating the whole process of missions helps determine how truly indigenous a church or contextual a congregation is. Its identity with the people group and its level in fully expressing Christ and the gospel to its own society are indispensable. Are adequate "functional substitutes" being employed for those crucial areas of culture that would leave voids apart from relevant application from the Bible? Does the church movement have indigenous missions reaching out to other people groups? The bottom line should be judged on the basis of three R's: Does it have the respect of the Buddhist community? Is it taking responsibility under the Lord for ministry to the society around it? Is it exhibiting resourcefulness in evangelizing its Buddhist neighbors and coping with opposition from within? Speaking out of painful honesty, until recently there have been no contextual congregations in the whole country of Myanmar. The vast majority of Christian leaders still favor the traditional approach of integrating Buddhist converts into existing culturally-removed congregations. Looking at the history of the early church in Acts, it is obvious that as men and women came to the savior, they immediately banded themselves together in small groups to form churches. They worshiped God and used the local assemblies as bases from which to evangelize the regions around them. Thus, the establishment of the contextual congregations should not be postponed. The goal should be to establish small house fellowships with converts, which will help them stay within their cultural community and culture, which will be more effective in attracting Buddhists to the gospel. The establishment of the contextual congregations cannot be postponed. Congregations should begin with the few converts. From this humble start, more contextual conversions need to be encouraged. All mission initiatives should be evaluated on the basis of their ability to organize contextual conversions into contextual congregations.

CONCLUSION

In fulfilling the Great Commission of Jesus Christ, one of the most challenging tasks for Christians in Myanmar is how to communicate Christ in life and action intelligible to their Buddhist neighbors. For Buddhists to make sense of Christ will inevitably include preaching the gospel in their own dharmic terms and faith-expressions, and relating Jesus' teachings to their thoughts and life experiences. It is encouraging that church and mission leaders and mission partners have expressed their commitment to do mission among the Buddhists all over the country. However, until now, churches and mission organizations have been primarily following the traditional mission principles and approaches in their mission works. Consequently, today, the estimated Buddhist convert membership of Christian churches in Myanmar still forms a tiny minority, without indigenous leaders. It appears to be oblivious of two critical concerns. First, there appears to be a general unawareness of the missiological lessons that should be learned from the efforts of missionaries in the past. Secondly, and perhaps more critically, there appears to be a general lack of interest among the churches in the sociocultural and religious history of the Burmese people. For indigenous leaders to emerge in the mission work to Burmese Buddhists, the church and mission leaders, mission partners, and volunteers must be empowered to follow Jesus Movements or indigenous movements. Only with the full understanding of the church and mission leadership can new approaches become effective. When it succeeds, we will see many Burmese Buddhist converts from different social classes taking refuge in Jesus as the liberator and compassionate savior. We will hear them reciting, "I take refuge in Jesus (Jesus *saranan gacchami*), the word of God is my dharma (the words of Jesus *saranan gacchami*), and the church is the *Sangha* of Christ (*athindaw saranan gacchami*)." We will see Burmese Buddhist converts worshiping him in their own language and expressing their new faith in their own cultural forms. At the end they will be saying, "Sadu, Sadu and Sadu."

References

Arn, Win, and Charles Arn. 1982. *The master's plan for making disciples: How every Christian can be an effective witness through an enabling church*. Pasadena: Church Growth Press.

Coleman, Robert E. 2000. The lifestyle of the Great Commission. In *Telling the Truth: Evangelizing Postmoderns*, ed. D. A. Carson, 255–69. Grand Rapids, MI: Zondervan.

Cosgrove Jr., Francis M. 1980. *Essentials of discipleship: Practical help on how to live as Christ's disciple*. Colorado Springs: NavPress.

Gilliland, Dean S. 1989. New Testament contextualization: Continuity and particularity in Paul's theology. In *The Word among us: Contextualizing theology for mission today*, ed. Dean S. Gilliland, 52–73. London: Word Publishing.Hesselgrave, David J. 1978. *Communicating Christ cross-culturally*. Grand Rapids: Baker Books.

Hiebert, Paul G. 1994. *Anthropological reflections on missiological issues.* Grand Rapids: Baker Books.

_____. 1997. Conversion and worldview transformation. *International Journal of Frontier Missions* 14/2 (April–June): 84–86.

Kasdorf, Hans. 1980. *Christian conversion in Christ.* Scottdale, PA: Herald Press.

Kraft, Charles H. 2005. Contextualization in three crucial dimensions. In *Appropriate Christianity,* ed. Charles H. Kraft, 99–116. Pasadena: William Carey Library.

_____. 1991b. What kind of encounters do we need in our Christian witness. *Evangelical Missions Quarterly* 27 (2): 258–268.

Jenson, Ron, and Jim Stevens. 1981. *Dynamics of church growth.* Grand Rapids: Baker Books.

Latt, Zau. 2006. Rereading the Great Commission. In *Our theological journey: writings in honor of Dr. Anna May Say Pa,* ed. Festschrift Committee of Myanmar Institute of Theology, 84–104. Insein: MIT.

Lim, David. 2010. Catalyzing "insider movements" in Buddhist context. In *Family and faith in Asia: The missional impact of social networks,* ed. Paul De Neui, 31–46. Pasadena: William Carey Library.

Lubeigt, Guy. 2004. Myanmar: A country modeled by Buddhist traditions. In *Traditions of knowledge in Southeast Asia part 2,* ed. Myanmar Historical Committee, 222–47. Yangon: University Press.

McGavran, Donald A. 1992. A church in every people: Plain talk about a difficult subject. In *Perspectives on the world Christian movement: A reader,* eds. Ralph D. Winter and Steve C. Hawthorne, d-100–d-106. Pasadena: William Carey Library.

_____. 1955. *The bridges of God: A study in the strategy of missions.* New York: Friendship Press.

Myanmar Council of Churches. 2002. *Collections of Professor U Khin Maung Din's papers & articles*. Yangon: MCC.

Smalley, William A. 1992. Cultural implications of an indigenous church. In *Perspectives on the world Christian movement: A reader*, eds. Ralph D. Winter and Steve C. Hawthorne, C-149–C-157. Pasadena: William Carey Library.

Soe, Tin. 2005. An economic interpretation of some Myanmar traditional concepts in the context of globalization. In *Traditions of knowledge in Southeast Asia part 3*, eds. Myanmar Historical Committee, 118–55. Yangon: University Press.

Thittila, Ashin. 2000. *Essential themes of Buddhist lectures*. Yangon: Department of Religious Affairs.

Van Rheenen, Gailyn. 1996. *Missions: Biblical foundations & contemporary strategies*. Grand Rapids: Zondervan.

Wa, Maung Shwe. 1963. *Burma Baptist chronicles*. Rangoon: Burma Baptist Convention.

Wilson, Carl. 1976. *With Christ in the school of disciple building: A study of Christ's method of building disciples*. Grand Rapids: Zondervan.

Wood, Rick. 2011. Muslim, Hindu and Buddhist followers of Jesus: How should we respond? *Missions Frontiers* (May–June): 4.

Index

Scripture Index